LEARNING MORE FROM SOCIAL EXPERIMENTS

LEARNING MORE FROM SOCIAL EXPERIMENTS

Evolving Analytic Approaches

Howard S. Bloom
Editor

AN MDRC PROJECT

Russell Sage Foundation • New York

The Russell Sage Foundation

The Russell Sage Foundation, one of the oldest of America's general purpose foundations, was established in 1907 by Mrs. Margaret Olivia Sage for "the improvement of social and living conditions in the United States." The Foundation seeks to fulfill this mandate by fostering the development and dissemination of knowledge about the country's political, social, and economic problems. While the Foundation endeavors to assure the accuracy and objectivity of each book it publishes, the conclusions and interpretations in Russell Sage Foundation publications are those of the authors and not of the Foundation, its Trustees, or its staff. Publication by Russell Sage, therefore, does not imply Foundation endorsement.

Library of Congress Cataloging-in-Publication Data

Learning more from social experiments : evolving analytic approaches / Howard S. Bloom, editor.
    p.   cm.
    Includes bibliographical references and index.
    ISBN 0-87154-127-0
    1. Social sciences—Experiments.   2. Social sciences—Research.
    3. Experimental design.   I. Bloom, Howard S.

H62.L392 2005
300'.72'4—dc22   2004061463

Text design by Suzanne Nichols.

RUSSELL SAGE FOUNDATION
112 East 64th Street, New York, New York 10021
10   9   8   7   6   5   4   3   2   1

Contents

Contributors

Howard S. Bloom is chief social scientist of MDRC.

Johannes M. Bos is president and CEO of Berkeley Policy Associates.

Lisa A. Gennetian is senior research associate at MDRC.

Carolyn J. Hill is assistant professor of public policy at the Georgetown Public Policy Institute.

Charles Michalopoulos is senior fellow at MDRC.

Pamela A. Morris is deputy director of MDRC's Family Well-Being and Children's Development policy area.

James A. Riccio is director of MDRC's Low-Wage Workers and Communities policy area.

Preface

This book is founded on a commitment to promote evidence-based policymaking in human affairs by developing and refining the research tools available to social scientists. Specifically, the book seeks to advance the science of evaluation research by presenting innovative ways to address the following high-stakes questions: What social programs, policies, and interventions work? For whom do they work, and under what conditions? And why do they work—or fall short? Answering these questions is a sine qua non for formulating effective responses to the many pressing social problems in our country and around the world.

The book's publication concludes the first stage of an ongoing initiative by MDRC—a nonprofit, nonpartisan social policy research organization—to improve methodologies for measuring the effects of welfare, employment, and education programs. Called the Research Methodology Initiative, this effort has three broad objectives: to push the frontiers of experimental methods that rely on random assignment research designs; to refine quasi-experimental methods that use creative approximations to random assignment; and to devise and expand methods for combining research on program effects with research on program implementation. Although such methodological research is most useful when performed in the context of ongoing evaluation projects, the stringent constraints of field studies usually leave little time or money for it to be carried out. Securing resources for the research in this book thus demanded considerable effort on the part of MDRC and exceptional dedication on the part of its funding partners.

The goals of the book are several. First, it seeks to advance and integrate theory and practice in the design and analysis of evaluation research. Thus, all the featured methods are examined with an eye both to the desirability of their theoretical properties and to their likely feasibility, cost, transparency, and credibility. Second, rather than contribute to the often heated and sometimes counterproductive debate between proponents of randomized experimental methods and proponents of nonexperimental methods, the book seeks opportunities to combine the two approaches in ways that get the best out of both and avoid the worst of each. Third, the book grounds its discussions of methodology in a wide range of examples from real-world evaluations. Much of the work reported here draws on MDRC projects, which supply many of the detailed illustrations, but the scope and applicability of the examined methodological approaches are broadened by the inclusion of numerous other examples from the literature. Finally, the book aspires to reach a wide audience of researchers in many fields of study with diverse methodological traditions. To this end, each chapter addresses its subject matter not only in a formal, mathematical way when needed but also in a conceptual, intuitive way.

Because the chapters in this volume owe their existence to a cast of literally thousands—program participants, administrators, and staff as well as researchers and research funders—numerous acknowledgments are in order. First and foremost is the debt of gratitude owed Judith Gueron, MDRC's president from 1986 to 2004 and the driving force behind the initiative on which the book is built. With unflagging enthusiasm and a passion for perfection, Judy made it a personal and organizational priority to garner the resources and free up the time needed for MDRC staff to launch the initiative and has been a continual source of encouragement and support for it.

Thanks are next due my collaborators on the book, starting with my coauthors: Johannes Bos, Lisa Gennetian, Carolyn Hill, Charles Michalopoulos, Pamela Morris, and James Riccio. Countless hours, endless revisions, and infinite patience were required of this group to achieve what we set out to accomplish, and it was a pleasure and a privilege to work with such creative and committed colleagues. In addition, all of us are most grateful to Valerie Chase for her extraordinary editorial contribution and for her personification of grace under pressure.

Thanks are due next to our colleagues at MDRC and elsewhere who contributed insights and information about the examples used in the book, facilitated access to the literature upon which the book builds, provided feedback on its chapters and produced its manuscript: Gordon Berlin, Susan Bloom, Christopher Bost, Thomas Brock, Stephanie Cowell, Fred Doolittle, Stephen Freedman, Barbara Gewirtz, Barbara Goldman, Robert Granger, Gayle Hamilton, James Kemple, Virginia Knox, Ying Lei, Winston Lin, Catherine Magnuson, Vanessa Martin, Cynthia Miller, Lashawn Richburg Hayes, Howard Rolston, and Leonard Sternbach.

Thanks are next due the distinguished scholars who gave generously of their time to serve as advisors on or reviewers of chapters in the book, projects on which the chapters are based, or both. Among those who provided invaluable advice on the design and planning of the research, the analysis and interpretation of the findings, and strategies for articulating the conclusions are Joshua Angrist, Robert Boruch,

Rebecca Blank, Gary Burtless, Thomas Cook, David Card, Rajeev Dehejia, Greg Duncan, Gerd Gigerenzer, Laurence Lynn, Robinson Hollister, Guido Imbens, Robert LaLonde, Lawrence Mead, Bruce Meyer, Robert Moffitt, Stephen Raudenbush, Philip Robins, and Robert Solow.

For their generous financial support, thanks are due the Pew Charitable Trusts, the Russell Sage Foundation, the William T. Grant Foundation, the Alfred P. Sloan Foundation, the U.S. Department of Health and Human Services, and the U.S. Department of Education, which fund the Research Methodology Initiative, and the Russell Sage Foundation and the Pew Charitable Trusts, which funded the book itself.

In closing, I should note, as is customary, that the content of the book does not necessarily represent the official positions of its funding organizations and that any errors are the responsibility of the editor and authors.

Howard Bloom
MDRC

Chapter 1

Precedents and Prospects for Randomized Experiments

WHEN FAMILIES move to low-poverty neighborhoods, their teenage children are less likely to commit crimes (Ludwig, Hirschfield, and Duncan 2001). Couples therapy and family therapy are equally effective at improving marital relationships (Shadish et al. 1995). Increasing welfare benefit amounts by 10 percent discourages 1 percent of low-income parents from working (Burtless 1987). Each of these statements answers a question about the effect, or impact, of a social policy or intervention on people's behavior. Does helping low-income families move to low-poverty neighborhoods affect their children's development? Does couples counseling bring more benefits than family therapy? What proportion of low-income parents would stop working if welfare benefits were increased by a certain amount?

These conclusions, like many others of importance to individuals and society as a whole, are based on studies that used a powerful research paradigm known as random assignment. In this book, such studies are referred to as randomized experiments or, simply, experiments (in medicine and other disciplines they are often called randomized trials or clinical trials). In randomized experiments, the units of analysis—usually individuals, but sometimes clusters of individuals—are assigned randomly either to a group that is exposed to the intervention or treatment being studied or to a control group that is not exposed to it. Because the groups do not differ systematically from one another at the outset of the experiment, any differences between them that subsequently arise can be attributed to the intervention or treatment rather than to preexisting differences between the groups. Random assignment also provides a means of rigorously determining the likelihood that subsequent differences could have occurred by chance rather than because of differences in treatment assignment.

1

Consider how researchers used random assignment in the studies cited in the opening paragraph. In the study of neighborhoods and juvenile crime, families living in public housing developments, all of them situated in high-poverty neighborhoods, were randomly assigned to three groups. Two groups received one of two types of housing voucher: one that could be used toward the cost of private housing provided that the family moved to a low-poverty neighborhood (this was called the conditional-voucher group), or another that could be used to pay for private housing in any neighborhood (the unconditional-voucher group). The third group received no private housing vouchers (the no-voucher group).

Random assignment ensured that the group a family was assigned to depended neither on the family's observable characteristics, such as the parents' age and race or the number of children in the family, nor on characteristics that would be difficult or impossible for a researcher to observe, such as the parents' motivation, ability, and preferences about where to live. In other words, because all the families in the study had an equal chance of being assigned to each of the three groups, the only systematic difference among them was the type of voucher (or no voucher) received. Consequently, when the researchers found a larger proportion of moves to low-poverty neighborhoods and a lower incidence of juvenile crime in the conditional-voucher group than in the other two groups, they were confident about attributing these changes to that single systematic difference.

By itself, however, random assignment would not have allowed these researchers to conclude that moving to a low-poverty neighborhood reduced criminal activity among children. The conditional vouchers affected many other outcomes that might have reduced juvenile crime. For example, they increased work and reduced welfare receipt among parents, and they also increased family income. To find out whether juvenile crime stemmed from living in a low-poverty neighborhood, the researchers went beyond random assignment in two ways: They relied on a strong theory linking neighborhoods to crime, and they used a statistical technique called instrumental variables to identify the effect on juvenile crime of a family's moving out of public housing to a low-poverty neighborhood.

The other two results mentioned in the opening paragraph likewise came from studies that built on random assignment. In the study exploring the effectiveness of psychotherapy in helping couples resolve their problems, the researchers looked at seventy-one random-assignment studies of two types. In one type, couples were randomly assigned to receive marital therapy or no therapy at all. In the other type, couples were randomly assigned to receive family therapy or no therapy at all.

Although the two types of therapy were never compared in a single experiment, the researchers were able to conduct cross-study comparisons using meta-analysis (Glass 1976), a statistical technique for systematically synthesizing quantitative results from multiple primary studies on the same topic. Though not as rigorous as a randomized experiment comparing the two types of therapy directly, this meta-analysis provided an immediate plausible answer to a question that had not yet been addressed using random assignment.

The study of the effect of welfare benefit levels on employment looked at a diverse low-income sample that included families who were not receiving public assistance. After being randomly assigned to one of several different welfare levels, each family was informed of the benefit amount for which it was eligible. A comparison of parental employment rates over a three-year period revealed that parents in families that were eligible for larger benefit amounts were less likely to work than were parents in families that were eligible for smaller amounts. The random-assignment design allowed the researchers to conclude that higher benefit levels caused parents to work less, but the design could not on its own indicate what proportion of parents would be moved to stop working if they were eligible for benefit levels not directly tested in the experiment. Using regression analysis to relate families' responses to the treatments they were assigned, the researchers extrapolated estimates of this proportion to unexamined benefit levels from the results of several different experiments.

Randomized experiments were a rarity in the social sciences until the second half of the twentieth century, but since then they have rapidly become a common method for testing the effects of policies, programs, and interventions in a wide range of areas, from prescription medicines to electricity prices. Written for a diverse audience of social scientists, the present book makes the case for enhancing the scope and relevance of social research by combining randomized experiments with nonexperimental statistical methods that leverage the power of random assignment. This chapter provides context for the rest of the book by describing how and why researchers in a variety of disciplines have gradually shifted from nonstatistical to statistical approaches and from nonexperimental to experimental methods. It also discusses the kinds of questions that are difficult to answer by means of randomized experimentation alone and explores ways in which nonexperimental statistical techniques can complement experimental designs to provide more or better answers than can either approach on its own. The authors of each of the four following chapters use detailed examples from their areas of research—welfare, education, and employment policy—to present four nonexperimental statistical approaches to maximizing the knowledge generated by experiments in the social sciences.

The Evolution of Impact Analysis

Ideas, individuals, and institutions all helped shape the evolution of statistics in science, especially statistical inference—which is the process of determining what data say about the world that generated them. In most disciplines, statistical inference did not become the norm until the twentieth century. Nowadays, not only scientific reports but popular-press accounts of discoveries in a wide range of fields mention statistical considerations, from significance levels in clinical medicine to margins of error in opinion research. To shed light on impact analysis today, this section presents a selective review of its historical development.[1]

Nineteenth-Century Approaches

> Despite historical roots that extend to the seventeenth century, the wide-spread use of systematic, data-based evaluations is a relatively modern development. The application of social research methods to evaluation coincides with the growth and refinement of the methods themselves, as well as with ideological, political, and demographic changes that have occurred during this century.
>
> —Peter H. Rossi and Howard E. Freeman (1993, 9–10)

One reason why statistical inference was less commonly used in nineteenth-century social science than today was the widely followed school of thought called determinism. In the deterministic view, uncertainty merely reflects human ignorance of the sequence of events that cause each subsequent event. Even in analyses of games of chance, where probability was perhaps most frequently applied in the nineteenth century, it was believed that every roll of a die or flip of a coin has a predetermined, if unknown, outcome.

Determinism led researchers to use statistical concepts such as the average to measure what they thought were fixed, knowable constants. For example, in estimating planetary orbits, astronomers took the average of calculations based on different observations of the planets because they saw each observation as providing information on constants implied by Isaac Newton's theories (Stigler 1999). They believed that different observations provided different information solely because errors had been made in those measurements.

This belief paved the way for major advances in the natural sciences, but it contributed little to the utility of statistics in the social sciences. Social scientists found that statistical aggregates describing humanity were stable over time and across places, and these social aggregates became the object of study for researchers such as the statistician Adolphe Quetelet (Gigerenzer et al. 1989). But social aggregates lacked the theoretical foundation that Newtonian theory provided astronomers, and they were therefore deemed inadequate for describing human behavior and outcomes.

Quetelet's 1835 study of conviction rates in French courts is a good example of the challenges faced by nineteenth-century social scientists. Quetelet compared criminal cases with respect to a number of factors hypothesized to influence conviction, including whether the crime had been committed against property or a person and whether the defendant was male or female and was under or over thirty years of age. Such comparisons led him to conclude that well-educated females over the age of thirty were least likely to be convicted (Stigler 1986).

Quetelet's approach met with criticism (Stigler 1986). Baron de Keverberg, who was advising the state on the matter, argued that data had to be separated into every possible category of characteristics that might be related to the outcome of interest. Not doing so would mean comparing groups that were otherwise not equivalent and perhaps drawing unwarranted conclusions. The economist Jean-Baptiste Say likewise argued that averaging measurements across people resulted in a meaningless jumble of disparate factors (Gigerenzer et al. 1989). In medicine, physicians argued that averages were useless because each patient was unique and each disease was specific to an individual (Gigerenzer et al. 1989). Perhaps for this reason, "As late as 1950, most physicians still thought of statistics as a public health domain largely concerned with records of death and sickness" (Marks 1997).

The German physicist and philosopher Gustav Fechner felt that his method of testing his theory of psychophysics (the science concerned with quantitative relations between sensations and the stimuli producing them) provided him with the theoretical justification for averaging observations that the social sciences had hitherto lacked (Stigler 1999). Specifically, Fechner developed the psychological measure known as the "just noticeable difference," which is the smallest observable difference between two stimuli. To measure the just noticeable difference between two weights, for example, Fechner had subjects pick up pairs of weights more and less similar in weight and observed the proportion of the time they correctly identified the heavier weight in each pair. For differences smaller than the just noticeable difference, they would be forced to guess, in which case they would correctly identify the heavier weight only half the time. Fechner's theory provided an objective, theoretically derived constant, .5, to which he could compare the proportion of times the heavier weight was correctly identified. Even more important for the present purpose, Fechner could manipulate environmental conditions such as the amount of weight that was lifted.

Although experimentation provided the phenomena to be measured, the deterministic view led researchers to believe that probability-based statistical inference was unnecessary. In other words, the experimental method was considered at odds with the use of statistical inference. Because uncertainty was thought to be due to measurement error, researchers focused on removing that uncertainty by increasing the quality and rigor of their studies. The physiologist Emil du Bois-Raymond thought that natural processes are constant over time and across individuals and therefore can be measured adequately by observing a small number of subjects in a well-designed, well-run study (Coleman 1987). The psychologist Wilhelm Wundt similarly argued that all individuals responded to psychological stimuli in the same way, justifying the study of the effects of a stimulus in a mere handful of subjects (Danziger 1987).

Nonexperimental Statistical Approaches

> Do slums make slum people or do slum people make the slums? Will changing the living conditions significantly change the social behavior of the people affected?
>
> —A. S. Stephan (quoted in Rossi and Freeman 1993, 12)

> The method of least squares is the automobile of modern statistical analysis: despite its limitations, occasional accidents, and incidental pollution, this method and its numerous variations, extensions, and related conveyances carry the bulk of statistical analyses, and are known and valued by nearly all.
>
> —Stephen M. Stigler (1999, 320)

As innovative as Fechner's method was, its utility did not immediately benefit social scientific fields, in which environmental conditions could not be manipulated as readily as in psychophysics (although economists have recently found ways to manipulate conditions in classroom settings to test basic economic theories; see Smith 1994). For example, Quetelet, in his investigations of who would be convicted of criminal behavior, could measure conviction rates for different groups, but he could not manipulate the judicial system to test his hypotheses about the factors that affected conviction rates.

What were the scientific and political changes that fostered the use of statistical inference in the social sciences? An important breakthrough for social scientists came in the 1890s with G. Udny Yule's theoretical reinterpretation of least squares, a method that the French mathematician Adrien-Marie Legendre had introduced to find the average of a series of observations that differed because of measurement error (Stigler 1986).[2] The technique was named "least squares" because it minimizes the sum of the squared deviations between the observed data and the estimated mean. Building on several decades of research by social scientists and statisticians, Yule realized that the method could also be used to estimate the parameters of a linear relationship among any number of factors. Further, he argued that the multivariate linear relationship provided a means of investigating how one factor varied with a second factor, with all other factors held constant. In this new framework, least squares provided social scientists with three essential ingredients of statistical inference: parameters that could be subjected to estimation and statistical inference (the parameters resulting from least squares), a way to adjust for all other observed differences across individuals (including them in the least-squares regression), and a technology for estimating a multivariate relationship (the least-squares method itself).

To appreciate the implications of these developments, imagine that it is 1900 and you are investigating the link between neighborhoods' economic prosperity and rates of juvenile crime. On the basis of your discovery that children in low-poverty neighborhoods commit fewer crimes than other children, you conclude that a family's living in a high-poverty neighborhood makes the children in that family more likely to commit crimes. Your critics object that families and children in the two types of neighborhoods may differ in other respects as well. For instance, the average family in low-poverty neighborhoods might be better educated or have different attitudes about criminal activity than the average family in high-poverty neighborhoods, which might affect children's chances of getting into trouble with the law. A decade earlier, your critics probably would have insisted, as did Baron de Keverberg, that you separate the data into every possible combination of characteristics that might be related to juvenile crime and show that only the type of neighborhood can explain the difference in crime rates. But thanks to Yule, you can now perform a multivariate regression analysis using as the dependent variable the likelihood that a particular child has committed a crime, and as the explanatory variables factors thought to affect juvenile crime such as whether the family lives in a high-poverty neighborhood, the family's income, the parents' education level, and the child's age. The estimated coefficient for the factor specifying whether a family lives in a high-poverty neighborhood gives you an estimate of the effect of the type of neighborhood on juvenile crime, independent of the other characteristics included in the regression.

In parallel with the advances in statistical theory sketched here, the shift toward statistical inference gained impetus when university researchers in medicine began calling for systematic scientific review of medical interventions such as drugs. The prevalent belief at the time that physicians could tell helpful drugs from harmful ones solely on the basis of their own observation and intuition allowed drug manufacturers to aggressively market products that had not been clinically proven (Marks 1997). Unfortunately, the rigorous assessment of drugs was not the norm in 1938, when 106 people died because a drug manufacturer unwittingly used a known toxin to buffer a new medicine. Although the U.S. Food and Drug Administration (FDA) was granted the authority to regulate drugs for effectiveness and safety in 1938, it still was unclear how benefits and hazards were to be measured. For example, when the FDA was considering whether to approve sulfapyridine as a treatment for pneumonia, although it knew there was evidence of negative side effects as well as benefits, it had no rigorous information on the size of either. The need for more—and more rigorous—evidence fueled the use of statistical inference.

In social policy as in medicine, the use of statistical inference grew with the need to make decisions about government policy. Because the social programs created as part of the New Deal of the 1930s were never evaluated, their descendants in the War on Poverty of the 1960s were designed without hard evidence about the earlier programs' effectiveness (Rossi and Williams 1972). The legislation that launched the War on Poverty mandated and funded evaluations of the policies it established. Thus, evaluation research took off during the twentieth century at least partly because, as publicly financed programs expanded, the government demanded more and better information as to whether it was investing its billions of dollars wisely.

Despite these theoretical advances and the desire for more rigorous evidence, social researchers soon came to realize that the effects of an intervention—estimated by comparing the differences in outcomes between two or more groups—reflect the influence not only of the intervention under study but also of other factors that could affect group membership. Failure to take account of these other factors in the statistical model leaves impact estimates at risk of deviating from true impacts because of selection bias—systematic differences between the groups in the study other than that arising from the intervention. A controversial analysis of the effects of parental alcoholism on children conducted by Karl Pearson in 1910 illustrates the problem. On the basis of his finding that, on average, children of alcoholic parents had about the same levels of intelligence and health as other children, Pearson concluded that parental alcoholism does not harm children (Stigler 1999). In support of this conclusion, he argued that the alcoholic and nonalcoholic parents in his analysis were comparable because the two groups' average hourly wages were similar. But prominent economists of the day challenged Pearson's study, arguing that the two groups probably differed in other ways that could not be ruled out. To them, the fact that the two groups earned the same average amount suggested that the alcoholic parents actually had higher average ability that had been suppressed by alcoholism, or else they would not have been able to "keep up" with the nonalcoholic parents. Because Pearson's critics believed that ability was partially inherited, they concluded that the children of alcoholic parents in the study probably would have performed at a higher level but for their parents' alcoholism.

Over time, researchers developed increasingly sophisticated methods to reduce selection bias. In social policy, most of these methods involve comparing a group that is exposed to the treatment under study, referred to in this book as the program group (it is sometimes called the experimental group or the treatment group), with a comparison group that is not. The simplest approach to reducing selection bias relies on multivariate regression methods to control for as many observed differences between the program group and the comparison group as possible. No matter how many such factors are included, however, this strategy is not likely by itself to overcome selection bias arising from unobserved factors.

An alternative approach to reducing selection bias focuses on choosing a comparison group that matches the program group with respect to as many observed characteristics as possible. If two groups have the same education, income, and employment history, it is hoped, they might also have the same motivation, attitudes, and other attributes that are difficult to measure. For example, to understand the effects of housing conditions on a range of outcomes, one study compared three hundred families that were placed in improved public housing with three hundred families with similar social and demographic characteristics that were chosen from a waiting list (Wilner et al. 1962, as described in Gilbert, Light, and Mosteller 1975).

Special cases of this method use comparison groups composed of people who applied for a program but subsequently withdrew (withdrawals), were accepted into a program but did not participate in it (noshows), or were screened out of a program for failing to meet eligibility criteria (screen-outs). Unfortunately, the strategy of choosing a comparison group on the basis of observed characteristics stumbles on the same problem as multivariate regression: Groups that are similar with respect to observed characteristics might be dissimilar with respect to unobserved characteristics that could influence both whether the treatment is received and subsequent outcomes.

Another method of reducing selection bias relies on comparing the program group to itself at two or more points in time. For example, medical researchers first realized that insulin might be the key to fighting diabetes by observing dramatic improvements in the health of diabetics who took insulin (Marks 1997). Similarly, evaluators have sometimes measured the effects of job training services by examining changes in trainees' earnings over time. Michael E. Borus (1964) used this method to study a 1960s federal program that trained workers who had lost their jobs because of technological change. Comparing the program group with itself holds constant all unobserved characteristics that do not change over time, but it opens the door to other biases. For example, William Shadish, Thomas D. Cook, and Donald T. Campbell (2002) pointed to potential biases from maturation and history. Maturation bias arises when outcomes would gradually change even without intervention, such as when ill people either get better or die. History bias arises when other policy or societal changes occur during the period of observation. For example, the economic growth of the 1990s made it difficult to estimate the effects of the federal welfare reform legislation passed in 1996.

Rather than focusing on how to select or construct a comparison group, some researchers devised statistical means to control for differences in unobserved characteristics between the program and comparison groups that give rise to selection bias (Barnow, Cain, and Goldberger 1980). Given some assumptions, this bias can be eliminated if the researcher has all relevant information regarding how a person was selected to receive a treatment (Cain 1975). Suppose, for example, that applicants to an employment training program are accepted solely on the basis of their earnings in the prior month. Although applicants with earnings just above the threshold receive no training from the program and applicants with earnings just below the threshold are accepted into the program, they should otherwise be quite similar. If the below-threshold applicants have very different earnings after they go through the program than the above-threshold applicants, it is plausible to conclude that the program affected earnings. This approach, first proposed by Donald L. Thistlewaite and Donald T. Campbell (1960), is sometimes called regression discontinuity. Unfortunately, participation in many programs is determined by factors that cannot be observed by researchers.

Selection bias can also be eliminated through the use of statistical assumptions about how observed and unobserved factors affect which treatment a person receives. The method is robust, however, only if a factor that is related to the selection of treatment but not to unobserved determinants of the outcome is identified, which can be very difficult.[3]

Despite their ingenuity, these efforts to overcome selection bias in studies of training, housing assistance, education, youth programs, and health care have met with considerable skepticism because even in the largest studies with the most sophisticated designs, different evaluators have come to different conclusions depending on the comparison groups and statistical methods selected (Barnow 1987; Kennedy 1988; Gilbert, Light, and Mosteller 1975; McDill, McDill, and Sprehe 1972; Glenman 1972). The essential problem is that selection bias can arise from variation in unobserved characteristics, making the bias difficult to detect and eliminate.

Random Assignment

> Let us take out of the Hospitals, out of the Camps, or from elsewhere 200, or 500, poor People, that have Fevers, Pleurisies, etc. Let us divide them in halfes, let us cast lots, that one halfe of them may fall to my share, and the other to yours; . . . we shall see how many Funerals both of us shall have.
>
> —John Baptista van Helmont (1662)

> Random assignment designs are a bit like the nectar of the gods; once you've had a taste of the pure stuff it is hard to settle for the flawed alternatives.
>
> —Robinson G. Hollister and Jennifer Hill (1995, 134)

There is one method that, when well implemented, is guaranteed to eliminate selection bias: random assignment of individuals or groups to treatments. In a typical experiment, half the study members are randomly assigned to the program group, and the other half are randomly assigned to the control group, a term reserved for the special case in which membership in the comparison group is randomly determined. Because random assignment ensures that unobserved factors such as motivation and ability are distributed about equally in the two groups, any differences that later emerge between them can be confidently attributed to differences in the groups to which they were assigned rather than to preexisting differences.

Widespread use of random assignment is relatively new in social policy research, but the idea has been around for much longer. The quotation at the beginning of this section shows that an understanding of the logic behind randomization—if not sensitivity to the rights of the sick and the poor—dates back at least to the seventeenth century. In an early application of the method, Charles S. Peirce and Joseph Jastrow (1884/1980) drew playing cards to determine the order of stimulus presentation in a study of Fechner's just noticeable difference.

Much of the foundation of the modern use of random assignment, however, can be traced back to Ronald A. Fisher's work in the early twentieth century. On becoming chief statistician at Rothamsted Experimental Station in England in 1919, Fisher found that data on crop yields had been collected for more than sixty years at the station but had not been rigorously analyzed (Gigerenzer et al. 1989). The Rothamsted researchers faced two problems discussed in the previous section: They did not know how to separate the effects of fertilizers from the effects of other factors influencing crop production, and they did not know how to assess the likelihood that fertilizers made a difference because crop yields varied even when the same fertilizer was used. Fisher realized that random assignment provided a way to deal with both problems. By randomly choosing which fields would receive fertilizers, he was able to convincingly argue that systematic differences in crop production between fertilized and unfertilized fields were due to the fertilizer. By repeating random assignment across many fields, he was able to compare the variation in crop production within each group (the unfertilized fields and the fertilized fields) to the difference in production between the two groups and assess the likelihood that the difference between groups was due to random variation—and, by extension, the likelihood that the choice of fertilizer made a real difference in production. Fisher (1925) helped other researchers understand how to use random assignment by providing them with information on how to implement random-assignment studies and how to conduct formal statistical inference with respect to their results.

Random assignment rules out alternative explanations for observed results so effectively that it is often called the "gold standard" in evaluation research, but this was not understood when Fisher first developed the method and began to promote it to his colleagues in agricultural research. Indeed, it was not until well after World War II that use of the approach became widespread in medical research (Marks 1997), and several more decades were to pass before random assignment would be used with any frequency in social policy research.

By one estimate, more than 350,000 randomized experiments have been conducted in medical science over the last fifty years (Cochrane Collaboration 2002). According to *The Digest of Social Experiments*, more than 800,000 people were randomly assigned in two hundred twenty studies of new or existing social policies between 1962 and 1997 (Greenberg and Shroder 1997). A number of other studies have involved the random assignment of larger entities, such as schools or municipalities (Boruch and Foley 2000). And within the last three years, the Administration for Children and Families within the U.S. Department of Health and Human Services alone has launched a number of major projects encompassing several dozen random-assignment studies to investigate the effects of policies designed to affect the employment, family structure, child-care choices, and marital relationships of low-income people.

The following are a few of the many social policy areas in which experimental studies have been performed:

Child health, nutrition, and education. In 1997, the government of Mexico launched a major experiment to measure the effects of substantial payments designed to encourage poor rural parents to send their children to school more regularly and over a longer period and to improve their children's health care and nutrition (Teruel and Davis 2000). This experiment randomized 320 rural communities to the program group and 186 rural communities to the control group.

Crime and juvenile delinquency. Random-assignment studies have been used extensively to study policies aimed at reducing juvenile delinquency and crime (Lipsey 1988; Sherman 1988). One of the most successful and oft-cited studies tested a policy of requiring alleged assailants in domestic assault cases to spend a night in jail.

Early child development. Random assignment has been used to study interventions to help children. For example, a number of experiments have investigated the effects of improvements in day care (Schweinhart and Weikart 1993; Ramey, Yeates, and Short 1984; Love et al. 2002) and of Head Start (Bell et al. 2003).

Education. Until the U.S. Department of Education made the use of random assignment a priority in evaluating new education approaches (Coalition for Evidence-Based Policy 2003), experimental designs were used only infrequently in education research. Earlier applications tested the effects of vouchers allowing low-income children to attend private schools (Mayer et al. 2002); of a high school reform in which students' learning is organized around a career theme (Kemple and Snipes 2000); and of smaller class sizes at the elementary school level (Mosteller, Light, and Sachs 1996).

Electricity pricing. Faced with increasing demand and limited supply, electricity policy analysts in the 1970s recommended making electricity more expensive during peak periods to induce consumers to shift their electricity use to off-peak periods. This approach, called "time-of-use pricing," was studied in a series of randomized experiments (Aigner 1985).

Health services. To investigate the link between health-care copayments and use of health-care services, one experiment randomly assigned different people to pay different proportions of their health-care expenditures (Newhouse 1996; Orr 1999). Random assignment has also been used to study the efficacy of mental health treatments (Ciarlo and Windle 1988).

Housing assistance. In the 1970s, the effects of direct cash low-income housing assistance in Pittsburgh and Phoenix were examined in a randomized experiment (Kennedy 1988). More recently, the U.S. Department of Housing and Urban Development launched an experiment investigating the effects of housing vouchers that require users to move to low-poverty neighborhoods (Goering et al. 1999; Orr et al. 2003).

Income maintenance. Among the earliest studies in the social sciences to use random assignment were the negative income tax experiments conducted in the 1960s and 1970s in Denver, Seattle, New Jersey, and Gary, Indiana. In these studies, different families were randomly assigned to different levels of income that would be guaranteed if the family had no other sources of income and to different "tax rates" that determined how much of the guaranteed level would be lost when the family's income from other sources increased (Munnell 1987).

Job training. A recent meta-analysis of voluntary education and training programs for low-skill adult workers and adolescents cites ten studies that used random assignment, most of them conducted after 1983 (for a list, see Greenberg, Michalopoulos, and Robins 2003). One of the best-known recent studies is a large-scale multisite experiment that measured the impacts of a national program to provide job training in a residential setting to adolescents and young adults at risk of economic failure and criminal behavior (Burghardt et al. 2001).

Unemployment insurance. Because many unemployed workers return to work only after their unemployment insurance benefits have been used up, random assignment has been used to explore the effects of financial incentives to return to work (Bloom et al. 1999; Woodbury and Spiegelman 1987; Spiegelman, O'Leary, and Kline 1992).

Welfare-to-work programs. Since 1980, dozens of experiments have been conducted to test programs designed to help welfare recipients move into employment (Gueron and Pauly 1991; Greenberg and Wiseman 1992; Bloom and Michalopoulos 2001).

As already discussed, random assignment has become more common in social policy research partly because nonexperimental statistical methods do not eliminate selection bias convincingly and do not provide widely persuasive estimates of policy effects. Another reason is that the sophisticated methods devised by statisticians and econometricians to reduce selection bias are often difficult for policy practitioners to understand—and easy for critics to challenge.

The logic of random assignment, in contrast, is straightforward to grasp and explain. At its most basic, a random-assignment analysis involves making simple comparisons between the average outcomes for the program group and the average outcomes for the control group. The simplicity and rigor of randomized experimentation have made it influential in policymaking. For example, experimental studies of welfare-to-work programs in the 1980s have been credited with influencing the debate that led to the Family Support Act of 1988 (Greenberg and Wiseman 1992), which paved the way for the landmark federal welfare reforms of 1996.

Learning More from Randomized Experiments

Despite its considerable strengths, random assignment of individuals or groups to treatments cannot answer all the important questions about what works best for whom and why.[4] For this reason, researchers have devised creative ways to combine experimental data with nonexperimental statistical methods. By doing so, they can capitalize on the strengths of each approach to mitigate the weaknesses of the other. The central premise of this book is that combining experimental and nonexperimental statistical methods is the most promising way to accumulate knowledge that can inform efforts to improve social interventions. This idea, articulated three decades ago by Robert F. Boruch (1975), is only now beginning to gain greater recognition.

Opening the Black Box

In some cases, random assignment is too blunt an instrument to be used to test theories about what makes a program effective. Budget limitations can also preclude the use of random assignment to compare different versions of a program model. Furthermore, randomized experiments are usually unable to disentangle the contributions of specific program components to the program's overall effects. In other words, they often do not reveal what happens inside the "black box" where their effects unfold. Figure 1.1 displays a model of the black box, which focuses on how program implementation, program participation, and intermediate impacts lead to the ultimate impacts of an intervention.

"Program implementation" represents the components of the program and the way in which they are carried out. For example, a mandatory welfare-to-work program might include features such as financial assistance for education and certain required activities, and might sanction those who do not engage in them. More generally, the effectiveness of any program depends on whether staff are enthusiastic about it, whether potential participants know about and understand it, and the management practices of the people running it.

A program's overall effects will depend on "program participation": how many people participate in it and how intensively they do so. For example, in a study of an antihypertensive drug, the drug's effects can be expected to increase as the percentage of patients who comply with the prescribed treatment increases. To help families earn more, a welfare-to-work program must engage parents in job search activities.

Figure 1.1   How Programs Create Impacts

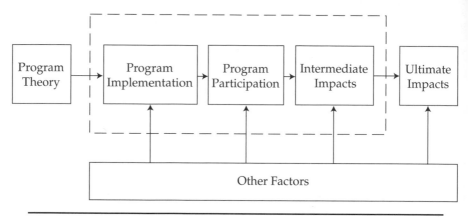

Source: Author's compilation.

Housing vouchers change the lives of more families both as the pro-portion of families using the vouchers increases and as the length of time that vouchers are used increases.

Participation in a program can have a variety of impacts on interme-diate outcomes. For example, an antihypertensive drug should lower blood pressure. A welfare-to-work program should increase employ-ment and reduce welfare use. A housing voucher program might bene-fit families not only by helping them move to lower-poverty neigh-borhoods per se but by bringing their children into closer contact with middle-class peers, who might be less likely to commit crimes, engage in premarital sex, and use illegal drugs.

Finally, program impacts on intermediate outcomes can lead to a range of impacts on ultimate outcomes. For example, the ultimate goal of antihypertensive medication is to help people live longer, healthier lives. Most welfare programs aim to improve the economic well-being of families and children. The ultimate objective of a housing voucher program might be to help families move into the middle class and to reap the financial and nonfinancial benefits associated with that status. In many cases, the distinction between intermediate and ultimate out-comes is not cut-and-dried. For example, increasing employment and reducing welfare use might be the ultimate objective of a policymaker rather than an intermediate objective. In other words, it might be viewed as an end in itself rather than a means to some other end.

Random assignment studies are typically designed to reveal whether a treatment affects intermediate and ultimate outcomes, not to eluci-date the role of implementation and program participation or the link between intermediate and ultimate outcomes. So how can going beyond random assignment using nonexperimental statistical methods help researchers open the black box of experiments to explore these issues?

Measuring Implementation Effects

One important question that randomized experiments have difficulty addressing directly is how various components of a program contribute to its effects. For example, if a three-component program reduces teen pregnancy rates, how can one infer whether and to what extent each component contributed to the program's overall success? To answer such questions, evaluators often turn to research synthesis, which is an attempt to draw lessons by looking across studies. A frequently applied example of this approach, narrative synthesis, entails qualitatively comparing results across sites or studies. For example, the final report in the six-county evaluation of a California welfare-to-work program called Greater Avenues to Independence (GAIN) found the largest effects in Riverside County. In their effort to synthesize results from the six counties and understand how Riverside differed from the other counties, the authors looked at how more than a dozen site characteristics were correlated with the variation in program impacts across sites. The evidence suggested that the Riverside program's strong emphasis on getting participants into employment set it apart from the others (Riccio, Friedlander, and Freedman 1994).

Narrative synthesis often leads to several possible conclusions. The National Evaluation of Welfare-to-Work Strategies (NEWWS) used random assignment to study the effects of eleven programs in seven sites, including Portland, Oregon, where the program was outstandingly effective. Evaluators were left to wonder why Portland's effects stand out. Was this attributable to the program's services, the message conveyed by its staff that participants should accept only "good" jobs, the strong local economy, exemptions given to welfare recipients who staff thought would not benefit from the program, its vigorous efforts to connect welfare recipients with specific employers, or something else (Hamilton et al. 2001)? Although both GAIN and NEWWS are excellent examples of the use of random assignment, the experimental design could take the researchers only so far in understanding why the policies under study were more or less effective.

These examples illustrate that simple experiments have a limited ability to separate policy from practice. More complex designs can help. The most common approach is to randomly assign entities to two or more interventions. In the evaluations of the Minnesota Family Investment Program (MFIP) and Canada's Self-Sufficiency Project (SSP), for example, families were assigned at random to three groups: a group that received financial incentives to work, a group that received job search assistance as well as the financial incentives, and a control group (Miller et al. 2000; Michalopoulos et al. 2002). The design was especially useful in MFIP. In that study, incentives alone did not increase employment, but they increased family income because financial payments were made to families that would have worked in the absence of the incentive. In addition, children in the incentives-only group were better off after three years than were children in the control group, providing evidence that increasing family income would help children.

Although three-group random-assignment designs are useful, they provide information on only two policy components. Early social experiments were much more ambitious (Greenberg and Robins 1986). For example, the negative income tax experiments of the 1970s assigned families to fifty-eight different combinations of tax rates and guarantee levels to study how people respond to changes in those policy parameters (Munnell 1987; Greenberg and Robins 1986). Similarly, the direct cash low-income housing assistance experiment randomly assigned people to receive housing subsidies equal to 0, 30, 40, 50, or 60 percent of their rent to understand how strongly people responded to different subsidy rates (Kennedy 1988). Finally, a health-care copayment experiment randomly assigned people to pay 0, 25, 50, or 95 percent of their health-care expenditures up to an annual maximum of $1,000 to allow researchers to extrapolate to other subsidy rates (Newhouse 1996). Exploiting such variation to extrapolate from experimental results to other types of policies was one of the original motivations behind using random assignment (Heckman 1992). But testing many policies at once also has a drawback: Testing more variants of a program with a given sample results in less precise estimates of the effects of any one variation because fewer people are assigned to each variation.

In the absence of random assignment to many different treatments, meta-analysis, another form of research synthesis, can be used to explore why some programs are more effective than others. Meta-analysis is a statistical technique for synthesizing quantitative results. For example, researchers in the United Kingdom conducted a meta-analysis of twenty-four random-assignment evaluations of mandatory welfare-to-work programs in the United States and concluded that job search is associated with larger effects on earnings and welfare receipt, that vocational training is associated with smaller effects on earnings and welfare receipt, and that programs with more white recipients have larger effects than other programs (Ashworth et al. 2001).[5] Obtaining statistically precise estimates of the determinants of program effects using meta-analysis, however, requires dozens of policy experiments (Greenberg et al. 2003).

A third type of research synthesis uses multilevel statistical modeling (which accounts for the grouping of individuals in aggregate units) to explore how the natural variation in program effects across sites in a single experiment or across experiments in a set of studies co-varies with features of the program, its participants, and its environment. This approach is illustrated by Howard Bloom, Carolyn Hill, and James Riccio in chapter 2 of the present volume, "Modeling Cross-Site Experimental Differences to Find Out Why Program Effectiveness Varies." Their analysis focuses on how the earnings effects of welfare-to-work programs vary with respect to how the programs were implemented, the specific services they provided, the characteristics of their participants, and local labor market conditions. This analysis was made possible by the fact that comparable data had been collected for three large-scale multisite randomized evaluations of welfare-to-work programs: the National Evaluation of Welfare to Work Strategies (NEWWS), the California GAIN program described earlier, plus Florida's welfare-to-work program Project Independence (Kemple and Haimson 1994).

Future random-assignment studies could likewise be set up to learn more about how programs achieve their effects. For example, a recently completed study of a vaccine to prevent infection with HIV (human immunodeficiency virus) that randomly assigned people in fifty-nine locations in the United States, Canada, and the Netherlands found that the vaccine worked better for African American and Hispanic sample members than for white sample members (Pollack and Altman 2003). If procedures varied from site to site, the variation could be used to help understand why the vaccine worked better for some people than for others. In fact, procedures in different sites in an experiment could be varied intentionally to assess the effects of different procedures. Even if an experiment is not conducted in dozens of sites, collecting information about each site might help future researchers investigate the role of program practices and inputs. For example, the GAIN, Project Independence, and NEWWS evaluations were not conducted at the same time, but they were conducted by a single research organization that collected comparable data across studies.

Assessing the Role of Participation

Randomized experiments are designed to measure the average effect of a treatment among all the people who are randomly assigned to it, but it is sometimes of interest to estimate the effect among those who actually receive the treatment. Consider a random-assignment study of a new vaccine that is otherwise unavailable. The effect of the intervention among all people who are assigned to receive the vaccine might represent the expected effect of introducing the vaccine in a real-world situation in which some patients do not comply with their treatment. The effect among people who actually receive the vaccine provides an estimate of the effect of the vaccine on compliant patients.

In many cases, an intervention is unlikely to have an effect on people who are not exposed to it. For example, a vaccine against a noncommunicable disease cannot benefit someone who does not receive it. In such cases, the effect among people who receive the treatment can be calculated by dividing the overall average effect by the proportion of program group members who actually received the treatment (Bloom 1984). Suppose the average effect of a welfare-to-work program on earnings is $500 per year, including participants and nonparticipants. If only half of program group members actually participate in the program, then the average effect on earnings per participant is twice as high since they generated the entire effect. The effect of a treatment on those who receive it, sometimes referred to as the effect of the treatment on the treated, is discussed in chapter 3.

It is even possible for an intervention to have effects on people who do not participate. For example, a requirement that welfare recipients attend a job club or face sanctions might increase employment even among people who do not attend the job club if the threat of sanctions encourages them to look for work on their own or to take a job they have already been offered. When an intervention might have effects among those who are assigned to the treatment but do not receive it, determining the effect of treatment on the treated or the effect of treatment assignment on those who do not receive the treatment is not straightforward. If the effect on each of the two groups is roughly constant across individuals within them, however, then the effect for each group can be derived (Peck 2002).

Exploring Causal Pathways

Increasing program participation is rarely the ultimate goal of a treatment, but understanding the link between program participation and other outcomes can inform practitioners' efforts to implement a treatment and policymakers' efforts to design a policy. Likewise, knowing how different outcomes are related to one another, especially whether changing one outcome is likely to cause changes in other outcomes, can help shed light on the question of which intermediate outcomes or mediators should be the target of future treatments and policies.

For example, mediators can help explain the effects on children of programs targeted at parents. To take one recent example, studies of policies that increase family income have been found to benefit school-age children (Morris et al. 2001; Clark-Kauffman, Duncan, and Morris 2003). Higher income might allow parents to purchase goods and services that directly help their children, such as more nutritious food or higher-quality child care. Programs that increase income typically have many effects, among them increasing parents' earnings and hours of work. Extra income might also affect parenting by reducing stress or influencing the likelihood that the parent will marry, which under certain conditions might help their children. Understanding whether extra income per se benefits children—and if so, how much each dollar of income helps—could help policymakers decide whether investments in programs such as the federal Earned Income Tax Credit are worthwhile or whether money should be spent on other objectives, such as improving the quality of child care used by low-income families.

Nonexperimental researchers have developed statistical methods to investigate the role of mediators. An approach that has generated much recent interest is instrumental variables analysis (Angrist and Krueger 2001). A researcher who wants to understand the effects of income on children's well-being could compare the children of wealthier and poorer families, but the comparison would probably be plagued by selection bias: wealthier families might have parents with more extensive social networks or higher levels of motivation, both of which might benefit children independent of income. To explore the relationship between income and children's well-being more rigorously, the researcher could find an instrumental variable, which in this example would be a factor that is correlated with both income and children's well-being but is not correlated with unobserved factors that also might affect these two variables (such as motivation and intelligence). The researcher would then explore the effects of income on children's well-being by comparing outcomes for children whose families have different values of the instrumental variable.

The biggest obstacle to using instrumental variables is finding an instrument. Myriad factors affect not only family income but also most other outcomes of interest. Random assignment, however, can provide the needed instrument. Because assignment to the program and control groups is random, it is not related to parents' intelligence, the extensiveness of their social network, or their motivation. Indeed, it is uncorrelated with every characteristic that exists before or at the time of random assignment.

Instrumental variables analyses of the effects of mediators require at least one instrument for each hypothesized intermediate outcome. In the study of housing vouchers mentioned in the introduction to this chapter (Ludwig, Hirschfield, and Duncan 2001), two intermediate outcomes were assumed to be important: whether the family moved at all and whether the family moved to a lower-poverty neighborhood. The random assignment of families to two program groups provided the two instruments needed. Families given unconditional vouchers were more likely to move out of public housing but were not more likely to move to lower-poverty neighborhoods than did control group families. Comparing the rate of juvenile crime in these two groups therefore indicated how much moving reduced juvenile crime. Families given conditional vouchers, in contrast, were not only more likely to move out of public housing but moved to lower-poverty neighborhoods than did control group families, providing a means of determining how much moving to lower-poverty neighborhoods reduced juvenile crime. Thus, the instrumental variables technique provided the method for calculating the effects of a key mediator.

The link between welfare-to-work programs and children's well-being might be affected by many mediators, and it is unlikely that one evaluation would include enough program groups to provide such a large number of instruments. However, the necessary instruments might be obtained by using data from a number of random-assignment studies. Different studies will have larger or smaller effects on income, employment, hours of work, and other mediators. An instrumental variables analysis essentially compares the variation in the programs' effects on the mediators with the variation in the programs' effects on children's well-being to infer the effects of the mediators on children's well-being.

Although instrumental variables techniques can be extremely useful when combined with random assignment, they do require making some assumptions. One assumption is that if data are pooled across studies to achieve the needed number of instruments, the effects of the mediators on the ultimate outcomes must be the same from place to place. For example, an extra dollar of income and an extra hour of work would have to have the same effect on children in California as it does in Minnesota.

Chapter 3 of the present volume ("Constructing Instrumental Variables from Experimental Data to Explore How Treatments Produce Effects," by Lisa Gennetian, Pamela Morris, Johannes Bos, and Howard Bloom) examines the use of instrumental variables with random assignment experiments to explore the causal paths (linkages among mediating variables) by which programs produce their impacts. The authors describe how the approach works, outline the assumptions that are necessary for it to do so, and illustrate its application to numerous real-world examples. They also consider how to make the approach operational given the realities of how randomized experiments are conducted.

Studying Place-Based Interventions

Most experiments randomly assign individuals to program and control groups because they seek to study the effects of programs on the outcomes and behavior of individuals, couples, or families. There are circumstances, however, in which random assignment of larger entities such as child-care providers, firms, schools, housing developments, or entire communities might be more appropriate. The aforementioned experiment that randomized whole communities in Mexico (Teruel and Davis 2000) is an example of a place-based intervention. Sometimes called group randomization, this method is referred to in this book as cluster randomization or cluster random assignment.

Cluster randomization is appropriate where an intervention is meaningful only at the level of a larger entity or when it is impractical or unacceptable to assign individuals randomly to different treatments. For example, an experimental study of a program that trains child-care providers to teach preschool children who are receiving child-care subsidies to read should probably conduct random assignment at the level of providers rather than individual children. Randomly assigning children within a classroom to the treatment or a control group would be logistically infeasible because control-group children in classrooms with a trained provider could not be prevented from benefiting from the provider's training. And randomly assigning children to a trained provider or an untrained provider might be politically infeasible because it would restrict their families' child-care choices, violating federal regulations governing child-care subsidies. For similar reasons, the effects of public-service advertisements designed to discourage smoking have been studied by randomly assigning everyone who might come across the same advertisements to the same group (Boruch and Foley 2000). If television advertising were being used, an entire viewing area would be randomly assigned to receive the advertising or not to receive it.

Cluster random assignment has also been recommended in cases where outcomes for people exposed to an intervention have the potential to "spill over" and affect outcomes for other people (Harris 1985; Boruch and Foley 2000; Garfinkel, Manski, and Michalopoulos 1992). Vaccinating some children against a communicable disease might protect unvaccinated children from the disease as well. A study that randomly assigned individual children in the same community to receive or not to receive the vaccine would underestimate the vaccine's effects if vaccinating children in the program group indeed lessened the chance that children in the control group would contract the disease. Similarly, a large-scale training program might help trainees find better jobs, but it might also displace others who would have taken those jobs. If the displaced workers are members of the control group in a random-assignment study, the program's estimated effects will exceed its true effects.[6] Finally, a study that randomly assigns welfare recipients to a pilot welfare program or a control group might underestimate the program's effects because the amount of word-of-mouth communication and public discussion about the program, which could influence current and potential recipients' behavior, would probably be lower than if the program were implemented at full scale as welfare policy. In each of these examples, measuring the full effects of an intervention requires randomly assigning larger communities, not individuals, to the program or a control group.

In certain contexts, cluster randomization is not only theoretically sound but also practical, as demonstrated by its application in many studies (for a review of such applications, see Boruch and Foley 2000). Among the interventions that have been studied using cluster random assignment are programs to reduce drug and alcohol use among high school students, public health campaigns, crime prevention initiatives, and new hospital procedures. The most commonly randomized entities have been schools or classrooms, but random assignment has also been conducted among industrial organizations, adult literacy centers, Goodwill service providers, hospitals, police patrol areas, and entire communities. This record of successful application casts doubt on arguments that experiments cannot be conducted on aggregate entities. Chapter 4 of the present volume ("Randomizing Groups to Evaluate Place-Based Programs," by Howard Bloom) presents a detailed discussion of this approach. The chapter outlines the main reasons for randomizing groups, describes the statistical properties of the approach, considers ways to improve the approach by using background information on the randomized groups and their members, and examines the statistical properties of subgroup findings produced by the approach. The chapter also considers the conceptual, statistical, programmatic, and policy implications of the fact that individuals move in and out of randomized groups over time.

Assessing Nonexperimental Statistical Methods

If many questions can be answered only by going beyond random assignment, it is natural to wonder whether one should start with an experimental design at all. Is the problem of selection bias in nonexperimental studies more theoretical than real? Fortunately, this question can be answered by reviewing research that has compared nonexperimentally derived impact estimates with impact estimates based on well-executed random-assignment studies. Overall, the findings indicate that, even under the most favorable circumstances, nonexperimental statistical methods are often far off the mark.

One group of studies has assessed nonexperimental statistical methods by comparing experimental and nonexperimental impact estimates on the basis of data collected from individuals who were randomly assigned to a treatment or a control group. Much of this research was based on data from the National Supported Work (NSW) Demonstration. Conducted by a consortium of organizations in the mid-1970s at twelve sites across the United States, the NSW study evaluated voluntary training and assisted work programs targeted at four groups of individuals with serious barriers to employment: long-term recipients of Aid to Families with Dependent Children (AFDC), which was the federal cash welfare program until 1996; former drug addicts; former criminal offenders; and young school dropouts. To assess nonexperimental estimators of the program's effects, the results of this randomized experiment have been compared with results obtained by comparing the NSW group's outcomes with the outcomes for comparison groups drawn from two national surveys: the Current Population Survey and the Panel Study of Income Dynamics.

The earliest assessment of nonexperimental estimators using NSW data sounded an alarm, revealing that large biases can arise from using nonexperimental comparison groups (LaLonde 1986; Fraker and Maynard 1987). But the most biased nonexperimental results were later identified and excluded by means of statistical tests used to reject comparison groups whose characteristics differed markedly from those of the program group at baseline (Heckman and Hotz 1989). Another method that produced estimates close to the experimental benchmark (Dehejia and Wahba 1999) is matching, in which differences between the groups at baseline are eliminated by selecting comparison group members similar to program group members with respect to such characteristics as gender, level of education, and employment history. A recent reanalysis, however, indicates that matching worked well only for a specific subsample of the NSW data (Smith and Todd 2005).

Inspired by the early studies of date from NSW, Daniel Friedlander and Philip K. Robins (1995) compared experimentally derived estimates of program effects with nonexperimentally derived estimates using data from random-assignment studies of mandatory state welfare-to-work programs operated in the early to mid-1980s. They examined comparison groups drawn from three sources: earlier cohorts of welfare recipients from the same local welfare offices, welfare recipients from other local offices in the same state, and welfare recipients from other states. The authors found that in-state comparison groups worked better than out-of-state comparison groups, although both were problematic. Furthermore, they found that the statistical tests suggested by James Heckman and V. Joseph Hotz (1989) did not adequately distinguish between good and bad estimators with their data—which later work by Heckman, Ichimura, and Todd (1997, 629) also indicates. A more recent analysis of a mandatory welfare-to-work program in Indiana confirmed that the bias can be quite large, even when the comparison sites have labor market characteristics similar to those in the program sites (Lee 2001).

Another comparison of nonexperimental and experimental results used data from an experimental study of a set of voluntary training and subsidized work programs for recipients of AFDC piloted in seven states in the mid- to late 1980s (Bell et al. 1995). Nonexperimental comparison groups were drawn from withdrawals, screen-outs, or no-shows. The authors found that estimates based on no-shows were the most accurate, those based on screen-outs were the next most accurate, and those based on withdrawals were the least accurate. In addition, the accuracy of estimates based on screen-outs improved over time, from being only slightly better than those for withdrawals at the beginning of the follow-up period to being almost as good as those for no-shows at the end.

The most comprehensive, detailed, and technically sophisticated assessment of nonexperimental estimators to date used a data set constructed for the evaluation of employment and training programs for economically disadvantaged adults and youth funded by the Job Training and Partnership Act (JTPA) of 1982 (Heckman, Ichimura, and Todd 1997, 1998; Heckman et al. 1998). Results from this study underscored the importance of choosing an appropriate comparison group, particularly one from the same local labor market as the program group and one for which comparable measures have been collected. But even the best methods left some amount of bias arising from selection on unobserved factors.

Although limited to a single policy area—namely, employment and training programs—the methodological research that has grown out of these four sets of experiments spans a lengthy period (from the 1970s to the 1990s); many different geographic areas representing different labor market structures; voluntary and mandatory programs, the characteristics of whose participants probably reflect very different selection processes; a wide variety of comparison group sources, including national surveys and past participants in the same program; and a vast array of statistical and econometric methods for estimating program effects using nonexperimental comparison groups (for a formal meta-analysis of the results, see Glazerman, Levy, and Myers 2003).

Two recent studies using a similar approach found that nonexperimental comparisons did not yield results similar to random-assignment evaluations of education programs (Agodini and Dynarski 2001; Wilde and Hollister 2002).

Another approach to comparing experimental and nonexperimental estimates is to use meta-analysis to summarize and contrast findings from a series of both types of studies. Beginning with Mary Lee Smith, Gene V. Glass, and Thomas I. Miller (1980), meta-analyses comparing findings from experimental and nonexperimental studies have had mixed results (Heinsman and Shadish 1996).

Perhaps the most extensive such comparison is a "meta-analysis of meta-analyses" that synthesizes past research on the effectiveness of psychological, behavioral, and education treatments (Lipsey and Wilson 1993). In one part of it, the authors compared the means and standard deviations of experimental and nonexperimental estimates drawn from seventy-four meta-analyses for which findings from both types of studies were available. This comparison, which represented hundreds of primary studies, showed virtually no difference in the mean effect as estimated on the basis of experimental statistical studies, as opposed to nonexperimental. Although some of the meta-analyses reported a large difference between average experimental and nonexperimental estimates, the differences were as likely to be positive as negative, and they canceled out across the seventy-four meta-analyses.

Meta-analytic comparisons of experimental and nonexperimental estimates have also been made for voluntary employment and training programs (Greenberg, Michalopoulos, and Robins 2003, 2004). According to these comparisons, the average impact estimate for men has been substantially larger for experimentally evaluated programs than for other programs, and the difference is statistically significant. This is consistent with the results using the NSW and JTPA evaluations that implied that nonexperimental statistical methods might be subject to substantial selection bias. For women and teens, by contrast, experimental and nonexperimental evaluations of voluntary employment-training programs yielded similar estimated effects. Moreover, the two types of evaluations indicated similar changes in the effectiveness of programs over time for all three groups. It is important not to make too much of these comparisons, however, since they include only six programs. In addition, most of the nonexperimental evaluations were conducted before 1975, but most of the random-assignment studies occurred later. Thus, the two sets of evaluations might not have analyzed comparable treatments.

In chapter 5 of the present volume, "Using Experiments to Assess Nonexperimental Comparison-Group Methods for Measuring Program Effects," Howard Bloom, Charles Michalopoulos, and Carolyn Hill use random-assignment studies of mandatory welfare-to-work programs to assess the utility of a variety of nonexperimental estimators of program impacts, some of which have been examined only in the context of voluntary programs. The chapter addresses the questions of which nonexperimental comparison group methods work best, under what conditions they do so, and under what conditions, if any, the best nonexperimental comparison group methods perform well enough to be used instead of random assignment.

Goal of This Book

Although the next four chapters in this volume deal with very different questions, they have two features in common: a recognition that random assignment provides valid and useful estimates of the effects of social interventions and a belief that more can be learned from experiments by combining them with nonexperimental statistical techniques. By no means a comprehensive survey of ways to integrate experimental and nonexperimental approaches, the book is meant to inspire researchers both to use randomized experiments and to go beyond experiments in their pursuit of answers to important social questions.

Notes

1. For a much more thorough treatment of the history of statistics, see Stephen M. Stigler (1986, 1989), Gerd Gigerenzer et al. (1989), and Lorenz Krüger et al. (1987). A particularly accessible and wide-ranging description of the development of statistical theory and empirical methods can be found in David Salsburg (2001).
2. Stigler's (1986) view is only one of many. As represented by Mary S. Morgan (1990), Theodore Porter (1986), for example, thought the key breakthrough in the social sciences was a philosophical shift toward interpreting individual differences in behavior as natural variation attributable to the complexity of human affairs, which in turn opened the door to the use of techniques such as correlation and regression. J. L. Klein (1986), in contrast, argued that economists began adapting and applying statistical methods used by astronomers and biometricians because it facilitated the modeling of economic time-series phenomena.
3. George S. Maddala (1983) provides a detailed discussion of the assumptions and methods of estimating the model, which is often credited to James J. Heckman (1974). The assumptions have been relaxed in statistical refinements of the model, but even the refinements demand identification of a factor that affects whether someone receives an intervention but does not influence the effect of the intervention.
4. Random assignment too has been criticized (see, for instance, Manski and Garfinkel 1992; Bloom, Cordray, and Light 1988; Hausman and Wise 1985). Among the most potent criticisms are the following: (1) The process of random assignment can affect implementation of the program under study such that the resulting estimates may not reflect the impacts of the actual program but rather of the program when it is under study; (2) being in a study affects people in ways unrelated to the treatment (often called the Hawthorne effect) by, for instance, encouraging program group members to adhere more closely to the treatment than they would if they received the treatment outside the study; (3) the program can affect the surrounding community (for example, through displacement, in which program group members take jobs that would otherwise be held by oth-

ers), causing experimental estimates of the program's impacts to systematically misestimate its true effects; and (4) some individuals do not receive the treatment to which they are randomly assigned, resulting in underestimates of the effect of the treatment. Because these concerns have been addressed in detail elsewhere and are tangential to the themes in this book, they are not discussed further here.

5. In this case, meta-analysis might have led to a misleading result. Analyses of the impacts of random assignment studies of U.S. welfare-to-work programs by subgroup show little systematic evidence that white welfare recipients fare better than black welfare recipients (Michalopoulos and Schwartz 2000; Michalopoulos 2004). This result suggests that neither race nor ethnicity per se is important but that the welfare-to-work programs operating in areas with higher proportions of white recipients happened to be more effective.

6. Although displacement of workers is often considered a potential source of bias in experimental estimates of the effects of employment programs, a number of empirical studies found little evidence for displacement resulting from such programs (Friedberg and Hunt 1995). However, a recent paper argues that displacement might be more problematic in some experiments (Lise, Seitz, and Smith 2004).

References

Agodini, Roberto, and Mark Dynarski. 2001. *Are Experiments the Only Option? A Look at Dropout Prevention Programs.* Princeton, N.J.: Mathematica Policy Research.

Aigner, Dennis J. 1985. "The Residential Time-of-Use Pricing Experiments: What Have We Learned?" In *Social Experimentation*, edited by Jerry A. Hausman and David A. Wise. Chicago: University of Chicago Press.

Angrist, Joshua D., and Alan B. Krueger. 2001. "Instrumental Variables and the Search for Identification: From Supply and Demand to Natural Experiments." *Journal of Economic Perspectives* 50(4): 69–85.

Ashworth, Karl, Andreas Cebulla, David Greenberg, and Robert Walker. 2001. "Meta-Evaluation: Discovering What Works Best in Welfare Provision." Unpublished paper. University of Nottingham, England.

Barnow, Burt S. 1987. "The Impact of CETA Programs on Earnings: A Review of the Literature." *The Journal of Human Resources* 22(Spring): 157–93.

Barnow, Burt S., Glen G. Cain, and Arthur S. Goldberger. 1980. "Issues in the Analysis of Selectivity Bias." In *Evaluation Studies Review Annual*, edited by Ernst Stromsdorfer and George Farkas. Volume 5. San Francisco: Sage Publications.

Bell, Stephen H., Larry L. Orr, John D. Blomquist, and Glen G. Cain. 1995. *Program Applicants as a Comparison Group in Evaluating Training Programs.* Kalamazoo, Mich.: W. E. Upjohn Institute for Employment Research.

Bell, Stephen, Michael Puma, Gary Shapiro, Ronna Cook, and Michael Lopez. 2003. "Random Assignment for Impact Analysis in a Statistically Representative Set of Sites: Issues from the National Head Start Impact Study." *Proceedings of the August 2003 American Statistical Association Joint Statistical Meetings (CD-ROM).

Bloom, Dan, and Charles Michalopoulos. 2001. How Welfare and Work Policies Affect Employment and Income: A Synthesis of Research. New York: MDRC.

Bloom, Howard. 1984. "Accounting for No-Shows in Experimental Evaluation Designs." Evaluation Review 8(2): 225–46.

Bloom, Howard S., David S. Cordray, and Richard J. Light, eds. 1988. Lessons from Selected Program and Policy Areas. San Francisco: Jossey-Bass.

Bloom, Howard, Saul Schwartz, Susanna Lui-Gurr, and Suk-Won Lee. 1999. Testing a Re-employment Incentive for Displaced Workers: The Earnings Supplement Project. Ottawa, Canada: Social Research and Demonstration Corporation.

Boruch, Robert F. 1975. "Coupling Randomized Experiments and Approximations to Experiments in Social Program Evaluation." Sociological Methods and Research 4: 31–53.

Boruch, Robert F., and Ellen Foley. 2000. "The Honestly Experimental Society: Sites and Other Entities as the Units of Allocation and Analysis in Randomized Trials." In Validity and Social Experimentation: Donald Campbell's Legacy, edited by Leonard Bickman. Thousand Oaks, Calif.: Sage Publications.

Borus, Michael E. 1964. "A Benefit-Cost Analysis of the Economic Effectiveness of Retraining the Unemployed." Yale Economic Essays 4(2): 371–430.

Burghardt, John, Peter Z. Schochet, Sheena McConnell, Terry Johnson, R. Mark Gritz, Steven Glazerman, John Homrighausen, and Russell Jackson. 2001. "Does Job Corps Work? Summary of the National Job Corps Study." Princeton, N.J.: Mathematica Policy Research.

Burtless, Gary. 1987. "The Work Response to a Guaranteed Income: A Survey of Experimental Evidence." In Lessons from the Income Maintenance Experiments, edited by Alicia Munnell. Boston: Federal Reserve Bank of Boston.

Cain, Glen G. 1975. "Regression and Selection Models to Improve Nonexperimental Comparisons." In Evaluation and Experiments: Some Critical Issues in Assessing Social Programs, edited by Carl A. Bennett and Arthur A. Lumsdaine. New York: Academic Press.

Ciarlo, James A., and Charles Windle. 1988. "Mental Health Evaluation and Needs Assessment." In Lessons from Selected Program and Policy Areas, edited by Howard S. Bloom, David S. Cordray, and Richard J. Light. San Francisco: Jossey-Bass.

Clark-Kauffman, Elizabeth, Greg J. Duncan, and Pamela Morris. 2003. "How Welfare Policies Affect Child and Adolescent Achievement." American Economic Review: Papers and Proceedings of the American Economic Association 93(2): 299–303.

Coalition for Evidence-Based Policy. 2003. Identifying and Implementing Educational Practices Supported by Rigorous Evidence: A User-Friendly Guide. Washington: U.S. Department of Education, Institute of Education Sciences.

Cochrane Collaboration. 2002. "Cochrane Central Register of Controlled Trials." Database. Available at The Cochrane Library: www.cochrane.org (accessed September 14, 2004).

Coleman, William. 1987. "Experimental Psychology and Statistical Inference: The Therapeutic Trial in Nineteenth-Century Germany." In The Probabilistic

Revolution, volume 2: *Ideas in the Sciences,* edited by Lorenz Krüger, Gerg Gigerenzer, and Mary S. Morgan. Cambridge, Mass.: MIT Press.

Danziger, Kurt. 1987. "Statistical Methods and the Historical Development of Research Practice in American Psychology." In *The Probabilistic Revolution,* volume 2: *Ideas in the Sciences,* edited by Lorenz Krüger, Gerd Gigerenzer, and Mary S. Morgan. Cambridge, Mass.: MIT Press.

Dehejia, Rajeev H., and Sadek Wahba. 1999. "Causal Effects in Nonexperimental Studies: Reevaluating the Evaluation of Training Programs." *Journal of the American Statistical Association* 94(488): 1053–62.

Fisher, Ronald A. 1925. *Statistical Methods for Research Workers.* Edinburgh, Scotland: Oliver & Boyd.

Fraker, Thomas M., and Rebecca A. Maynard. 1987. "The Adequacy of Comparison Group Designs for Evaluations of Employment-Related Programs." *Journal of Human Resources* 22(2): 194–227.

Friedberg, Rachel M., and Jennifer Hunt. 1995. "The Impact of Immigrants on Host Country Wages, Employment and Growth." *Journal of Economic Perspectives* 9(2): 23–44.

Friedlander, Daniel, and Philip K. Robins. 1995. "Evaluating Program Evaluations: New Evidence on Commonly Used Nonexperimental Methods." *American Economic Review* 85(4): 923–37.

Garfinkel, Irwin, Charles F. Manski, and Charles Michalopoulos. 1992. "Micro Experiments and Macro Effects." In *Evaluating Welfare and Training Programs,* edited by Charles F. Manski. and Irwin Garfinkel. Cambridge, Mass.: Harvard University Press.

Gigerenzer, Gerd, Zeno Swijtink, Theodore Porter, Lorraine Daston, John Beatty, and Lorenz Krüger. 1989. *The Empire of Chance: How Probability Changed Science and Everyday Life.* Cambridge: Cambridge University Press.

Gilbert, John P., Richard J. Light, and Frederick Mosteller. 1975. "Assessing Social Innovations: An Empirical Basis for Policy." In *Evaluation and Experiment,* edited by Carl A. Bennett and Arthur A. Lumsdaine. New York: Academic Press.

Glass, Gene V. 1976. "Primary, Secondary, and Meta-Analysis of Research." *Educational Researcher* 5(10): 3–8.

Glazerman, Steven, Dan M. Levy, and David Myers. 2003. "Nonexperimental versus Experimental Estimates of Earnings Impacts." *Annals of the American Academy of Political and Social Science* 589: 63–93.

Glenman, Thomas K. 1972. "Evaluating Federal Manpower Programs." In *Evaluating Social Programs,* edited by Peter H. Rossi and Walter Williams. New York: Seminar Press.

Goering, John, Joan Kraft, Judith Feins, Debra McInnis, Mary Joel Holin, and Huda Elhassan. 1999. *Moving to Opportunity for Fair Housing Demonstration Program: Current Status and Initial Findings.* Washington: U.S. Department of Housing and Urban Development.

Greenberg, David H., Robert Meyer, Charles Michalopoulos, and Michael Wiseman. 2003. "Explaining Variation in the Effects of Welfare-to-Work Programs." *Evaluation Review* 27(4): 359–94.

Greenberg, David H., Charles Michalopoulos, and Philip K. Robins. 2003. "A

Meta-Analysis of Government-Sponsored Training Programs." *Industrial and Labor Relations Review* 50(1): 31–53.

———. 2004. "What Happens to the Effects of Government-Funded Training Programs over Time?" *Journal of Human Resources* 39(1): 277–93.

Greenberg, David H., and Philip K. Robins. 1986. "Social Experiments in Policy Analysis." *Journal of Policy Analysis and Management* 5(2): 340–62.

Greenberg, David, and Mark Shroder. 1997. *The Digest of Social Experiments.* Washington, D.C.: Urban Institute Press.

Greenberg, David H., and Michael Wiseman. 1992. "What Did the OBRA Demonstrations Do?" In *Evaluating Welfare and Training Programs*, edited by Charles F. Manski and Irwin Garfinkel. Cambridge, Mass.: Harvard University Press.

Gueron, Judith M., and Edward Pauly. 1991. *From Welfare to Work.* New York: Russell Sage Foundation.

Hamilton, Gayle, Stephen Freedman, Lisa A. Gennetian, Charles Michalopoulos, Johanna Walter, Diana Adams-Ciardullo, Anna Gassman-Pines, Sharon McGroder, Martha Zaslow, Jennifer Brooks, and Surjeet Ahluwalia. 2001. *How Effective Are Different Welfare-to-Work Approaches? Five-Year Adult and Child Impacts for Eleven Programs.* Washington: U.S. Department of Health and Human Services and U.S. Department of Education.

Harris, Jeffrey E. 1985. "Macroexperiments and Microexperiments for Health Policy." In *Social Experimentation*, edited by Jerry A. Hausman and David A. Wise. Chicago: University of Chicago Press.

Hausman, Jerry A., and David A. Wise, eds. 1985. *Social Experimentation.* Chicago: University of Chicago Press.

Heckman, James J. 1974. "Shadow Prices, Market Wages, and Labor Supply." *Econometrica* 42(4): 679–94.

———. 1992. "Randomization and Social Policy Evaluation." In *Evaluating Welfare and Training Programs*, edited by Charles F. Manski and Irwin Garfinkel. Cambridge, Mass.: Harvard University Press.

Heckman, James J., and V. Joseph Hotz. 1989. "Choosing Among Alternative Nonexperimental Methods for Estimating the Impact of Social Programs: The Case of Manpower Training." *Journal of the American Statistical Association* 84(408): 862–74.

Heckman, James J., Hidehiko Ichimura, Jeffrey Smith, and Petra Todd. 1998. "Characterizing Selection Bias Using Experimental Data." *Econometrica* 66(5): 1017–98.

Heckman, James J., Hidehiko Ichimura, and Petra Todd. 1997. "Matching as an Econometric Evaluation Estimator: Evidence from Evaluating a Job Training Program." *Review of Economic Studies* 64(4): 605–54.

———. 1998. "Matching as an Econometric Evaluation Estimator." *Review of Economic Studies* 65(2): 261–94.

Heinsman, Donna T., and William R. Shadish. 1996. "Assignment Methods in Experimentation: When Do Nonrandomized Experiments Approximate Answers from Randomized Experiments?" *Psychological Methods* 1(2): 154–69.

Hollister, Robinson G., and Jennifer Hill. 1995. "Problems in the Evaluation of Community-Wide Initiatives." In *New Approaches to Evaluating Community Initiatives: Concepts, Methods, and Contexts*, edited by James P. Connell, Anne

C. Kubisch, Lisbeth B. Schorr, and Carol H. Weiss. Washington, D.C.: Aspen Institute.

Kemple, James, and Joshua Haimson. 1994. *Florida's Project Independence: Program Implementation, Participation Patterns, and First-Year Impacts*. New York: MDRC.

Kemple, James J., and Jason Snipes. 2000. *Career Academies: Impacts on Students' Engagement and Performance in High School*. New York: MDRC.

Kennedy, Stephen D. 1988. "Direct Cash Low-Income Housing Assistance." In *Lessons from Selected Program and Policy Areas*, edited by Howard S. Bloom, David S. Cordray, and Richard J. Light. San Francisco: Jossey-Bass.

Klein, J. L. 1986. "The Conceptual Development of Population and Variation as Foundations of Econometric Analysis." Ph.D. diss., City of London Polytechnic.

Krüger, Lorenz, Gerd Gigerenzer, and Mary S. Morgan, eds. 1987. *The Probabilistic Revolution*, volume 2: *Ideas in the Sciences*. Cambridge, Mass.: MIT Press.

LaLonde, Robert J. 1986. "Evaluating the Econometric Evaluations of Training Programs with Experimental Data." *American Economic Review* 76(4): 604–20.

Lee, Wang S. 2001. "Propensity Score Matching on Commonly Available Nonexperimental Comparison Groups." Unpublished paper. Bethesda, Md.: Abt Associates.

Lipsey, Mark W. 1988. "Juvenile Delinquency Intervention." In *Lessons from Selected Program and Policy Areas*, edited by Howard S. Bloom, David S. Cordray, and Richard J. Light. San Francisco: Jossey-Bass.

Lipsey, Mark W., and David B. Wilson. 1993. "The Efficacy of Psychological, Educational, and Behavioral Treatment." *American Psychologist* 48(12): 1181–1209.

Lise, Jeremy, Shannon Seitz, and Jeffrey Smith. 2004. "Equilibrium Policy Experiments and the Evaluation of Social Programs." NBER working paper 10283. Cambridge, Mass.: National Bureau of Economic Research.

Love, John M., Ellen Eliason Kisker, Christine M. Ross, Peter Z. Schochet, Jeanne Brooks-Gunn, Dianne Paulsell, Kimberly Boller, Jill Constantine, Cheri Vogel, Allison Sidle Fuligni, and Christy Brady-Smith. 2002. *Making a Difference in the Lives of Infants and Toddlers and Their Families: The Impacts of Early Head Start*. Washington: U.S. Department of Health and Human Services.

Ludwig, Jens, Paul Hirschfield, and Greg J. Duncan. 2001. "Urban Poverty and Juvenile Crime: Evidence from a Randomized Housing-Mobility Experiment." *Quarterly Journal of Economics* 116(2): 655–79.

Maddala, G. S. 1983. *Limited-Dependent and Qualitative Variables in Econometrics*. Cambridge: Cambridge University Press.

Manski, Charles F., and Irwin Garfinkel, eds. 1992. *Evaluating Welfare and Training Programs*. Cambridge, Mass.: Harvard University Press.

Marks, Harry M. 1997. *The Progress of Experiment: Science and Therapeutic Reform in the United States, 1900–1990*. Cambridge: Cambridge University Press.

Mayer, Daniel P., Paul E. Peterson, David E. Myers, Christina Clark Tuttle, and William G. Howell. 2002. *School Choice in New York City After Three Years: An Evaluation of the School Choice Scholarships Program*. Princeton, N.J.: Mathematica Policy Research.

McDill, Edward L., Mary S. McDill, and J. Timothy Sprehe. 1972. "Evaluation in Practice: Compensatory Education." In *Evaluating Social Programs*, edited by Peter H. Rossi and Walter Williams. New York: Seminar Press.

Michalopoulos, Charles. 2004. "What Works Best for Whom: The Effects of Welfare and Work Policies by Race and Ethnicity." *Eastern Economic Journal* 30: 53–79.

Michalopoulos, Charles, and Christine Schwartz. 2000. *What Works Best for Whom: Impacts of 20 Welfare-to-Work Programs by Subgroup.* Washington: U.S. Department of Health and Human Services and U.S. Department of Education.

Michalopoulos, Charles, Douglas Tattrie, Cynthia Miller, Philip K. Robins, Pamela Morris, David Gyarmati, Cindy Redcross, Kelly Foley, and Reuben Ford. 2002. *Making Work Pay: Final Report on the Self-Sufficiency Project for Long-Term Welfare Recipients.* Ottawa, Canada: Social Research and Demonstration Corporation.

Miller, Cynthia, Virginia Knox, Lisa A. Gennetian, Martey Dodoo, JoAnna Hunter, and Cindy Redcross. 2000. *Reforming Welfare and Rewarding Work: Final Report on the Minnesota Family Investment Program.* New York. MDRC.

Morgan, Mary S. 1990. *The History of Econometric Ideas.* Cambridge: Cambridge University Press.

Morris, Pamela A., Aletha C. Huston, Greg J. Duncan, Danielle A. Crosby, and Johannes M. Bos. 2001. *How Welfare and Work Policies Affect Children: A Synthesis of Research.* New York: MDRC.

Mosteller, Frederick, Richard J. Light, and Jason A. Sachs. 1996. "Sustained Inquiry in Education: Lessons from Skill Grouping and Class Size." *Harvard Educational Review* 66(4): 797–842.

Munnell, Alicia, ed. 1987. *Lessons from the Income Maintenance Experiments.* Boston: Federal Reserve Bank of Boston.

Newhouse, Joseph P. 1996. *Free for All? Lessons from the RAND Health Insurance Experiment.* Cambridge, Mass.: Harvard University Press.

Orr, Larry L. 1999. *Social Experiments.* Thousand Oaks, Calif.: Sage Publications.

Orr, Larry, Judith D. Feins, Robin Jacob, Erik Beecroft, Lisa Sanbomatsu, Lawrence F. Katz, Jeffrey B. Liebman, and Jeffrey R. Kling. 2003. *Moving to Opportunity: Interim Impacts Evaluation.* Washington: U.S. Department of Housing and Urban Development.

Peck, Laura. 2002. "Subgroup Analyses in Social Experiments." Unpublished paper. Arizona State University, School of Public Affairs.

Peirce, Charles S., and Joseph Jastrow. 1884/1980. "On Small Differences of Sensation." Reprinted in *American Contributions to Mathematical Statistics in the Nineteenth Century*, volume 2, edited by Stephen M. Stigler. New York: Arno Press.

Pollack, Andrew, and Lawrence K. Altman. 2003. "Large Trial Finds AIDS Vaccine Fails to Stop Infection." *New York Times*, February 24, 2003, p. A1, 1.

Porter, Theodore M. 1986. *The Rise of Statistical Thinking, 1820–1900.* Princeton: Princeton University Press.

Ramey, Craig T., Keith Owen Yeates, and Elizabeth J. Short. 1984. "The Plasticity of Intellectual Development: Insights from Preventive Intervention." *Child Development* 55: 1913–25.

Riccio, James, Daniel Friedlander, and Stephen Freedman. 1994. *GAIN: Benefits, Costs, and Three-Year Impacts of a Welfare-to-Work Program.* New York: MDRC.

Rossi, Peter H., and Howard E. Freeman. 1993. *Evaluation: A Systematic Approach.* Thousand Oaks, Calif.: Sage Publications.

Rossi, Peter H., and Walter Williams. 1972. *Evaluating Social Programs.* New York: Seminar Press.

Salsburg, David. 2001. *The Lady Tasting Tea: How Statistics Revolutionized Science in the Twentieth Century.* New York: Henry Holt.

Schweinhart, Lawrence J., and David P. Weikart. 1993. "Success by Empowerment: The High/Scope Perry Preschool Study through Age 27." *Young Children* 49(1): 54–58.

Shadish, William R., Thomas D. Cook, and Donald T. Campbell. 2002. *Experimental and Quasi-Experimental Designs for Generalized Causal Inference.* Boston: Houghton Mifflin.

Shadish, William R., Kevin Ragsdale, Benita R. Glaser, and Linda M. Montgomery. 1995. "The Efficacy and Effectiveness of Marital and Family Therapy: A Perspective from Meta-Analysis." *Journal of Marital and Family Therapy* 21: 345–60.

Sherman, Lawrence W. 1988. "Randomized Experiments in Criminal Sanctions." In *Lessons from Selected Program and Policy Areas*, edited by Howard S. Bloom, David S. Cordray, and Richard J. Light. San Francisco: Jossey-Bass.

Smith, Jeffrey, and Petra Todd. 2005. "Does Matching Overcome LaLonde's Critique of Nonexperimental Estimators?" *Journal of Econometrics* 125(1–2): 305–53.

Smith, Mary Lee, Gene V. Glass, and Thomas I. Miller. 1980. *The Benefits of Psychotherapy.* Baltimore: Johns Hopkins University Press.

Smith, Vernon. 1994. "Economics in the Laboratory." *Journal of Economic Perspectives* 8(1): 113–31.

Spiegelman, Robert G., Christopher J. O'Leary, and Kenneth J. Kline. 1992. *The Washington Reemployment Bonus Experiment: Final Report.* Unemployment Insurance occasional paper 92–6. Washington: U.S. Department of Labor.

Stephan, A. S. 1935. "Prospects and Possibilities: The New Deal and the New Social Research." *Social Forces* 13(4): 515–21.

Stigler, Stephen M. 1986. *The History of Statistics: The Measurement of Uncertainty Before 1900.* Cambridge, Mass.: Belknap Press.

———. 1999. *Statistics on the Table: The History of Statistical Concepts and Methods.* Cambridge, Mass.: Harvard University Press.

Teruel, Graciela M., and Benjamin Davis. 2000. *Final Report: An Evaluation of the Impact of PROGRESA Cash Payments on Private Inter-Household Transfers.* Washington, D.C.: International Food Policy Research Institute.

Thistlethwaite, Donald L., and Donald T. Campbell. 1960. "Regression Discontinuity Analysis: An Alternative to Ex Post Facto Experiment." *Journal of Educational Psychology* 51(6): 309–17.

van Helmont, John Baptista. 1662. *Oriatrik or, Physick Refined: The Common Errors Therein Refuted and the Whole Art Reformed and Rectified.* London: Lodowick-Lloyd. Available at the James Lind Library web site: www.jameslindlibrary .org/trial_records/17th_18th_Century/van_helmont/van_helmont_kp.html (accessed January 3, 2005).

Wilde, Elizabeth Ty, and Robinson Hollister. 2002. "How Close Is Close Enough? Testing Nonexperimental Estimates of Impact Against Experimental Estimates of Impact with Education Test Scores as Outcomes." Discussion paper 1242–02. Madison, Wis.: Institute for Research on Poverty. Available at the University of Wisconsin—Madison web site: www.ssc.wisc.edu/irp/pubs/dp124202.pdf (accessed January 3, 2005).

Wilner, Daniel M., Rosabelle P. Walkley, Thomas C. Pinkerton, and Mathew Tayback. 1962. *The Housing Environment and Family Life*. Baltimore: Johns Hopkins University Press.

Woodbury, Stephen A. and Robert G. Spiegelman. 1987. "Bonuses to Workers and Employers to Reduce Unemployment: Randomized Trials in Illinois." *American Economic Review* 77(4): 513–30.

Chapter 2

Modeling Cross-Site Experimental Differences to Find Out Why Program Effectiveness Varies

C HARGED WITH planning a new social program, senior administrators in a state human services agency pore over stacks of evaluation research, seeking knowledge and insights that can help them design the new initiative. The evaluations provide them with lots of information about the effects of particular programs on particular people in particular settings. And having used random assignment to measure program effects, or impacts, the studies also afford considerable confidence in the reported results.

Yet the research evidence is not as useful to the program designers as they had hoped. For all the studies' rigor, many of them are not directly applicable to the situation that the program designers face. Not only are the people to be targeted by the program not directly comparable to the people studied, but the social and economic conditions under which the program will operate also differ from those under which the programs under study were implemented. What if these differences in target population and local conditions influence program effects? Another limitation of the experiments is that although they measure the impacts of each program as a whole, they do not provide readily interpretable evidence about what made a given program more or less effective. Was the intensive orientation provided in the studied programs the key to their beneficial effects, or could the same success be achieved without this costly component? In the absence of systematic crosscutting analysis, the body of information available—despite its heft—may not provide the guidance needed to design and implement the new program.[1]

How can knowledge about what works for whom, and under what conditions, be gathered for use by the people who design, analyze, and implement new social policies? And how can this knowledge be brought to bear on efforts to improve the effectiveness of existing social policies? In this chapter we present a way to generate such knowledge that entails pooling data from randomized experiments conducted in a variety of settings and synthesizing these data with the aid of a multi-level statistical model. The approach models the relationships between experimental estimates of the impacts of programs operated in different settings and the characteristics of the programs and individuals in those settings. The term "experimental" in this context means based on a random assignment research design.

The approach presented in this chapter, empirically grounded in detailed data from underlying experiments, is an example of secondary analysis of primary data. This type of research synthesis provides greater flexibility, precision, and analytic power than do meta-analyses, which depend on summary statistics from published studies and attempt to characterize the overall pattern of results. Primary experimental data confer another advantage as well: They protect research syntheses from the fallacy of ecological correlation (Robinson 1950), which can occur when statistical inferences about individual-level processes or behaviors are drawn from analyses of aggregate-level data, which reflect group factors as well as individual factors.

The principal strength of the present approach is its grounding in valid estimates of program impacts within sites. Its principal limitation is its reliance on natural, as opposed to experimentally manipulated, variation in the determinants of impacts across sites. Using this natural variation leaves the approach open to model misspecification, that is, to generating findings that are inaccurate because some of the factors that influence impacts have not been included in the model or have not been measured correctly. But the approach also enables researchers to tackle policy questions that could not otherwise be addressed because it is generally impossible to measure the effects of the myriad factors that can influence program impacts by randomly varying each one. Furthermore, the potential hazards of the approach can be minimized through the use of high-quality experimental data and careful model specification informed by theory in the social sciences, past empirical research, and practitioner knowledge.

Because very few research syntheses of this type have been conducted (for an exception, see Heinrich 2002), we describe the requisite steps in detail, identify special challenges that can arise, and suggest ways to address the challenges. The research synthesis process has three stages: articulating the research questions, developing the model, and constructing and assessing the measures. We then present the findings from a specific research synthesis, and, finally, consider the broader applicability of the approach and the preconditions for its successful application in other policy areas.

Each element of the approach is first described in general terms (often with reference to a familiar example from an education context) and is then illustrated using a research synthesis conducted by Howard S. Bloom, Carolyn J. Hill, and James A. Riccio (2003).[2] The synthesis is based on three random assignment evaluations of mandatory welfare-to-work programs operated in the United States in the late 1980s and 1990s: California's Greater Avenues for Independence (GAIN) program, Florida's Project Independence (PI), and the eleven programs studied in the six-state, seven-site National Evaluation of Welfare-to-Work Strategies (NEWWS). By pooling data from large-scale evaluations of programs with similar components and goals, we obtained sample sizes large enough to permit estimation of a statistical model that controls for many variables. The primary data pertain to a total of 69,399 female single parents (sample members) who were randomly assigned to a program group or a control group in fifty-nine local program offices (sites).

Articulating the Research Questions

Are some types of social programs more effective than others? If so, under what conditions? Are particular types of programs more effective for some target groups than for others? Program effectiveness needs definition before the factors thought to influence it can be identified and tested.

What Is Program Effectiveness, and What Factors Influence It?

Program effectiveness is difficult to define because of the diversity of goals that social programs, most of them run by public or nonprofit organizations, are designed to realize. For example, schools are expected to teach literacy, numeracy, and reasoning skills; impart subject area knowledge; socialize young people; and prepare children to enter the labor market as adults. These goals, or the means of achieving them, can conflict with one other, and different stakeholders may not agree on their relative importance. A lack of coherence or consensus can make it difficult to measure the effectiveness of a social program using a single scale.

Measuring program effectiveness is also difficult when at least some of the desired outcomes are intangible. For example, standardized tests of student achievement do not fully reflect the educational, social, and developmental goals that schools have for their students. Furthermore, some desired outcomes occur long after a program has been implemented, which can make it difficult to measure them and to make changes in the program in response. For example, one desired effect of an eighth-grade math curriculum may be increased productivity in the labor market, but this outcome cannot be measured until years after students complete the curriculum. Finally, program effectiveness cannot be assessed solely on the basis of the outcomes for program participants. It is also necessary to estimate what is known as the counterfactual: the outcomes as they would have occurred in the absence of the program. The difference between participants' outcomes and the counterfactual provides an estimate of the impact of the program on the people for whom it was designed.

The most rigorous way to measure the impacts of a program is to conduct an experiment in which members of the target population are randomly assigned to a program group (whose members can or must participate in the program being tested) or a control group (which cannot participate in the program). In large samples, this approach ensures that the program and control groups are virtually identical to one another, on average, with respect to every variable except access to the program. The control group's subsequent outcomes thus provide a valid counterfactual for the program group, and the difference between the two groups with respect to an outcome is a valid measure of the program's impact on that outcome. For example, if two years after random assignment 70 percent of children in a reading program can read at grade level, whereas only 40 percent of children in the control group can do so, the impact of the program on this outcome (its effectiveness) is 30 percentage points.

Researchers and practitioners have long debated about the relative contributions of four basic types of factors to the effectiveness of social programs: the way the program is implemented, the activities and services it provides, the socioeconomic environments in which it is operated, and the types of people it serves. To see how these factors play out in a specific area, consider the following example from our research synthesis of welfare-to-work programs.

A Detailed Example

Targeted to low-income parents who qualify for cash welfare benefits, the primary goals of welfare-to-work programs are to increase enrollees' employment and earnings, reduce their dependence on welfare, alleviate their poverty, and improve their lives and those of their children. The effectiveness of individual programs in realizing these goals has been measured in many ways (Gueron and Pauly 1991; Friedlander and Burtless 1995), and the GAIN, PI, and NEWWS experiments together use a range of effectiveness measures. To sharpen the focus of this research synthesis, we examined a single measure: sample members' total earnings during the two years after they were randomly assigned to the welfare-to-work program under study or to a control group. We thus sought to assess the influence of program implementation,[3] program activities, program environment, and individual characteristics on this short-run impact.

Program implementation concerns how programs are organized and how they deliver services (Mead 1983; Bane 1989; Behn 1991). For a welfare-to-work program, implementation factors include the size of each staff member's caseload (the number of program enrollees for whom he or she is responsible), the degree to which the program is personalized, the degree to which enrollees are closely monitored, the forcefulness with which employment is emphasized, and the extent to which staff members agree among themselves and with their supervisors about these issues.

The main activities provided by welfare-to-work programs are job-search assistance, basic education, and vocational training. Differences from program to program in the mix of offered activities reflect different beliefs about how best to promote economic self-sufficiency among welfare recipients. The labor-force attachment approach is based on the belief that on-the-job experience is the shortest, surest path to higher wages and long-term employment, and thus emphasizes immediate job placement. The human capital development approach is based on the belief that skills in reading, math, and other basic academic subjects are the key to labor market success, and thus emphasizes education and training before job placement.

There are also opposing views about how program environment, defined as local economic conditions, influences the effects of welfare-to-work programs. One view is that in weak labor markets with high unemployment rates, it is especially difficult to help welfare recipients find jobs because of intense competition for the few jobs available. Those holding this view predict that a high unemployment rate will reduce program impacts. An alternative view is that promoting employment among welfare recipients is actually more difficult in strong labor markets with low unemployment rates, in which people who depend on welfare are disproportionately unlikely to be prepared for the labor force (or else they would already be employed). Those holding this view predict that a low unemployment rate will reduce program impacts.

With respect to how individual characteristics influence the effectiveness of welfare-to-work programs, most attention has been given to factors that represent barriers or, conversely, stepping-stones to employment such as education level, work experience, and welfare history. At one extreme are people with few or no barriers to employment.

Although they have the smallest margin for improvement, they may have the greatest ability to respond to a program. At the other extreme are people with many barriers to employment. They have the largest margin for improvement, but they may have the least ability to respond to a program. Thus, some researchers argue that people with a moderate number of barriers to employment are more likely than people at either extreme to benefit from a welfare-to-work program (Friedlander 1988).

The question driving our research synthesis was: How do these four sets of factors affect the ability of welfare-to-work programs to increase enrollees' short-run earnings?

Developing the Model

Ideally, the relationships between each type of factor and desired outcomes would be estimated in an experimental design. Several welfare-to-work experiments have indeed used multigroup research designs, in which sample members are randomly assigned to a control group or to one or more program groups, to test the relative effectiveness of different program features or alternative program approaches. These experiments include tests of labor-force attachment versus human capital development strategies (Hamilton et al. 2001); of lower versus higher client-to-staff ratios (Riccio, Friedlander, and Freedman 1994); and of financial work incentives alone versus a combination of financial work incentives, participation mandates, and employment-related services (Knox, Miller, and Gennetian 2000).

In principle, experiments may be ideal for estimating the causal effects of program implementation, program activities and services, the socioeconomic environment, and the types of people served. But the approach can be costly, and often it is not feasible to explore the many possible factors that influence outcomes in a fully experimental design. When this ideal is unattainable in practice, statistical models can be used to measure nonexperimentally the independent effects of multiple factors on program effectiveness. The relationships between these factors and effectiveness can be characterized as a production process comprising multiple levels.

Multilevel Production Functions

Production functions examine relationships between the inputs and outputs of processes for producing public and private goods and services. They have been used for decades. Recent applications of the production function approach are referred to as value-added models

(Meyer 1997). Typically, production functions are estimated with ordinary least squares (OLS) regression and do not model specific hierarchical relationships in the production system. Among the many applications of the approach are studies of the linkages between education inputs (characteristics of students, teachers, parents, and schools) and education outputs (students' attitudes, behavior, and achievement; for an overview in the education context, see Hanushek 1997 and Taylor 2001).

Multilevel models are a fairly recent innovation. One strength of these models is their ability to represent explicitly how observations at one level are clustered within observational units at higher levels of aggregation (Raudenbush and Bryk 2002). They apply to multilevel systems such as students clustered within classes, classes clustered within schools, and schools clustered within school districts (four levels); employees clustered within departments and departments clustered within firms (three levels); and individuals clustered within households and households clustered within neighborhoods (three levels). Also known as hierarchical, random-effects, mixed, or variance-components models, multilevel models make it possible to estimate the effects on an outcome of every independent variable at every level and simultaneously to control for all other independent variables at all levels.

A multilevel production function for a program is thus a regression model for a production process that accounts for the clustering of inputs and outputs within programs, sites, or other operational entities. For simplicity, we focus on two-level production models in this chapter, but the basic approach can be generalized to models with any number of levels.

Consider a simple two-level model of a reading program that is being evaluated in twenty schools by randomly assigning each first-grader to the program group or to a control group at the beginning of the school year.[4] At the end of the school year, the evaluation measures the program's impact on reading test scores. It also examines how this impact varies with student characteristics, school characteristics, and the program's implementation in different schools.

In this example, the unit of observation at the first level is the individual student. Thus, the level 1 model is a regression equation specifying first-graders' reading scores as a function of individual characteristics, program status (whether the student has been randomly assigned to the program group or to the control group), and interactions between individual characteristics and program status. Using this regression, one can estimate the conditional program impact and the control group's conditional mean score for each school, controlling for the characteristics of students in the school. These two school-specific parameters are random effects that vary in ways specified by the second level of the model.[5]

The unit of observation at the second level is the school. There are two level 2 regression equations. One specifies that the conditional program impacts depend on school characteristics and the program's implementation in each school, and the other specifies that the control group's conditional mean scores depend on school characteristics.

To summarize, the full model comprises three separate but related regressions: one accounting for how test scores vary across individual students within schools, a second accounting for how program impacts vary across schools, and a third accounting for how control-group mean scores vary across schools. Each parameter in these regressions represents an effect of a given variable on a given student or on a given school outcome, controlling for all other variables in the model.

Multilevel production functions, which are estimated simultaneously instead of separately or sequentially, have several important advantages (Raudenbush and Bryk 2002).[6] First, by accounting for the clustering of lower-level units (such as students) within higher-level aggregate units (such as schools), they give accurate estimates of the standard errors of the model's parameters. In samples that are clustered, standard errors can be grossly misestimated by methods that do not account for the clustering.[7] Second, they allow interactions between levels to be estimated. For example, the relationship between student gender and test scores may differ between public and private schools. Third, multilevel production functions boost efficiency by using all the information, even for aggregate units for which only a few observations are available. Fourth, they provide a helpful framework for conceptualizing how the characteristics of clients, programs, and program environments influence program effectiveness. The heuristic value of multiple levels is considerable when one is trying to develop or convey intuitions about a model of a social program.

The several advantages of multilevel production functions can be garnered, however, only if both the amount of variation in the variables included and the number of degrees of freedom are sufficient to estimate the parameters. It is particularly important to ascertain whether there is variation in program impacts or, more specifically, whether there is variation in the conditional program impacts across aggregate units in the multilevel model. A χ^2 test can be used to assess the statistical significance of cross-site variation in program impacts and cross-site variation in the factors that influence program impacts (Raudenbush and Bryk 2002). Even if every impact estimate is large and statistically significant, there is nothing for aggregate characteristics to explain if the estimates do not vary across aggregate units.

The number of degrees of freedom available for a multilevel model depends on the number of aggregate units in the sample relative to the number of aggregate independent variables in the model. Thus, when specifying the model, one must find a balance between model misspecification (because of too few variables) and insufficient statistical power (because of too many variables; for a detailed discussion of statistical power in multilevel models, see Raudenbush and Bryk 2002, 158, 159, 267, and Snijders and Bosker 1999, 140–54). The best way to strike a balance between misspecification on the one hand and insufficient power on the other is to construct a parsimonious model that includes only variables that are believed—on the basis of past empirical studies, practitioner knowledge, theory in the social sciences, or other reliable sources of information—to have a strong influence on program effectiveness.

A Detailed Example

We used a two-level linear production function to model the dependence of program impacts on earnings on the implementation, activities, environment, and target population of the programs included in our synthesis of welfare-to-work experiments. The unit of analysis for level 1 of the model was the female single-parent welfare recipient, sometimes referred to here as the client, of which there were 69,399. The unit of analysis for level 2 of the model was the local welfare-to-work program office, of which there were fifty-nine. The full model comprises a single level 1 regression and three level 2 regressions, all of which were estimated simultaneously. The regression models are described below, and the measures in the regressions are described in a later section.

Individual-Level Factors That Affect Earnings (Level 1)   Equation 2.1 specifies that sample members' total earnings during the two years after random assignment depend on their program status, their characteristics, interactions between their program status and characteristics, their local random assignment cohort (explained shortly), and a random component,

$$Y_{ji} = \alpha_j + \beta_j P_{ji} + \sum_k \delta_k CC_{kji} + \sum_k \gamma_k CC_{kji} P_{ji} + \kappa_j RA_{ji} + \varepsilon_{ji}, \qquad (2.1)$$

where:

Y_{ji} = total earnings in dollars during the two years after random assignment for each sample member i in office j

P_{ji} = a binary indicator of program status for each sample member i in office j that was set equal to 1 for program-group members and to 0 for control-group members

CC_{kji} = the value of client characteristic k for each sample member i in office j (grand mean–centered)

RA_{ji} = a binary indicator of random assignment cohort for each sample member i in office j

α_j = control-group conditional mean earnings for each office j

β_j = the conditional program impact on earnings for each office j

δ_k = the effect of client characteristic k on control-group mean earnings

γ_k = the effect of client characteristic k on the program impact on earnings

κ_j = a random assignment cohort coefficient for each office j

ε_{ji} = a random component of earnings for each sample member i in office j

Because client characteristics were grand mean–centered—measured as deviations from their mean values for the full sample—β_j represents local office j's program impact for the average member of the full sample, that is, for a hypothetical individual whose values with respect to all client characteristics match the mean values for the full sample (for a discussion of different ways to center the variables and how each way affects interpretation of the coefficients, see Raudenbush and Bryk 2002, 31–35).

Office-Level Factors That Affect Conditional Impacts on Earnings (Level 2)
Equation 2.2 specifies that the conditional program impact β_j for each local office depends on its program implementation, program activities, economic environment, and a random component:

$$\beta_j = \beta_0 + \sum_m \pi_m PI_{mj} + \sum_n \phi_n PA_{nj} + \psi EE_j + \mu_j, \qquad (2.2)$$

where:

β_j = the conditional program impact for each office j

PI_{mj} = the value of program implementation feature m for each office j (grand mean–centered)

PA_{nj} = the value of program activity n for each office j (grand mean–centered)

EE_j = a measure of the economic environment for each office j (grand mean–centered)

β_0 = the grand mean impact

π_m = the effect of program implementation feature m on program impacts

ϕ_n = the effect of program activity n on program impacts

ψ = the effect of the economic environment on program impacts

μ_j = a random component of the program impact for each office j

Because all the independent variables in the equation were grand mean–centered, or measured as deviations from the mean value for all fifty-nine offices, β_0 in equation 2.2 represents the grand mean impact for the average sample member in the average office.

Office-Level Factors That Affect the Control Group's Conditional Mean Earnings (Level 2)   Equation 2.3 specifies that the conditional mean earnings of the control group in each office depend on the local economic environment and a random component, producing a different counterfactual for each office:

$$\alpha_j = \alpha_0 + \lambda EE_j + \upsilon_j, \qquad (2.3)$$

where:

α_j = control-group conditional mean earnings during the two years after random assignment for each office j

EE_j = a measure of the economic environment for each office j (grand mean–centered)

α_0 = the grand mean of control-group earnings

λ = the effect of economic environment on control-group mean earnings

υ_j = a random component of control-group mean earnings for each office j

Because the economic environment variable is grand mean-centered, the coefficient α_0 represents the mean outcome for the average control-group member in the average office.

Random Differences in Counterfactuals for Different Cohorts in Each Office (Level 2)   Because some local offices in the original experiments altered the ratio between the number of program-group members and the number of control-group members over time in response to administrative concerns, we controlled for possible effects of the cohort one had been randomly assigned to on earnings using a cohort indicator, the coefficient of which varied as a random effect across offices (Bloom, Hill, and Riccio 2001, 23):

$$\kappa_j = \kappa_0 + \eta_j, \tag{2.4}$$

where:

κ_j = a random-assignment cohort coefficient for each office j

κ_0 = the grand mean random-assignment cohort coefficient

η_j = a random component of the cohort coefficient for each office j

Constructing and Assessing the Measures

Having clearly specified a multilevel model of the factors that determine program impacts, one must define and construct operational measures for each variable in the model. There are different ways to construct such measures and to assess their quality.

Individual Outcomes and Program Impacts (Dependent Variables)

Constructing a dependent variable requires having an appropriate outcome measure for each sample member, which for an education program might be standardized test scores; for a substance-abuse program, self-reported drug use; and for a correctional program, criminal convictions. Data for such measures often can be obtained from the administrative records of public agencies and nonprofit organizations or from surveys of sample members. When data are pooled across experiments, it is crucial that they be based on the same definitions, conventions, and sources in every experiment. This standardization eliminates the possibility that measurement procedures that differ across aggregate-level units produce reported differences in outcomes that are confounded with unmeasured actual differences across programs.

The foregoing types of individual-outcome data provide the dependent variable for level 1 of a program impact model. The next step in the modeling process is to create appropriate dependent variables for the higher levels. As already described in the section on developing the model, the random effects specified at level 1 of the multilevel model become dependent variables at the higher levels.

Individual and Aggregate Unit Characteristics (Independent Variables)

Independent variables for sample members typically include socioeconomic characteristics such as gender, age, race, ethnicity, and education level. When possible, a baseline measure of the outcome variable (for example, past test scores, past drug use, or past convictions) is also included. The main purposes of collecting these data in experiments are to increase the precision of impact estimates by reducing their standard errors and to specify interactions between individual characteristics and program impacts.

Independent variables for aggregate units in multilevel models often pose greater challenges with regard to conceptualization and measurement. These variables can be grouped into three broad categories, each of which is discussed in turn: aggregate summaries of individual characteristics, measures of the program-services contrast, and observers' and participants' assessments of contextual factors.

In certain settings, the context in which people experience a program is partly shaped by the other people involved, and the resulting differences in context may influence the impacts experienced. For example, students' education experiences have been shown to depend on the types of students who are their classmates. Thus, one way to characterize an education program is through summary measures of the characteristics of its students.

Another way to characterize programs is with respect to the difference in the activities or services to which program-group members and control-group members are exposed. In an experimental design, this program-services contrast is responsible for any systematic differences between the program- and control-group outcomes that arise after randomization. If a program is effective, one would expect to see larger program impacts in the presence of larger program-services contrasts. The magnitude of the program-services contrast depends on two factors, which can vary across aggregate units: the proportion of program-group members who receive the program's services and participate in its activities and the proportion of control-group members who are exposed to the program's services and activities (perhaps inadvertently) or to similar services and activities from other providers.[8] When one is modeling program effectiveness on the basis of data pooled across experiments conducted under real-world conditions, one should pay close attention to both aspects of the program-services contrast.

How programs are organized, managed, and implemented may substantially influence their impacts. Some information, such as caseload, class size, and budget size, may be obtainable from administrative data. Other information can be gleaned only from people who work in, participate in, or observe the programs being studied. Often, firsthand feedback is obtained from multiple observers who rank or rate multiple aspects of a program or the outcomes associated with it. Relevant examples include teachers' perceptions of organizational climate in schools, paid observers' perceptions of housing conditions in neighborhoods, and residents' perceptions of crime and violence in communities. Documentation of these factors raises the following questions: How should multiple questions about a construct such as organizational climate be combined into a single scale? How should responses from multiple observers in an aggregate unit be combined into a single descriptor? And how should the possibility that different types of observers perceive the same situation differently be adjusted for?

Measurement Quality

Having constructed some of or all the preceding types of measures, one should assess their quality in terms of reliability and validity. The reliability of a measure is the degree to which it produces consistent information instead of random error (its signal-to-noise ratio). The validity of a measure is the degree to which it systematically reflects the construct that it is intended to reflect.[9]

Two considerations affect the reliability of measures based on multiple observers' responses to multiple assessment items (Nunnally 1967). One consideration is whether different items used to assess the same aggregate feature yield similar information. A standard index of inter-item consistency is Cronbach's alpha, which ranges from 0 (no consistency) to 1 (perfect consistency). A second consideration is whether different observers of the same unit have similar responses to it. One useful index of inter-rater consistency, which also ranges from 0 (no consistency) to 1 (perfect consistency), is the proportion of the total observer variation that is attributable to average observer differences across units rather than to individual observer differences within units.[10]

Measurement validity also depends on two considerations, face validity and construct validity. The face validity of a measure is the degree to which the specific items on which it is based appear to capture what the measure is supposed to reflect. To be valid in this sense is to accord with common sense. The construct validity of a measure is the degree to which it correlates with other measures in ways that would be expected given the constructs to be measured. A simple way to assess the construct validity of one's measures is to observe their pattern of bivariate correlations (Campbell and Fiske 1959). If the signs and relative magnitudes of these correlations accord with one's prior expectations, the measures are judged to have adequate construct validity.

A Detailed Example

The construction and assessment of key measures in our welfare-to-work research synthesis illustrate most of the issues outlined above.

Individual Earnings and Local Office Earnings Impacts (Dependent Variables)   The GAIN, PI, and NEWWS experiments used data from unemployment insurance wage records maintained by the states to measure sample members' earnings. Although these records do not reflect all possible categories of earnings, such as unofficial employment, they are a commonly used source of earnings information (Kornfeld and Bloom 1999). To construct our level 1 dependent variable, we adjusted the earnings measures for inflation by converting them into 1996 dollars (because 1996 was the last year of follow-up used) using the Consumer Price Index for Urban Consumers (U.S. Department of Labor, Bureau of Labor Statistics 2001). By estimating parameters in the multilevel model system, we then produced the three level 2 dependent variables defined in equations 2.2, 2.3, and 2.4. As noted, the dependent variable of primary interest in our analysis is the impact of each local program on client earnings during the two years after random assignment.

The unconditional impact estimates—unconditional in that they do not control for client characteristics—ranged from –$1,412 to $4,217 across the fifty-nine local offices in the sample and averaged $879, or 18 percent of control-group mean earnings. Of the thirteen impact estimates that were negative, many were small, and none were statistically significant. Of the forty-six impact estimates that were positive, by contrast, twenty were statistically significant, and many were large. Hence, there was no evidence of real negative impacts, whereas there was substantial evidence of real positive impacts. More important, because the cross-office variation in the unconditional and conditional impact estimates was unlikely to be due to chance alone (it was statistically significant at the 0.0001 level), there was plenty of real variation for the model to explain.

Client Characteristics (Level 1 Independent Variables)   Data on client characteristics were obtained from background information forms completed before random assignment in the original experiments. Guided by previous research, we included the following client characteristics in level 1 of our model: education level, recent past earnings, recent past welfare receipt, age, race and ethnicity, and number and age of children. The characteristics were specified as binary indicator variables, and the percentage of sample members with each characteristic is listed in the first column in table 2.1. The second column lists the range of these percentages across local offices, showing that client characteristics varied considerably from site to site. Thus, to the extent that client characteristics influence program impacts and are correlated with local program characteristics, it is important to control for them when estimating how program characteristics affect program effectiveness.

Table 2.1   Client Characteristics in the Multilevel Analysis

Client Characteristic (at Random Assignment)	Full Sample (Percentage)	Cross-Office Range (Percentage)
Was a high school graduate or had a GED	56	17 to 74
Had one child	42	30 to 56
Had two children	33	28 to 50
Had three or more children	25	11 to 39
Had a child under six years old	46	7 to 73
Was younger than twenty-five years old	19	1 to 42
Was twenty-five to thirty-four	49	23 to 57
Was thirty-five to forty-four	26	14 to 45
Was forty-five or older	6	2 to 34
Was white, non-Hispanic	41	1 to 87
Was black, non-Hispanic	41	0 to 98
Was Hispanic	14	0 to 92
Was Native American	2	0 to 21
Was Asian	2	0 to 23
Was some other race or ethnicity	<1	0 to 5
Was a welfare applicant	17	0 to 99
Had received welfare continuously for the past twelve months	44	0 to 96
Had no earnings in the past year	56	29 to 81
Had earned $1 to $2,499	21	10 to 30
Had earned $2,500 to $7,499	14	6 to 26
Had earned $7,500 or more	9	2 to 27
Sample size	69,399	

Source: Authors' calculations based on GAIN, PI, and NEWWS administrative records data and baseline survey data.

Program Characteristics (Level 2 Independent Variables)   We included six program-implementation measures, three program-activity (program-services contrast) measures, and one program-environment measure as independent variables in the level 2 model of local program impacts. A program-environment measure was also included in the level 2 model of control-group conditional mean earnings. Table 2.2 presents summary statistics for these variables, each of which is described briefly below (for details about the rationale behind and the construction of these variables, see Riccio, Bloom, and Hill 2000 and Bloom, Hill, and Riccio 2001).

Table 2.2   Program Characteristics in the Multilevel Analysis

Program Characteristic	Mean	Cross-Office Range
Implementation		
Emphasis on quick job entry	0.0	−1.7 to 2.5
Emphasis on personalized attention	0.0	−2.0 to 2.3
Closeness of monitoring	0.0	−2.8 to 1.9
Staff caseload size	136	70 to 367
Staff disagreement	0.0	−2.1 to 4.5
Staff-supervisor disagreement	0.0	−1.5 to 3.2
Activity differential		
Basic education	11	−11 to 50
Job-search assistance	17	−13 to 47
Vocational training	5	−21 to 35
Economic environment		
Unemployment rate	7.4	3.5 to 14.3

Source: Authors' calculations based on GAIN, PI, and NEWWS staff survey data and follow-up survey data.

Program Implementation   The six program-implementation measures were based on data from staff surveys administered in local program offices in the GAIN, PI, and NEWWS experiments.[11] These measures reflect the perceptions of frontline workers about how their programs were operated. The questions were based on hypotheses about what works best drawn from the welfare-to-work research literature and from views widely expressed by practitioners in the field. The number of respondents per office ranged from one to eighty-three caseworkers and from zero to fourteen supervisors, averaging twenty-one caseworkers and three supervisors. In most offices, the survey completion rates exceeded 90 percent.

Three of the implementation measures constructed from these surveys are multiquestion scales that were standardized to have a mean value of 0 and a standard deviation of 1 across offices. "Emphasis on quick job entry" reflects the employment message conveyed by the office, that is, the degree to which clients were encouraged to take a job quickly or to be more selective by waiting for a better job or by pursuing education and training to improve their employment prospects. "Emphasis on personalized attention" is the degree of emphasis placed by each office on understanding clients' personal histories and circumstances in an effort to accommodate their needs and preferences. "Closeness of monitoring" refers to how closely staff members in each office tracked clients' participation in assigned activities and clients' changing needs. To show the thinking behind these measures, table 2.3 presents the survey questions used to construct them.

Table 2.3   Staff Survey Questions for the Program Implementation Scales

Scale and Questions	Response Scale		
Emphasis on moving clients into jobs quickly			
Based on the practices in your unit, what would you say is the more important goal of your unit: to help clients get jobs as quickly as possible or to raise the education or skill levels of clients so that they can get jobs in the future?	1 skills	. . . .	7 jobs
In your opinion, which should be the more important goal of your unit: to help clients get jobs as quickly as possible or to raise the education or skill levels of clients so that they can get jobs in the future?	1 skills	. . . .	7 jobs
After a short time in the program, an average welfare mother is offered a low-skill, low-paying job that would make her slightly better off financially. Assume she has two choices: either to take the job and leave welfare or to stay on welfare and wait for a better opportunity. If you were asked, what would your personal advice to this client be?	1 welfare	. . . .	7 jobs
What advice would your supervisor want you to give to a client of this type?	1 welfare	. . . .	7 jobs
Emphasis on personalized client attention			
In our program, there is more emphasis on the number of clients served than on the quality of services.	1 strongly agree	. . . .	7 strongly disagree
Do you feel that in your unit not enough time or enough time is being spent with clients during the intake process?	1 not enough	. . . .	7 enough

Table 2.3   *Continued*

Scale and Questions	Response Scale		
During intake, how much effort does the staff make to learn about the client's family problems in depth?	1 very little	. . . .	7 a great deal
During intake, how much effort does the staff make to learn about the client's goals and motivation to work in depth?	1 very little	. . . .	7 a great deal
In your opinion, how well is the program tailoring the educational, training, and work experience services that clients receive to their particular needs, circumstances, and goals?	1 very poorly	. . . .	7 very well
Closeness of client monitoring			
How closely would you say the staff of your unit is monitoring clients?	1 not very	. . . .	7 very
Suppose a client has been assigned to basic education but has not attended it at all. How long would it usually take for staff to learn about this situation from the service provider?	1 1 or fewer weeks	. . . .	5 5 or more weeks
Suppose a client has been assigned to vocational education but has not attended it at all. How long would it usually take for staff to learn about this situation from the service provider?	1 1 or fewer weeks	. . . .	5 5 or more weeks
Suppose a client has a part-time job that deferred her from other program obligations. How closely would you say your agency is monitoring whether clients quit or lose part-time jobs?	1 not very	. . . .	7 very
Once your agency learned that a client lost or quit a part-time job, how long on average would it take before the client was assigned to another program component?	1 1 or fewer weeks	. . . .	8 8 or more weeks

Source: GAIN, PI, and NEWWS staff surveys.

"Staff caseload size" refers to the average number of clients for whom each frontline staff member was responsible, based on members' responses to a single question about the current size of their caseload. The values of this measure ranged widely across offices, from 70 clients to 367 clients per staff member; the average was 136 clients per staff member.

"Disagreement among frontline staff" indicates the variation in staff members' perceptions of the first three aspects of program implementation. A value for the measure was obtained for each office by averaging the variances of frontline staff responses for the three scales. "Disagreement between frontline staff and supervisors" refers to the difference between the perceptions of frontline staff and supervisors with respect to the same three aspects of program implementation. Thus, the last two measures of implementation, each standardized to have a mean of 0 and a standard deviation of 1 across offices, reflect the degree to which frontline staff members and supervisors had a common vision of the program.

Program-Activity Differential   The next set of office-level independent variables are differences between the program group and the control group with respect to the rate of participation in the three main types of activities sponsored by welfare-to-work programs: job-search assistance, basic education, and vocational training.[12] These general categories encompass many specific activities. Basic education includes adult education classes, preparation for the General Educational Development (GED) certificate, and courses in English as a second language. Job search assistance includes self-directed job search and job clubs. Vocational training includes classroom training in basic occupational skills, on-the-job training, unpaid work experience, and postsecondary education or training.

The data used to construct the measures of the program-services contrast were obtained from surveys administered in the original experiments to a random subsample of program and control-group members roughly two years after random assignment. The size of the subsamples ranged from 27 sample members to 2,159 sample members across offices, averaging 258 sample members. The response rates, which were not computed at the office level, ranged from 70 percent to 93 percent across the counties represented in the studies.

The differences between the percentages of program-group members and control-group members who participated in each activity reflect the degree to which the programs increased clients' exposure to them. These program-activity differentials thus represent three facets of the program-services contrast, to which any program impacts are attributable.

Program Environment   The final independent variable in level two of our model was the unemployment rate for each office, which was computed—in a way that accounted for the fact that different sample members entered the studies at different times—as the average monthly unemployment rate during the two-year period after random assignment in the county where the office was situated. County-level unemployment statistics were obtained from publicly available information provided by the Bureau of Labor Statistics and the California Employment Development Department.

Assessment of the Measures   Before using the office-level independent variables, we assessed their variability, reliability, and validity.

Variability. The cross-office variances for 8 of the 10 office-level independent variables were statistically significant at the 0.001 level (Bloom, Hill, and Riccio 2001). The variance for the staff-supervisor disagreement measure was not statistically significant (probably because there were only one or two supervisors in most of the offices), and the statistical significance of the variance for the staff disagreement measure could not be determined. Nevertheless, we included all ten measures in our model because they were conceptually important.

Reliability. Both forms of reliability were high for the three measures for which it could be assessed, namely, emphasis on quick job entry, emphasis on personalized attention, and closeness of monitoring. The inter-item reliability coefficients for these measures ranged from 0.76 to 0.84, and the corresponding inter-rater reliability coefficients ranged from 0.76 to 0.83 (Bloom, Hill, and Riccio 2001).

Validity. Both the face validity and the construct validity were high. In terms of face validity, there is a prima facie case that the staff survey questions used to measure implementation (see table 2.3), for example, tap into the constructs that they purport to measure. There are equally strong cases for the caseload size indicator, program-activity differentials, and unemployment rate.

To assess construct validity, we correlated the measures with each other and found the pattern that one would expect in light of the constructs they are intended to represent (Bloom, Hill, and Riccio 2001). For example, program emphasis on quick job entry is positively correlated with increased participation in job search assistance and negatively correlated with increased participation in basic education or vocational training. In addition, program emphasis on personalized attention and closeness of monitoring are positively correlated with each other and negatively correlated with average caseload size. Furthermore, local unemployment rates are negatively correlated with the control group's mean earnings.

Presenting the Findings

To present findings based on any statistical model correctly, completely, and concisely is as much an art as a science. This is especially true for multilevel models, the parameters of which relate to different entities at different levels. Using our welfare-to-work research synthesis, we illustrate one of several appropriate ways to present such findings.

As a point of departure, recall that the programs we studied increased client earnings by an average of $879, or 18 percent, during a two-year period. The unconditional impacts varied from -$1,412 to $4,217 across offices, and the total cross-office variation was unlikely to have occurred by chance alone.

The results for our model indicate that only 16 percent of the cross-office variation in unconditional program impacts is attributable to client characteristics, whereas client and program characteristics together account for 80 percent. These findings suggest that our model was successful at explaining local variation in program effectiveness and that program characteristics were more influential than client characteristics in this regard.

Program Characteristics and Program Effectiveness

Table 2.4 presents estimates of how each program characteristic in our model affected program impacts on two-year earnings, controlling statistically for client characteristics and the other program characteristics. The estimated regression coefficient for each program characteristic (from equation 2.2), shown in the first column, represents the change in impact per unit change in the characteristic, holding constant all other client and program characteristics. The partially standardized regression coefficient for each program characteristic, shown in the second column, represents the change in impact per standard deviation change in the characteristic, holding constant all other client and program characteristics. The statistical significance level, or p-value, for each estimated regression coefficient appears in the third column. The smaller the p-value is, the less likely it is that the coefficient would have its estimated value (or a larger one in absolute value) if the characteristic it represents did not influence program impacts. The standard error for each regression coefficient, shown in the fourth column, can be used to construct confidence intervals.

The fifth column in table 2.4 expresses the findings as conditional

Table 2.4 Effects of Program Characteristics on Program Impacts

Program Characteristic	Regression Coefficient (Dollars)	Partially Standardized Regression Coefficient (Dollars)	Statistical Significance (p-value)	Standard Error (Dollars)	Conditional Impact Interval (Dollars)
Implementation					
Emphasis on quick job entry	720***	720***	0.000002	$134	$397 to 1,361
Emphasis on personalized attention	428***	428***	0.0002	107	592 to 1,166
Closeness of monitoring	–197	–197	0.110	121	1,011 to 747
Staff caseload size	–4***	–268***	0.003	1	1,058 to 700
Staff disagreement	124	124	0.141	83	796 to 962
Staff-supervisor disagreement	–159*	–159*	0.102	96	986 to 772
Activities					
Basic education	–16**	–208**	0.017	6	1,017 to 741
Job-search assistance	1	12	0.899	9	871 to 887
Vocational training	7	71	0.503	11	831 to 927
Economic environment					
Unemployment rate	–94***	–291***	0.004	30	1,074 to 684

Source: Authors' calculations based on GAIN, PI, and NEWWS administrative records data, staff survey data, and follow-up survey data.
Notes: Regression coefficients are reported in 1996 dollars per unit change in each independent variable. Partially standardized regression coefficients are reported in 1996 dollars per standard deviation change in each independent variable. These coefficients are estimated simultaneously with those reported in table 2.5. The grand mean impact is $879, or 18 percent of the counterfactual. Two-tailed statistical significance is indicated as * for the 0.10 level, ** for the 0.05 level, and *** for the 0.01 level.

impact intervals. Developed for the purposes of this study, this way of presenting the results reveals how predicted program impacts vary when the value of one program characteristic spans its interquartile range—that is, when the value of that characteristic shifts from the 25th percentile to the 75th percentile—and all other independent variables remain at their mean values.[13] In other words, it represents the conditional response of program impacts to a standardized change in a program characteristic for the average sample member in the average program office.

The following are five examples of findings from the multilevel analysis shown in table 2.4 (for a more complete discussion of the findings, see Bloom, Hill, and Riccio 2003).

A Strong Employment Message from Program Staff is a Powerful Catalyst for Change in Client Earnings   The emphasis placed by welfare-to-work program staff on quick job entry had a substantial influence on program impacts that is unlikely to be due to chance. Indeed, this factor appears to have had a larger influence on client earnings than did any program characteristic that was considered in our model. The coefficient for this multiquestion survey scale indicates that when emphasis on quick job entry increases by one unit, program impacts increase by $720, when all other client and program characteristics are held constant. To place this finding in perspective, recall that the mean program impact (when all independent variables are at their mean values) is $879. If the quick job entry scale were increased by one unit and all other variables remained constant, the estimated impact would increase from $879 to $1,599, or from 18 percent to 33 percent of the average counterfactual (that is, of the control group's mean earnings, which were $4,871).

Because the employment message scale is defined to have a standard deviation of 1, the partially standardized regression coefficient in the second column in table 2.4 for this variable equals its unstandardized coefficient in the first column and therefore adds no new information. Thus, a one-unit change in the scale equals a change of one standard deviation. This is not the case for some of the other program characteristics in the model.

The third column indicates that the statistical significance, or p-value, for quick job entry equals 0.000002. Hence, the observed relationship between program emphasis on quick job entry and program impacts would be extremely unlikely to occur if this message did not matter. The fifth column shows that the conditional impact interval for the quick job entry scale is $397 to $1,361, or 8 percent to 28 percent of the average counterfactual. For a two-quartile (fifty-percentage-point) difference in the value of the scale, this is a substantial difference in impacts.

The finding for emphasis on quick job entry indicates that, without additional funding, managers of welfare-to-work programs might markedly improve program performance by inculcating in their staff the importance of focusing on getting clients into jobs quickly.

Larger Staff Caseloads Result in Smaller Impacts on Client Earnings   The estimated influence of caseload size on program impacts is negative, large, and unlikely to have occurred by chance alone. The regression coefficient for this variable indicates that, on average, program impacts decline by $4 with each additional client per caseworker, holding constant all other client and program characteristics. It is more useful, however, to view this result through the lens of a partially standardized regression coefficient. This parameter implies that if caseload size were increased by one standard deviation (sixty-seven clients), program impacts would decline by $268. Thus, increasing caseload size by one standard deviation would reduce the mean program impact on earnings from $879 to $611, or from 18 percent to 13 percent of the average counterfactual.

The conditional impact interval for this variable indicates that impacts are predicted to range from $1,058 (when average caseload size is 91 clients per caseworker and all other independent variables are at their mean values) to $700 (when average caseload size is 181 clients per caseworker and all other independent variables are at their mean values). This interval implies a range of impacts from 22 percent to 14 percent of the average counterfactual.

This finding underscores the importance of focusing attention on the most important human resource for such programs: caseworkers. While this finding is consistent with conventional wisdom, it is not consistent with prior results from the Riverside GAIN caseload experiment (Riccio, Friedlander, and Freedman 1994). Our analysis examines caseloads that are much larger and vary much more than those in the Riverside GAIN experiment. It is possible, then, that the findings are consistent because program impacts may erode substantially only when caseloads approach the higher end of the range. The implication is that policymakers should make sure that funding levels are adequate to maintain suitably low caseload levels.

Increasing the Emphasis on Basic Education Reduces Earnings Impacts, at Least in the Short Run   The regression coefficient for the basic education measure is negative and statistically significant. It implies that program impacts decline by $16 for each one-point increase in the percentage of clients who receive basic education as a result of the program, holding constant all other client and program characteristics. The partially standardized regression coefficient indicates that program impacts decline by $208 when the percentage of clients who receive basic education as a result of the program increases by one standard deviation (thirteen percentage points). The conditional impact interval for this variable is $1,017 to $741, or 21 percent to 15 percent of the average counterfactual.

This finding regarding the short-run effects of basic education is consistent with the original findings from the GAIN and NEWWS evaluations (Hamilton et al. 2001; Riccio, Friedlander, and Freedman 1994). It has important practical implications both for policymakers who design programs and for local managers and frontline workers who have discretion over clients' program-activity options. Where basic education often does not have a clear employment focus or make a direct connection to the world of work, vocational training usually does both. The opportunity costs of vocational training—the difference between the benefits accrued as a result of engaging in one activity and the benefits forgone as a result of not engaging in alternative activities—are similar to those of basic education. In our model, however, the conditional effect of vocational training on earnings impacts was not statistically significant ($p = 0.503$).

Welfare-to-work clients are often mandated to attend basic education classes as an initial activity. Basic education might be less effective for such people than for people who choose this option for themselves (Hamilton and Brock 1994). Thus, an extreme emphasis on immediate mandatory basic education might be detrimental to client earnings but when undertaken in moderation and on a voluntary basis, it might be beneficial for some clients.[14]

It Is Difficult to Increase Client Earnings When Jobs Are Scarce   The regression coefficient for the unemployment rate is negative, large, and unlikely to have occurred by chance. It implies that a one-percentage-point increase in unemployment reduces program impacts by $94, when all other client and program characteristics are held constant. The partially standardized regression coefficient indicates that an increase in unemployment of one standard deviation (3.1 percentage points) reduces program impacts by $291. The conditional impact interval is $1,074 to $684, or 22 percent to 14 percent of the average counterfactual. Although a meta-analysis by David H. Greenberg, Charles Michalopoulos, and Philip K. Robins (2003) found no relationship between the unemployment rate and program impacts on earnings for women or men, it did reveal a negative relationship between the two variables for youth. The negative relationship between the unemployment rate and program impacts in both the meta-analysis and in our study thus indicates that a high unemployment rate can reduce the effectiveness of welfare-to-work programs, implying that welfare recipients are likely to face especially stiff competition in weak labor markets. Further, this finding suggests that state and local government agencies striving to set equitable standards for judging the performance of programs they fund should hold programs harmless against conditions that, like the unemployment rate, affect impacts but lie outside programs' control.

It Is Probably More Useful to Look at Program Characteristics in Constellations Than in Isolation   Perhaps the most illuminating way to apply findings like those in table 2.4 is to use them to predict the likely impacts of alternative approaches to designing programs, managing programs, or both. Alternative program approaches typically reflect different belief systems about the nature of the social problem in question and thus about the likely effectiveness of various solutions to it. Each approach typically comprises a constellation of characteristics rather than a set of unrelated characteristics. Consider the following realistic examples of alternative program approaches in the welfare-to-work context:

Close Direction of Staff and Clients

Staff members encourage clients to get jobs quickly.

Staff members support this strategy through personal client attention.

Staff members monitor client progress closely.

Staff members share this vision with each other.

Staff members share this vision with their supervisors.

Laissez-Faire Management of Staff and Clients

Caseload sizes are large.

Clients do not receive personal attention.

Client progress is not monitored closely.

Staff members do not share a common vision of the program.

Staff members do not share a common vision of the program with their supervisors.

Assuming that close direction of staff members and clients means that each program characteristic listed is one standard deviation above its mean value (or below it, depending on how the variable was defined) and that all client and other program characteristics are at their mean values, our model predicts that the first approach would increase client earnings by $1,865, or 38 percent of the average counterfactual. Assuming that laissez-faire management of staff and clients means that each program characteristic listed is one standard deviation below its mean value (or above it, depending on how the variable was defined) and that all client and other program characteristics are at their mean values, our model predicts that the second approach would increase client earnings by $345, or 7 percent of the average counterfactual. Clearly, the difference between these two impacts represents an enormous difference in program effectiveness.[15] Thus, it is likely to be well worth the effort of program funders and managers to influence the factors underlying this difference.

Client Characteristics and Program Effectiveness

Table 2.5 shows how program impacts vary with each client characteristic in our model, when all the other client and program characteristics are held constant. As noted earlier, client characteristics as a group explain 16 percent of the variation in impacts across local program offices. Because client characteristics are defined as categories and represented by binary indicator variables, it is necessary to report only the regression coefficient for each category, its p-value, and its standard error. (Partially standardized regression coefficients are not informative.) The coefficients represent the regression-adjusted difference between the mean program impact for a sample member with the specified characteristic and the mean program impact for a sample member who does not have that characteristic, with all the other client and program characteristics held constant.

For example, the regression coefficient of $653 for clients with a high school diploma or GED at the time of random assignment implies that the impact for sample members with this credential is $653 larger than that for clients without it, where all other client and program characteristics are held constant. This finding is highly statistically significant (p = 0.001).

Extending this type of interpretation to client characteristics with more than two categories is straightforward. Consider, for example, the number of children whom clients had at the time of random assignment. The regression coefficient for sample members who had three or more children (which is highly statistically significant) indicates that program impacts for clients in this category are $591 larger than for clients who are comparable to this group in every way except that they had one or no children.

The only other statistically significant coefficient in table 2.5 is for sample members who received welfare during all twelve months be-

Table 2.5   Effects of Client Characteristics on Program Impacts

Client Characteristic at Random Assignment	Regression Coefficient (Dollars)	Statistical Significance (p-value)	Standard Error (Dollars)
Was a high school graduate or had a GED	653***	0.001	187
Had two children	301	0.160	214
Had three or more children	591***	0.003	199
Had a child under six years old	34	0.841	171
Was younger than twenty-five	206	0.557	351
Was twenty-five to thirty-four	105	0.707	281
Was thirty-five to forty-four	305	0.376	345
Was black, non-Hispanic	−178	0.369	199
Was Hispanic	−213	0.527	337
Was Native American	−696	0.115	442
Was Asian	353	0.560	606
Was some other race or ethnicity	726	0.487	1,044
Was a welfare applicant	−145	0.532	232
Had received welfare continuously for the past twelve months	444*	0.085	258
Had earned $1 to $2,499	−186	0.222	152
Had earned $2,500 to $7,499	72	0.787	267
Had earned $7,500 or more	22	0.965	501

Source: Authors' calculations based on GAIN, PI, and NEWWS administrative records data and baseline survey data.
Notes: Each regression coefficient represents the change in mean impacts on earnings for the category specified, relative to the implied omitted category (and conditional on all other variables in the model). These coefficients are estimated simultaneously with those reported in table 2.4. The grand mean impact is $879, or 18 percent of the counterfactual. Two-tailed statistical significance is indicated as * for the 0.10 level, ** for the 0.05 level, and *** for the 0.01 level.

fore random assignment and were thus more welfare-dependent than average. This coefficient indicates that program impacts for sample members in this group were $444 larger than for those who were less welfare-dependent, when all other client and program characteristics were held constant.

The findings in table 2.5 paint a variegated picture of how client characteristics affect the impacts of welfare-to-work programs. Most characteristics do not seem to make much difference, and the few that do make a difference suggest that the programs are not consistently more or less effective for clients who are more or less job-ready. These findings have two important implications for policymakers and program planners. First, it appears that welfare-to-work programs can be effective for many types of clients, not just for those with a few particular characteristics. Second, it appears that targeting clients according to how hard or easy they are to serve will not necessarily influence program effectiveness.

Robustness of the Findings

A final, key, step in any modeling process is to assess the robustness of the findings that it produces. Especially for policy purposes, it is helpful to understand whether the findings are driven by, or sensitive to, a few unique observations. We therefore addressed three questions related to the robustness of our research synthesis.

Did the Highest- and Lowest-Performing Offices Drive the Results?   To test robustness with respect to outliers (extreme values) of the dependent variable, we deleted the offices with the most positive impact estimates and the offices with the most negative impact estimates and reestimated the model.[16] The main findings held even when these extreme cases were omitted.

For example, the regression coefficient for emphasis on quick job entry started at $720 for the full sample, dropped to $601 with the three highest-performing and the three lowest-performing offices omitted, and declined to $399 (an impact that was still highly statistically significant) with the five highest-performing offices and the five lowest-performing offices omitted. Thus, although the magnitude of this coefficient estimate changed, its meaning and statistical significance remained consistent, even with ten of fifty-nine offices absent from the sample. Other coefficient estimates that were statistically significant for the full sample also passed this test of robustness.

Did the Offices with the Most Extreme Program Characteristics Drive the Results?   Our second strategy for testing robustness focused on outliers with respect to the independent variables (program characteristics) that had large and statistically significant regression coefficients for the full sample. For each of these program characteristics, we deleted local offices with the most extreme values and reestimated the model. We repeated this process until the five offices with the highest values and the five offices with the lowest values were eliminated. The magnitudes of the estimated coefficients changed very little during this process, and in all but a few cases they remained statistically significant at the 0.10 level at every stage.

Did Higher-Level Aggregate Programs Drive the Results?   The third strategy that we used to test the robustness of our findings was to check whether local offices that represented particular umbrella programs (GAIN, PI, or NEWWS) or local offices that represented particular state programs (California GAIN, California NEWWS, Florida PI, Georgia NEWWS, Michigan NEWWS, Ohio NEWWS, Oklahoma NEWWS, or Oregon NEWWS) drove the results. In other words, we tested for higher-order aggregate program influences on program effectiveness.

To test for umbrella program effects, we added binary indicator variables for two of the three programs to our level 2 regressions (equations 2.2, 2.3, and 2.4) and reestimated the model. To test for state program effects, we added binary indicators for seven of the eight state programs in our sample and reestimated the model. The results of these sensitivity tests were encouraging. The regression coefficients for emphasis on quick job entry, personalized attention, and unemployment rate maintained approximately the same magnitude and statistical significance when the variables for umbrella programs or state programs were included in the model. The only exception was staff caseload size, which showed a pattern of findings that was difficult to interpret.[17]

The robustness of the findings to this extensive series of sensitivity tests bolstered our confidence in the model and the general modeling approach that it represents.

Future Extensions of the Model

Even given the considerable strengths of the model presented here, we acknowledge that it probably does not fully capture the subtleties of the ways in which program and client characteristics influence the effectiveness of welfare-to-work programs. This is because we kept the analysis simple (minimizing the number of parameters estimated) both to keep its interpretation clear and to maximize its statistical power. We see this work not as the last word but as a first step in a larger research agenda.

One way in which the model simplifies reality is its specification that each program characteristic have the same effect on program impacts regardless of its value. Another simplification is the specification that each program characteristic have the same effect on program impacts regardless of the other program and client characteristics. In other words, the model assumes that the influence of program characteristics on program impacts is linear and additive. These assumptions may be reasonable for the purpose of predicting the implications of small differences in program characteristics, but they are probably less suitable when one aims to predict the effects of large differences in program characteristics.

Another way to think about these two simplifications is to note that they imply the absence of thresholds and interactions. A threshold, sometimes referred to as a tipping point, is the point below (or above) which a program characteristic does not affect impacts and above (or below) which it does affect impacts.[18] For example, staff caseload size might not affect program impacts until it exceeds a particularly high level. An interaction reflects a synergy among program characteristics. For example, vocational training provided in conjunction with minimal job-search assistance might have no effect on program impacts, whereas it might have a substantial effect when job-search assistance is more strongly emphasized, helping to convert skills into jobs. Similarly, certain program features might interact with client characteristics, making a difference for certain types of clients but not for others.

The present model also does not account for the possibility that program activity differentials are intermediate factors that affect the relationships between program impacts and other program and client characteristics. In other words, the model does not account for the possibility that implementation practices, economic conditions, and client characteristics have indirect effects on program impacts through their effects on what program activities are received by sample members.

Finally, the present model does not consider how program and client characteristics affect program impacts on other labor market and welfare-related outcomes in the short run or in the long run. Although the focus of this analysis was on a single short-run program outcome—total earnings during the two years after random assignment—different types of outcomes may respond differently to variation in the same program characteristics. Furthermore, long-run impacts may look different than short-run impacts.

For all these reasons, this research synthesis is only one piece of a larger puzzle. Fortunately, if appropriate data are collected in experiments evaluating social programs, the present analytic strategy can be extended to help fill in the missing pieces.

Identifying Conditions for Applying the Approach

This chapter focuses on how to use randomized experiments to learn what works best for whom and under what conditions. Theoretically, the ideal research design for this purpose is random assignment of a very large number of individuals to many different combinations of program characteristics. An experimental design would allow one to directly measure the effectiveness of different program strategies for different target groups under different conditions. In practice, however, such an approach is rarely—if ever—feasible.

When a fully experimental design is infeasible, we propose an alternative approach that builds directly on the methodological strengths of randomized experiments by pooling impact and implementation data to model natural cross-site variation in program implementation, activities, environments, and clients. Having outlined the general issues and the steps to be taken in this modeling process and illustrated the process with a detailed empirical example, we now discuss what is needed to apply the approach successfully in other fields and the implications of the approach for future evaluation research.

Several conditions must be met for the approach that we propose to be applied successfully. These conditions concern the adequacy of the model as a conceptual and statistical framework, the quality and consistency of the data that make the model operational, the appropriateness of the analyses used to estimate the model's parameters, and the statistical properties of these parameters.[19]

Although our approach builds on a solid foundation of experimental impact estimates, it relies heavily on a nonexperimental model of natural variation in program impacts and characteristics. The findings are therefore only as valid as the model that produces them. To maximize validity, one must include in the model all four major categories of factors that can influence program effectiveness: implementation, activities, environment, and clients. And within each category, one must include as many as possible of the specific factors judged by researchers and practitioners to have a substantial influence on program impacts while at the same time striving for statistical power and clarity of interpretation. Striking this balance requires a deep understanding of the relevant theoretical and empirical literatures as well as broad exposure to the relevant policy and administrative debates about best practice. Because these types of knowledge span disciplines and professions, a closely knit research team with diverse backgrounds and skills is most likely to be successful at properly grounding a research synthesis model in theory and practice.

In all the experiments being pooled, the primary data must be consistently defined and carefully collected and must reflect the key characteristics of the sample members and the program sites. In addition, the data must be highly variable, reliable, and valid. These criteria are unlikely to be met without a concerted, coordinated effort to develop and refine measures across a series of studies. Although a number of strategies may promote such development and refinement, it is likely that a single large research organization with a stable, focused mission and long-term senior staff can provide the institutional memory needed to maintain momentum and quality over long periods of time. Moreover, major funders of evaluation research could increase the likelihood of adequate data being available for research synthesis by designing their funding efforts and requirements accordingly.

Measuring the determinants of program effectiveness is an inherently multilevel modeling problem. When addressing multilevel problems, it is crucial to capture the main levels of observation and analysis involved in an appropriate way to ensure the model's efficiency, accuracy, and conceptual clarity. Fortunately, the statistical methods for such modeling are increasingly well developed and understood, and the software for using these methods is becoming more widely available.

Implications for Future Research

We have presented a way to accumulate knowledge about what makes social programs effective that uses multilevel production functions, primary data from randomized experiments, and natural cross-experiment variation in individual and program characteristics. It is important to bear in mind that this approach to research synthesis relies on the careful collection of comprehensive and consistent data in randomized experiments that represent a large number and broad range of circumstances. Thus, as social scientists and policy researchers develop their research agendas and government agencies and foundations make their funding plans, we would urge them to adopt a long-run strategy that emphasizes the following: random-assignment designs that yield valid, reliable estimates of program effectiveness; multisite experiments that reflect the natural variation in program effectiveness; careful specification of the likely determinants of program effectiveness based on theory in the social sciences, past empirical research, and practitioner knowledge; careful and consistent measurement of the hypothesized determinants of program effectiveness across studies and sites; adequate support for and attention to quantitative syntheses of this information; and a concerted effort to compare the findings from nonexperimental and experimental research so that the limitations, opportunities, and tradeoffs may be better understood.

Improving the performance of social programs calls for an understanding of how best to organize, manage, and implement them. If expressly supported and developed, the type of research synthesis described here holds considerable promise as a way to arrive at such an understanding in many social policy fields.

Notes

1. The strengths and limitations of random-assignment experiments are well known. For further discussion see, for example, Gary Burtless (1995) and James J. Heckman and Jeffrey A. Smith (1995).
2. Additional information about the measures and methods used can be found in Riccio, Bloom, and Hill (2000) and Bloom, Hill, and Riccio (2001).
3. In working papers presenting this research, we used the term "program

management" rather than "program implementation" to reflect the fact that all the local office characteristics examined in this study lay within program managers' potential sphere of control (Riccio, Bloom, and Hill 2000; Bloom, Hill, and Riccio 2001). Because we expect most readers of this chapter to be accustomed to referring to such factors as implementation, however, we use the latter term here.

4. For simplicity, we ignore the fact that this design would result in spillover effects (as discussed in chapter 4 in this volume) and that the program would probably be provided in separate classes, creating a three-level situation in which students are clustered within classes and classes are clustered within schools.

5. More complex models might specify additional random effects, but for illustrative purposes we focus on the simplest plausible model.

6. Among the several software packages that allow for estimation of such models are HLM, SAS (PROC MIXED command), Stata (gllamm command), MLwiN, and VARCL.

7. Ita G. Kreft (1996) reviewed evidence comparing multilevel models with alternative estimation procedures; Stephen Raudenbush and Xiaofeng Liu (2000) discussed standard errors for coefficient estimates in hierarchical models of multisite random assignment experiments; and Carolyn J. Heinrich and Laurence E. Lynn (2001) compared results from multilevel, individual-level OLS, and aggregate-level OLS estimation for various outcomes in Job Training Partnership Act programs.

8. Note that the analysis sample considered here includes all the program-group members, not only those who participated in particular components of the program. Thus, the impact being modeled is that of the *intent to treat* rather than that of the *treatment on the treated* (for a detailed discussion of this distinction, see chapter 3 in this volume).

9. Concerns about reliability and validity generally pertain both to dependent and to independent variables; in the discussion here, we focus on the independent variables involving multiple raters and multiple items.

10. In a multilevel context, the reliability coefficient "measures the ratio of the *true score* or parameter variance, relative to the *observed score* or total variance of (each aggregate unit's sample mean outcome). The reliability . . . will be close to 1 when (a) the group means . . . vary substantially across level-2 units (holding constant the sample size per group); or (b) the sample size . . . is large" (Raudenbush and Bryk 2002, 46; emphasis in original).

11. Bloom, Hill, and Riccio (2001, 88) described how these averages were regression-adjusted to control for office differences in staff characteristics. Although the adjustments were minimal, they helped hold constant differences in the perceptions of different types of staff members.

12. Bloom, Hill, and Riccio (2001, 91) described how these participation differences were regression-adjusted to control for minor differences in the background characteristics of program and control group members in each office. This procedure was performed to increase the precision of the program-activity measures and to allow them to be estimated in a way that is consistent with the estimation of the program impacts.

13. To ensure consistent treatment of each independent variable, this calculation proceeds as if the independent variables were distributed normally across offices and sets the lower value of the interquartile range equal to 0.67 standard deviation below the mean and the upper value equal to 0.67 standard deviation above the mean. In a normal distribution, these are the 25th and 75th percentile values, respectively.

14. It is also worth noting that we find no effect of job search on program impacts.

15. Note that these predictions do not account for such possible nonlinearities as interaction effects or thresholds, which we discuss briefly later in the chapter.

16. As described in Bloom, Hill, and Riccio (2001, appendix D), first the two highest- and the two lowest-performing offices were removed; then the three highest- and lowest-performing offices were removed; and the testing continued until the five highest- and lowest-performing offices were deleted from the sample (leaving forty-nine in the estimated model). Because GAIN's Riverside office and NEWWS's Portland office were known to be especially high performers in their respective evaluations, we conducted a separate analysis omitting only the offices in each of these sites, separately and together. The basic findings were robust to the deletion of offices using all the above strategies.

17. These are unpublished results.

18. The best-known example of a tipping point involves transitions in the racial composition of neighborhoods, but the concept applies to a broad range of other phenomena (Gladwell 2000).

19. Lynn, Heinrich, and Hill (2001) discussed these and other concerns in their call for more rigorous, quantitative analyses of the influence of public governance and management on the performance of public policies and programs. Greenberg et al. (2003) suggested specific steps one can take to obtain more reliable estimates of the effects of program and client characteristics on program effectiveness.

References

Bane, Mary Jo. 1989. "Welfare Reform and Mandatory Versus Voluntary Work: Policy Issue or Management Problem?" *Journal of Policy Analysis and Management* 8(2): 285–89.

Behn, Robert. 1991. *Leadership Counts: Lessons for Public Managers from the Massachusetts Welfare, Training and Employment Program.* Cambridge, Mass.: Harvard University Press.

Bloom, Howard S., Carolyn J. Hill, and James Riccio. 2001. *Modeling the Performance of Welfare-to-Work Programs: The Effects of Program Management and Services, Economic Environment, and Client Characteristics.* New York: MDRC.

———. 2003. "Linking Program Implementation and Effectiveness: Lessons from a Pooled Sample of Welfare-to-Work Experiments." *Journal of Policy Analysis and Management* 22(4): 551–75.

Burtless, Gary. 1995. "The Case for Randomized Field Trials in Economic and Policy Research." *Journal of Economic Perspectives* 9(2): 63–84.

Campbell, Donald T., and Donald W. Fiske. 1959. "Convergent and Discriminant Validation by the Multitrait-Multimethod Matrix." *Psychological Bulletin* 56(1): 81–105.

Friedlander, Daniel. 1988. *Subgroup Impacts and Performance Indicators for Selected Welfare Employment Programs.* New York: MDRC.

Friedlander, Daniel, and Gary Burtless. 1995. *Five Years After: The Long-Term Effects of Welfare-to-Work Programs.* New York: Russell Sage Foundation.

Gladwell, Malcolm. 2000. *The Tipping Point.* Boston: Little, Brown.

Greenberg, David H., Robert Meyer, Charles Michalopoulos, and Michael Wiseman. 2003. "Explaining Variation in the Effects of Welfare-to-Work Programs." *Evaluation Review* 27(4): 359–94.

Greenberg, David H., Charles Michalopoulos, and Philip K. Robins. 2003. "A Meta-Analysis of Government-Sponsored Training Programs." *Industrial and Labor Relations Review* 57(1): 31–53.

Gueron, Judith M., and Edward Pauly. 1991. *From Welfare to Work.* New York: Russell Sage Foundation.

Hamilton, Gayle, and Thomas Brock. 1994. *The JOBS Evaluation: Early Lessons from Seven Sites.* Washington: U.S. Department of Health and Human Services and U.S. Department of Education.

Hamilton, Gayle, Steven Freedman, Lisa Gennetian, Charles Michalopoulos, Johanna Walter, Diane Adams-Ciardullo, Anna Gassman-Pines, Sharon McGroder, Martha Zaslow, Jennifer Brooks, and Sirjeet Ahluwalia. 2001. *How Effective Are Different Welfare-to-Work Approaches? Five-Year Adult and Child Impacts for Eleven Programs.* Washington: U.S. Department of Health and Human Services and U.S. Department of Education.

Hanushek, Eric A. 1997. "Assessing the Effects of School Resources on Student Performance: An Update." *Educational Evaluation and Policy Analysis* 19(2): 141–64.

Heckman, James J., and Jeffrey A. Smith. 1995. "Assessing the Case for Social Experiments." *Journal of Economic Perspectives* 9(2): 85–110.

Heinrich, Carolyn J. 2002. "Outcomes-Based Performance Management in the Public Sector: Implications for Government Accountability and Effectiveness." *Public Administration Review* 62(6): 712–25.

Heinrich, Carolyn J., and Laurence E. Lynn, Jr. 2001. "Means and Ends: A Comparative Study of Empirical Methods for Investigating Governance and Performance." *Journal of Public Administration Research and Theory* 11(1): 109–38.

Knox, Virginia, Cynthia Miller, and Lisa Gennetian. 2000. *Reforming Welfare and Rewarding Work: A Summary of the Final Report on the Minnesota Family Investment Program.* New York: MDRC.

Kornfeld, Robert, and Howard S. Bloom. 1999. "Measuring Program Impacts on Earnings and Employment: Do Unemployment Insurance Wage Reports from Employers Agree with Surveys of Individuals?" *Journal of Labor Economics* 17(1): 168–97.

Kreft, Ita G. 1996. "Are Multilevel Techniques Necessary? An Overview, Including Simulation Studies." Working paper. California State University, Los Angeles.

Lynn, Laurence E., Jr., Carolyn J. Heinrich, and Carolyn J. Hill. 2001. *Improving Governance: A New Logic for Empirical Research.* Washington, D.C.: Georgetown University Press.

Mead, Lawrence M. 1983. "Expectations and Welfare Work: WIN in New York City." *Policy Studies Review* 2(4): 648–61.

Meyer, Robert H. 1997. "Value-Added Indicators of School Performance: A Primer." *Economics of Education Review* 16(3): 283–301.

Nunnally, Jum C. 1967. *Psychometric Theory.* New York: McGraw-Hill.

Raudenbush, Stephen W., and Anthony S. Bryk. 2002. *Hierarchical Linear Models: Applications and Data Analysis Methods.* 2nd edition. Thousand Oaks, Calif.: Sage Publications.

Raudenbush, Stephen W., and Xiaofeng Liu. 2000. "Statistical Power and Optimal Design for Multisite Randomized Trials." *Psychological Methods* 5(2): 199–213.

Riccio, James, Howard S. Bloom, and Carolyn J. Hill. 2000. "Management, Organizational Characteristics, and Performance: The Case of Welfare-to-Work Programs." In *Governance and Performance: New Perspectives,* edited by Carolyn J. Heinrich and Laurence E. Lynn, Jr. Washington, D.C.: Georgetown University Press.

Riccio, James, Daniel Friedlander, and Stephen Freedman. 1994. *GAIN: Benefits, Costs, and Three-Year Impacts of a Welfare-to-Work Program.* New York: MDRC.

Robinson, W. 1950. "Ecological Correlations and the Behavior of Individuals." *American Sociological Review* 15(3): 351–57.

Snijders, Tom A. B., and Roel J. Bosker. 1999. *Multilevel Analysis: An Introduction to Basic and Advanced Multilevel Modeling.* London: Sage Publications.

Taylor, Corrine. 2001. "The Relationship Between Student Performance and School Expenditures: A Review of the Literature and New Evidence Using Better Data." In *Improving Educational Productivity,* edited by David H. Monk and Herbert J. Walberg. Greenwich, Conn.: Information Age Publishing.

U.S. Department of Labor. Bureau of Labor Statistics. 2001. *Consumer Price Index.* Available at: www.bls.gov/cpi (accessed January 7, 2005).

Chapter 3

Constructing Instrumental Variables from Experimental Data to Explore How Treatments Produce Effects

A RANDOM-ASSIGNMENT study can provide the most compelling evidence possible about how an intervention—be it social, economic, legal, or medical—affects the people to whom it is targeted. Randomization entails using a lotterylike process to assign each eligible sample member either to a group that is offered the intervention or to a group that is not. This process ensures that the two groups are the same in every way (in statistical expectation), except that one group is assigned to the intervention and the other is not. Any statistically significant differences between the two groups that are subsequently observed can be confidently attributed to the intervention.

This is why randomization, often referred to as the gold standard for studying cause-and-effect relationships, is now widely used in many fields of research. In medicine, more than 350,000 randomized clinical trials have been conducted during the last fifty years (Cochrane Collaboration 2002). In social policy, a total of more than 800,000 people were randomly assigned in two hundred twenty studies between 1962 and 1997 (Greenberg and Shroder 1997). Reflecting and reinforcing these trends, the Institute of Education Sciences was created within the U.S. Department of Education in 2002 in the belief that amassing rigorous, credible evidence about the effects of education interventions calls for randomized control trials (U.S. Department of Education 2003). The spread of randomization in social policy research has not been confined to the United States. In the developing world, the effectiveness of a variety of poverty-reduction programs, particularly ones focused on improving children's education attainment, are increasingly likely to be evaluated using random-assignment designs (see, for example, Schultz

2001). Here we refer to any study that uses random assignment as an experiment.

Problems related to sample selection, randomization, and attrition can undermine experimental designs, thereby preventing researchers from drawing valid causal inferences and reducing the policy relevance of the research. Although these problems deserve careful consideration, this chapter does not address them. Key assumptions underlying the present discussion are that an experiment's random-assignment process is well designed and successfully executed and that data collection is complete (or nearly complete) for the individuals or other entities under study.

But even well-realized experiments have limitations that are important to recognize if one is to interpret findings correctly and to design studies that provide the highest-quality, most policy-relevant information possible. We briefly review these limitations before introducing the methodological approach that is the centerpiece of this chapter.

First, even when random assignment is feasible, full compliance with its outcome usually cannot be assured. For example, one can randomize the offer of a new medical treatment to patients afflicted with a particular type of cancer, but one cannot guarantee full randomization of its receipt without forcing some patients to accept it against their will, which is unethical. Similarly, one can randomize the offer of subsidized child care for low-income families, but one cannot guarantee full randomization of its use because families have the right to choose their children's care. And one can randomize the offer of an education voucher that enables people to move their children to a better school, but one cannot randomize such moves without encountering tremendous political resistance. This limitation of the experimental approach is often not fully appreciated or understood. The questions at its heart—namely, who has the opportunity to take advantage of an offered treatment and who actually takes advantage of it—are fundamentally different from the question of what dosage of the treatment is offered.

A second limitation of experimental research is that it can be used to study only interventions to which entities can be randomly assigned. Because randomization is sometimes impossible or unacceptable, many important questions cannot be directly addressed using the experimental approach. To take a clear-cut example, the effects of birth parents' demographic characteristics on their children cannot be studied by randomly assigning children to parents or parents to children.

Finally, although experiments are the most powerful known way to assess the causal effects of an intervention on an outcome, they do not by themselves provide much insight into how these effects are brought about. This issue is particularly important for interventions that consist of numerous components, any combination of which might be responsible for an observed effect. For example, testing a multifaceted reading curriculum by randomly assigning each member of a sample of first-grade students to a group that is exposed to the new curriculum or to a group that is not is an excellent way to measure any subsequent changes in reading achievement caused by the curriculum (relative to the curriculum to which students would have otherwise been exposed). However, without more information, additional assumptions, or both, the experiment will not provide compelling evidence about how or why the curriculum does or does not improve reading achievement or about the relative effectiveness of its various components. This limitation of the experimental paradigm is often referred to as the "black box" problem. Simply put, the problem is that experiments are good at documenting the linkages, or the lack thereof, between an intervention (the input to the black box) and outcomes (the output of the black box), but they provide little or no direct information about why the intervention did or not did affect the outcome.

The goal of this chapter is to present an analytic approach that combines randomized experiments with a well-known nonexperimental method from econometrics called instrumental-variables estimation. Although coupling the instrumental-variables approach with experimental data is not new, we extend it to enable researchers to address questions about how the outcomes observed in an experiment might have been affected by multiple factors associated with the treatment. As discussed in the literature review that follows, the technique holds promise as a way to mitigate the three limitations of experimental research already noted.

Appropriately used, the instrumental-variables approach can broaden the range of policy issues that can be effectively addressed to include questions such as the following: What is the effect of taking small daily doses of aspirin on the incidence and severity of future heart attacks among men over fifty? What is the effect of serving in the military on the future earnings of people who render military service during wartime? What is the effect of families' moving from an impoverished neighborhood to a better-off neighborhood on the future criminal behavior of their adolescent children? What is the effect of attending job training on the future earnings of young school dropouts? What are the effects on children of policy-induced increases in their parents' future earnings and income?

In the next section of this chapter, we lay out a conceptual and statistical framework that will allow us to describe the limits of experimental evidence (even in well-realized random assignment designs), illustrate how research analysis can be extended beyond these limits, and delineate the conditions under which such extension is possible. To introduce the framework, we present and discuss a series of effect estimators that may be used to answer different policy questions of interest. These estimators form the foundation of the instrumental-variables analysis presented in the third section of the chapter, in which we illustrate how the technique can be applied to experimental data to explore the causal paths by which an intervention produces its observed effects. In the concluding section, we reflect on the potential of the instrumental-variables approach and the conditions necessary for its success.

Using Experiments to Measure Treatment Effects

Because application of instrumental-variables analysis to experimental data presupposes that the program under study had effects, or impacts, on an outcome of interest, we begin by presenting a conceptual framework for measuring the effects of programs using random-assignment studies.[1] Often referred to as the Rubin Causal Model (Holland 1986), this framework begins with the idea that each individual experiences a certain outcome if she participates in the program and a different outcome if she does not participate. Definitions of average impacts on groups start by defining impacts for individuals, thereby building in the flexibility needed to account for the fact that most (if not all) programs affect different people differently. This flexibility makes it possible to distinguish among the alternative impact questions that are addressed by alternative impact estimators.

In this chapter, we refer to an intervention, program, or policy as a treatment, to its impact on an outcome as a treatment effect, to the group of individuals randomly assigned to receive the treatment as the treatment group, and to the group of individuals randomly assigned not to receive the treatment as the control group. We depart from the other chapters in this volume in using the term "treatment," rather than "program" because "treatment" is the more prevalent term in the literature on instrumental-variables estimation with randomized experiments.

Defining Individual Effects and Average Effects

The basic building block of any measure of a treatment effect is how much the treatment influences a given individual with respect to a particular outcome. In each case, we can denote the value of the outcome variable (future earnings, test scores, crimes committed, or heart attacks) for an individual as $Y_i(1)$ if she receives the treatment and $Y_i(0)$ if she does not. By definition, the individual treatment effect (ITE) is the difference between these two potential outcomes, or $Y_i(1) - Y_i(0)$. For example, if an individual would earn $5,000 during the year after participating in a job-training program but only $4,000 without the program, her individual treatment effect would be $5,000 minus $4,000, or $1,000. As already noted, this effect can vary from individual to individual.

In practice, we can observe only one of the two potential outcomes for any given individual. If she receives the treatment, we observe $Y_i(1)$, and if she does not receive the treatment, we observe $Y_i(0)$. Thus, we cannot observe the treatment effect or the difference in potential outcomes for an individual. Nevertheless, under certain circumstances, we can observe the average treatment effect (ATE) for some groups. This average effect equals the expected value of the individual treatment effects for all members of the group. In symbols, and dropping the subscript i for convenience:

$$ATE = E[Y(1) - Y(0)] = E[Y(1)] - E[Y(0)] \qquad (3.1)$$

For example, if expected annual earnings would be $4,500 if everyone to whom a program is targeted participated in a job-training program but only $3,000 if no one participated, then the average treatment effect for the target group would be $4,500 minus $3,000, or $1,500.

Measuring the Average Treatment Effect with Full Compliance

In view of the fact that we can observe only one of the two potential outcomes for any given individual, how can we measure the average treatment effect for a target group? The best way is to randomly assign each target-group member to the treatment group, T, or to the control group, C. Doing so creates two random subsamples of target-group members, each of whose expected potential outcomes equal those for the target group as a whole. Expressed in symbols:

$$E[Y(1)]_T = E[Y(1)]_C = E[Y(1)] \qquad (3.2a)$$

$$E[Y(0)]_T = E[Y(0)]_C = E[Y(0)] \qquad (3.2b)$$

In an ideal world, there is full compliance with randomization. In other words, all target-group members randomly assigned to the treatment group participate in the treatment, and all target-group members randomly assigned to the control group do not. Under these conditions, and setting Z, a measure of assignment to the treatment group, equal to 1 or 0 for treatment- or control-group members, respectively:

$$E[Y(1)] = E(Y \mid Z = 1) \tag{3.3a}$$

$$E[Y(0)] = E(Y \mid Z = 0) \tag{3.3b}$$

The difference in expected outcomes for the treatment group and for the control group equals the average treatment effect for the target group because:

$$E(Y \mid Z = 1) - E(Y \mid Z = 0) = E[Y(1)] - E[Y(0)] = ATE \tag{3.4}$$

Thus, assuming full compliance with randomization, the observed difference between mean outcomes for the treatment group and for the control group provides an unbiased estimate of the average treatment effect for the target group.

Measuring the Average Effect of the Intent to Treat with No-Shows

In the real world, experiments cannot ensure that everyone randomized to the treatment receives it. We refer to treatment-group members who do not receive the treatment as "no-shows," a term coined by Howard Bloom (1984) for those who do not receive treatment, regardless of the reason (forgot to do so, refused to do so, were kept from doing so by others, moved away before they could do so, or died before they could do so).

Figure 3.1 illustrates this situation. The bar on the left side represents the treatment group, and the bar on the right side represents the control group. The variable D equals 1 for people who receive the treatment being tested and 0 for people who do not receive the treatment. In this example, no control-group members receive the treatment (for them, D equals 0), most treatment-group members receive the treatment (for them, D equals 1), and some treatment-group members do not receive the treatment (for them, D equals 0). Note that the value of D indicates whether the treatment was received, whereas the value of Z indicates treatment assignment—whether the treatment was offered.

The treatment contrast is the difference between the treatment group and the control group with respect to exposure to the treatment. No-shows dilute the treatment contrast and reduce the corresponding difference in expected outcomes for the treatment and control groups, so that it no longer represents the average treatment effect. Expressed in symbols:

$$E(Y \mid Z = 1) - E(Y \mid Z = 0) \neq E[Y(1)] - E[Y(0)] \neq ATE \tag{3.5}$$

Figure 3.1   A Hypothetical Experiment Including No-Shows

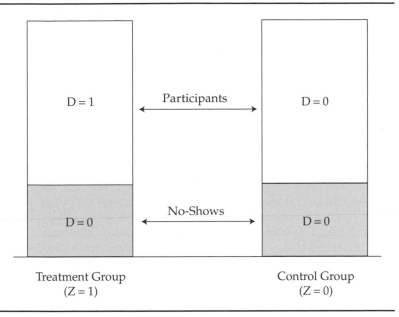

Source: Authors' compilation.
Note: D equals 1 if the treatment would be received and 0 otherwise.

This inequality stems from the fact that E[Y(1)] and E[Y(0)] represent average outcomes for the treatment and control groups, respectively, assuming that everyone in the treatment group receives the intended treatment, whereas $E(Y \mid Z = 1)$ and $E(Y \mid Z = 0)$ represent the average effects for the treatment and control groups, respectively, even when some treatment-group members do not receive the intended treatment.

Because most social programs and participation in experiments are voluntary, all one can do is make them available to potential recipients. Therefore it is important to answer the question: What is the average effect of making the treatment available to its target-group members? In medical research, the corresponding question is: What is the average effect of offering to treat target-group members? An unbiased answer is provided by the difference in the mean outcomes for the treatment and control groups. This finding is often referred to as the effect of intent to treat (ITT). Expressed in symbols:

$$ITT = E(Y \mid Z = 1) - E(Y \mid Z = 0) \qquad (3.6)$$

Consider the implications for the job-training example already introduced, where the target group's expected annual earnings are $3,000 without the program. Now assume that the treatment group's expected annual earnings are $4,100. In this case, the average effect of intent to treat equals $4,100 minus $3,000, or $1,100, per person to whom the program is offered. This amount is lower than the actual average treatment effect because not every member of the program group participated in job training.

Measuring the Average Effect of the Treatment on the Treated with No-Shows

Although policy-relevant in its own right, the average effect of the intent to treat is an amalgam of treatment effects for participants and null effects for nonparticipants. Furthermore, it departs from how most people think of program effectiveness, which is usually in terms of effects on participants. The focus in medicine, for example, is on how treatments affect patients who actually receive them. This more intuitive concept of impacts is often referred to as the average effect of treatment on the treated (TOT).

When there are no-shows, it is not feasible to estimate the effect of treatment on the treated directly from experimental data because one cannot confidently determine which control-group members are the counterparts of the treatment-group members who receive the treatment. Hence, estimating the average effect of treatment on the treated requires a nonexperimental extension of the experimental design.

Bloom (1984) proposed a nonexperimental extension that works well when no-shows experience (at least approximately) no treatment effect. This extension assumes that randomization does not influence the outcome for an individual unless she receives the intended treatment, which is most plausible in the case of treatments that are voluntary, substantial, and without close substitutes.[2] For example, an innovative new reading curriculum probably would help only students who received it. The mere experience of being randomized for receipt or nonreceipt of the curriculum might alter some facets of a student's behavior, but any such changes would probably not be comparable to those wrought by exposure to the curriculum itself. Likewise, being randomized to a potent new anticancer drug is unlikely to affect the future progression of the disease in a patient if the drug is not administered to him, unless the placebo effect is comparable in size to the effect of the drug.

In contrast, this assumption is unlikely to hold for mandatory programs that influence the behavior of all treatment-group members. For example, many welfare-to-work programs impose sanctions for nonparticipation; in these cases, the mere threat of sanctions can influence the behavior of, and thus the outcomes for, target-group members. Similarly, the assumption may not hold in voluntary programs in which the treatment offer affects treatment-group members irrespective of whether they participate (for example, if a participant's failure to take up the offer negatively affects his emotional well-being).

The logic behind Bloom's no-show correction is straightforward. It allocates the difference between the outcome for treatment-group members and the outcome for control-group members to the fraction of treatment-group members who received the treatment. Thus, if half the treatment-group members receive treatment, the outcome difference is allocated only to this half. This is achieved by doubling the observed experimental difference. More generally, the reallocation is accomplished by dividing the treatment and control-group outcome difference (the effect of intent to treat) by the proportion of treatment-group members who receive the treatment. This calculation is equivalent to summing the outcomes for treatment-group members and control-group members separately, computing the difference in the two groups' total outcomes, and dividing this difference by the number of treatment-group members who receive the treatment. It thus represents the average change in the outcome per recipient of the treatment.

If D equals 1 for treatment-group members who receive the treatment, the proportion of treatment-group members receiving the treatment is $E(D \mid Z = 1)$. In symbols (with TOT_1 indicating the special case of noncompliance attributable only to no-shows), the extension is written as follows:

$$TOT_1 = \frac{E(Y \mid Z = 1) - E(Y \mid Z = 0)}{E(D \mid Z = 1)} \tag{3.7}$$

$$= \frac{ITT}{E(D \mid Z = 1)} \tag{3.8}$$

Building on the solid methodological foundation provided by randomization, this adjustment for participation rests on a single assumption that is transparent enough for researchers to assess its validity readily.

Consider how this procedure might apply to the job-training example, where the effect of intent to treat is $1,100. Assume that 60 percent of treatment-group members received the treatment and that only recipients of the treatment experienced a treatment effect. In this case, we can reallocate the full effect of intent to treat to the 60 percent of treatment-group members who are recipients. To do so, we divide $1,100 by 0.60, obtaining $1,833.[3]

It is important to note several points about this finding. First, it represents an average effect for an identifiable subgroup. Second, there can be substantial individual variation around this average. Third, the average treatment effect for current participants might differ from what no-shows would experience if they were somehow induced to participate. Hence, the average effect of treatment on the treated need not equal the average treatment effect for a target group. (In the job-training example, ATE equals \$1,500, and TOT_1 equals \$1,833.) Fourth, this adjustment affects the magnitude, but not the statistical significance, of any observed effects. In other words, an insignificant ITT effect cannot yield a significant TOT effect.

Fifth, although measuring the average effect of treatment on the treated when no-shows are the only noncompliers is often possible, it is much more difficult to do when some control-group members also receive the treatment. Such control-group members are referred to as crossovers. Finally, because Bloom's no-show correction is a nonexperimental extension of the experimental approach, there are some situations (for example, where it is difficult to argue plausibly that no-shows experience virtually no treatment effect) when ITT is preferred to TOT as an estimate of the treatment effect.

Measuring the Local Average Treatment Effect

To address the more complex situation including crossovers, we use a formulation developed by Joshua Angrist, Guido Imbens, and Don Rubin (1996) that distinguishes between individuals for whom randomization can and cannot influence receipt of treatment. These two groups are further subdivided into four mutually exclusive and collectively exhaustive theoretical subgroups that, because of random assignment, are represented in the treatment group and the control group in equal proportions.

Figure 3.2 illustrates the formulation. The bar on the left side of the figure represents a hypothetical distribution of the subgroups in the treatment group (for which Z equals 1). The bar on the right side represents the subgroups' counterparts in the control group (for which Z equals 0). For sample members who receive the treatment, D equals 1; for those who do not receive the treatment, D equals 0.

Consider first the subgroups of sample members whose receipt of the treatment can be influenced by random assignment. Compliers, represented by the top portion of each bar in the figure, are people who would receive the intended treatment if they were randomized to the treatment group but would not receive it if they were randomized to the control group. In figure 3.2 this is the largest of the four groups, illustrating a situation in which compliance with randomization is high. If compliers in the treatment group and in the control group could be identified—which they cannot—the effect of the treatment on their outcomes could be estimated directly.

Figure 3.2   A Hypothetical Experiment Including No-Shows and Crossovers

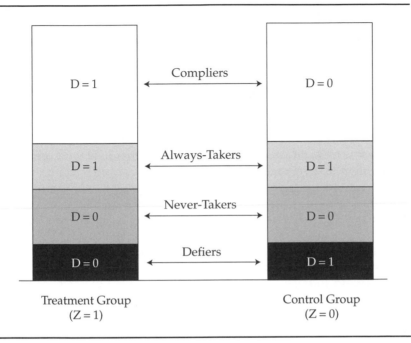

Source: Authors' compilation.
Note: D equals 1 if the treatment would be received and 0 otherwise.

Defiers, represented by the bottom portion of each bar in the figure, are people who would not receive the treatment if they were randomized to the treatment group but would receive it if they were randomized to the control group. In many situations, such contrarians are unlikely to exist, at least not in large numbers. When they do exist, however, the effect of treatment on their outcomes—an effect that cannot be observed—tends to offset that for compliers in the observed difference between the average outcomes for the treatment group and the control group.

The middle two portions of each bar in figure 3.2 represent, respectively, always-takers, who would receive the treatment regardless of whether they were assigned to the treatment group or to the control group, and never-takers, who would not receive the treatment regardless of whether they were assigned to the treatment group or to the control group. Because the treatment-induced difference in these subgroups' potential outcomes is independent of random assignment, the experimental design reveals nothing about the treatment's effects on them. In the absence of a way to influence these subgroups' receipt of treatment, the treatment effect on their outcomes cannot be easily estimated.

How should we measure treatment impacts given the latter two forms of noncompliance? The first step is to measure the average effect of the intent (or offer) to treat, which, as already noted, is usually policy-relevant in its own right. The next step requires narrowing the focus to the impact of treatment receipt on compliers and defiers—on whose outcomes the treatment's effect is found—resulting in an estimator that Angrist, Imbens, and Rubin (1996) called the local average treatment effect (LATE). Equivalent to an instrumental-variables estimate, as will be shown momentarily, LATE equals the difference in mean outcomes for the treatment group and the control group divided by the difference in treatment-receipt rates for the two groups:[4]

$$\text{LATE} = \frac{E(Y \mid Z = 1) - E(Y \mid Z = 0)}{E(D \mid Z = 1) - E(D \mid Z = 0)} = \frac{\Delta Y}{\Delta D} \tag{3.9}$$

This calculation is equivalent to dividing the average effect of intent to treat by the difference between the treatment group and the control group in treatment-receipt rates.

Equation 3.9 is based solely on the experience of compliers and defiers because always-takers and never-takers contribute nothing to the difference between the treatment group and the control group in treatment-receipt rates or in outcomes. The local average treatment effect thus represents the change per person in the outcome produced by experimentally induced receipt or nonreceipt of the treatment.

Returning to the job-training example, assume that 60 percent of the treatment-group members and 10 percent of the control-group members receive the treatment. Assume further that the average outcome is $3,900 for the treatment group and $3,000 for the control group. In this case, ITT is $3,900 – $3,000, or $900, and LATE is $900/(0.60 – 0.10), or $1,800.

Comparing ITT, TOT, LATE, and ATE with No-Shows and Crossovers

Each of the preceding estimators addresses a different impact question, represents a different group of sample members, rests on a different set of assumptions, and is empirically observable in the presence of the two types of experimental noncompliance (no-shows and crossovers) to a different degree. Each is also best suited to answer a different policy question, as summarized below:

Average treatment effect (ATE). What is the average effect of the treatment if all members of the target group received it?

Intent to treat (ITT). What is the average effect of the treatment per person offered it, regardless of how many target-group members received it?

Treatment on the treated (TOT). What is the average effect of the treatment per person actually receiving it?

Local average treatment effect (LATE). What is the average effect of the treatment per person induced by randomization to receive it?

Consider first the group of sample members represented by each estimator. The average treatment effect and the average effect of intent to treat both concern the entire target group that is subject to the experiment. The average effect of treatment on the treated looks at an observable subgroup of individuals who receive the treatment independent of random assignment. The local average treatment effect pertains to an unobservable subgroup of individuals who are induced by random assignment to receive the treatment.

Now consider the assumptions underlying each estimate. All the estimates assume that randomization is executed properly and that the treatment and control groups are therefore identical in expectation. This is the only assumption necessary for measuring the average effect of intent to treat, which can be observed directly from experimental data.

Estimating the local average treatment effect requires making two additional assumptions. The first is that the treatment causes statistically detectable effects, and the second is that the average treatment effect on compliers and the average treatment effect on defiers are the same (or have a known relationship to one another) or that there are no defiers. Given these assumptions, LATE can be inferred from experimental data.

The average effect of treatment on the treated and the average treatment effect cannot be observed or inferred from experimental data but rather must be extrapolated. If the average effect of treatment for always-takers is the same as that for compliers and defiers, then TOT equals LATE. Given the additional assumption that never-takers would experience the same average effect of treatment if they were induced to receive it, this estimate can be extrapolated to the full target group. In this special case, ATE also equals LATE.

There are many reasons, however, to expect that always-takers and never-takers (whose receipt of treatment is not influenced by randomization) might differ from compliers and defiers (whose receipt of treatment is influenced by randomization). Extrapolations between these pairs of subgroups should therefore be made with care and interpreted with caution. In many cases, it is preferable to limit impact findings to

ITT and LATE, which can be observed or inferred from experimental data.

Finally, the choice of impact estimate should depend not only on whether its underlying assumptions are met and whether estimates are observed, inferred, or extrapolated but also on the policy question to be answered. For example, when one aims to capture the effectiveness of a mandatory employment program or the effects of a pilot program if it were implemented on a larger scale, ITT may be the most relevant estimate. When one aims to capture the cost-effectiveness of a program offering a child-care subsidy or of a housing or education voucher targeted to a particular population, however, TOT may be the most relevant estimate. (For a discussion of the relevance of ITT as compared with other estimators in the context of a housing voucher experiment, see Kling and Liebman 2003.) Debates about the possible benefits to children's development of directly providing earnings supplements to low-income parents or making such supplements available only to those who work full time may be best informed by LATE.

Using Instrumental Variables with Experimental Data to Measure the Effects of Mediators

For all the estimators so far described, treatment receipt is the link in the causal chain—called the mediator—between randomization status (random assignment to the treatment group or to the control group) and an outcome such as earnings. But these estimators and extensions thereof can also be used to shed light on the causal links between other mediators and the outcome, affording researchers a glimpse into the black box of randomized experiments. In fact, the local average treatment effect in equation 3.9 is equivalent to an estimator developed by Abraham Wald (1940) that is a special case of instrumental variables.[5]

Instrumental-variables estimates can quantify the relationship between two outcomes—here, the mediator (or intermediate outcome), which is participation, and a more distal outcome such as earnings—that were both affected by the treatment. Thus, instrumental-variables estimates allow researchers to ask not only how randomizing people to a program designed to improve job skills affects earnings, for example, but also how improved job skills affect earnings.[6]

Because instrumental variables are traditionally presented in the context of regression analysis, we now reformulate LATE in terms of regression.

Recasting LATE as an Instrumental Variables Estimator

Consider the following bivariate regression model of the relationship between an outcome measure, Y, and an indicator of treatment receipt, D:

$$Y_i = B_0 + B_1 D_i + \varepsilon_i, \qquad (3.10)$$

where ε is a random error term, B_0 is an intercept, and B_1 is a regression coefficient. B_0 represents the mean value of the outcome (for instance, employment, education achievement, or health status) for sample members who do not receive the treatment, and B_1 represents the difference between the mean value of the outcome for people who receive the treatment and the mean value for those who do not.

If ε is independently and identically distributed, B_1 represents the causal effect of the treatment on the outcome and can be estimated using ordinary least squares. But if ε is correlated with D—that is, if people who receive the treatment differ from those who do not in ways related to the outcome—then ordinary least squares will produce a biased estimate of B_1. In the context of a program evaluation, this problem is referred to as selection bias. In the context of regression analysis more generally, it is referred to as model specification bias or omitted-variable bias.

The instrumental-variables approach to solving this problem entails finding another variable, Z, that is correlated with D and uncorrelated with ε. Referred to as an instrument, Z is used to purge D of the portion of its variation that is correlated with ε. The remaining, exogenous, portion of D's variation is then used to estimate its causal relationship to Y.[7]

This approach is easiest to understand when presented in the form of two-stage least squares, although it can also be executed in one stage. The first stage of the procedure is to estimate an ordinary least squares regression model of D as a linear function of Z:

$$D_i = \Pi_0 + \Pi_1 Z_i + \mu_i, \qquad (3.11)$$

where μ is a random error term, Π_0 is an intercept, and Π_1 is a regression coefficient. The estimated first-stage model is used to compute a predicted value $\hat{D}_i$ for each sample member, which is then substituted for D_i in equation 3.10. This second-stage equation is then estimated using ordinary least squares.[8] Because the values of $\hat{D}_i$ are a linear function of the values of Z_i, the variation in $\hat{D}_i$ is uncorrelated with ε_i when Z_i is uncorrelated with ε_i. Using this method of dissociating the indicator of treatment receipt from the random error in the outcome, one can eliminate selection bias from estimates of the effect of treatment receipt on the outcome.[9]

The two-stage least-squares instrumental-variables estimator just described is equivalent to the local average treatment effect in equation 3.9. This is because the difference in mean outcomes for the treatment group and for the control group, ΔY, equals the covariance between Y and Z, and the difference in treatment receipt rates for the treatment group and for the control group, ΔD, equals the covariance between D and Z. Hence, the instrumental-variables estimator of B_1 equals the ratio between the two covariances, and thus the ratio between the two differences. Expressed in symbols:

$$\frac{COV\,(YZ)}{COV\,(DZ)} = \frac{\Delta Y}{\Delta D} \tag{3.12}$$

Now consider the two conditions that an instrument must meet to provide a precise, consistent estimate of a causal relationship between the mediator and the distal outcome. The first is that the instrument must co-vary with the independent variable that it is supposed to represent. The strength of this covariation, which can be observed empirically, captures the strength of the instrument. In an experiment, the covariation equals the difference in the treatment receipt rate induced by randomization (ΔD). The larger the difference is, the more precise the impact estimator will be.

Because the strength of instruments is often low, the precision of resulting instrumental-variables estimators is also often low. Efforts to increase precision therefore play an important role in the application of instrumental variables. The most common approach is to add covariates to the regression model. These covariates, denoted X_k, should represent background characteristics of sample members that predict D, Y, or both. Adding the same set of covariates to both stages of the model obviates the need to make the further, and possibly erroneous, assumption that the covariates are exogenous to D but not to Y or that the covariates are exogenous to Y but not to D. Adding covariates yields the following equation:

$$D_i = \Pi_0 + \Pi_1 Z_i + \sum_{k>1} \Pi_k X_{ki} + \mu_i \tag{3.13}$$

$$Y_i = B_0 + B_1 D_i + \sum_{k>1} B_k X_{ki} + \varepsilon_i \tag{3.14}$$

The second condition for a good instrument, that it be uncorrelated with ε, determines the validity of the estimator of a causal relationship. Unfortunately, there is no way to observe this correlation empirically.[10] Thus, for nonexperimental applications of instrumental variables, one can judge whether the condition is met only from the nature of the instrument selected. For experiments, however, treatment assignment is a

Figure 3.3   A Causal Model Underlying an Instrumental-Variables Analysis with One Mediator

Source: Authors' compilation.

natural choice of instrument because randomization leaves it uncorrelated (in expectation) with every variable at the time of random assignment. If the only way that treatment assignment (Z) affects the outcome (Y) is by influencing treatment status (D), then Z is a valid instrument. This essential condition is often referred to as the exclusion restriction, presumably because it excludes all causal paths between Z and Y except that through D. Figure 3.3 illustrates the causal model implied by a situation in which the exclusion restriction is met.

Measuring the Effects of Mediators Other Than Treatment Receipt

Up to this point, we have focused on how to apply the instrumental-variables approach to experimental data to measure the local average effect of receiving a treatment. For this purpose, treatment receipt was measured as a binary variable and modeled as an intervening variable, or mediator, in the causal path between treatment assignment and the outcome of interest.

Instrumental variables can be applied to experimental data to estimate the causal effects of many other kinds of mediators as well. The mediators can be binary variables, such as attendance or nonattendance at a child-care facility, or continuous variables, such as the number of hours of attendance at a child-care facility. But the approach to measuring their effect on an outcome is the same in either case. First, treatment assignment is used as an instrument in a first-stage regression model to predict the values of the mediator. Next, the predicted values of the mediator are used as an independent variable in a second-stage regression of the outcome measure as a function of the mediator with the covariates that were used in the first stage.

This approach has been used to study, among other things, the effect on adults' earnings of obtaining a general educational development (GED) certificate (Bos et al. 2001), the effect on young people's mental health of moving out of a high-poverty neighborhood into a low-poverty neighborhood (Kling and Liebman 2003), the effect on men's future health and wealth of serving in the military (Angrist 1990), and the effect on children's academic achievement of using an education voucher (Mayer et al. 2002; Krueger and Zhu 2003).

The model underlying each of these applications is the same as that shown in figure 3.3, and the instrumental-variables (IV) procedure is similar to that already described. What differs across applications of IV are the definitions of Y, Z, and D. Consider, for example, the procedure for estimating the effect of receiving a GED on adults' earnings on the basis of an experimental study of an education and employment program. In this context, Y would represent future earnings, Z would represent random assignment to the program or to the control group, and D would represent receipt or nonreceipt of a GED during the follow-up period. It would be straightforward to estimate a first-stage regression of the likelihood of receiving a GED on treatment assignment. The predicted values of GED receipt could then be used in a second-stage regression of future earnings as a function of GED receipt, permitting one to estimate the effect of receiving a GED on future earnings.

Extending the Approach to Multiple Mediators

For programs that are comprehensive and multifaceted, it is important to understand the separate effects of the individual components, each of which is a possible mediator of the program's effects. One promising way to disentangle these effects is to use multiple instruments constructed from a multitreatment experiment, a multisite experiment, or pooled data from multiple experiments. For this procedure to work properly, there must be at least as many instruments as there are mediators. If the number of instruments is less than the number of mediators, the model is "underidentified" because not all the causal relationships that it represents can be determined. If the number of instruments equals the number of mediators, the model is "just identified" or "exactly identified." In the latter case, there is just enough information to estimate all the causal relationships in the model provided that the instruments have adequate independent variation (as discussed later). If the number of instruments in the model exceeds the number of mediators, the model is "overidentified."[11] Overidentified models permit estimation of all the causal relationships involved, but they can give rise to technical problems if they include a large number of weak instruments, a weak instrument being one that has a low correlation with the mediating variable that it is being used to represent (for discussion, see Bound, Jaeger, and Baker 1995; Staiger and Stock 1993). Because of

**Figure 3.4   A Causal Model for Estimating the Effects of Maternal
Employment on Child Behavior**

Source: Authors' compilation.

these problems, just-identified models are often preferred to overidentified models (Angrist and Krueger 2001).

To understand how multiple instrumental variables can be used to estimate the effects of multiple mediators, consider a hypothetical study of a welfare-to-work program that uses a random-assignment design to measure the effect of low-income parents' employment on their children's behavior. Figure 3.4 illustrates a simple causal model of this situation, where Z represents random assignment of eligible welfare recipients to the treatment group or to a control group, D is a discrete or continuous measure of sample members' subsequent employment, and Y is a measure of their children's subsequent behavior. The model specifies that treatment assignment influences parents' employment, which in turn affects their children's behavior. Thus, treatment assignment can be used as an instrument to estimate the effect of parental employment on child behavior.

For this analysis to be valid, the exclusion restriction requires that parental employment be the only causal pathway through which treatment assignment affects child behavior. Many welfare-to-work programs, however, provide additional services (such as child-care subsidies) that can influence child behavior through other pathways as well. Figure 3.5 presents a causal model of this more complex situation, where both parental employment and use of child care affect child behavior. (The figure also includes an effect of parental employment on child-care use.) As the figure makes clear, it would be incorrect to attribute all the program's effect on child behavior to its effect on parental employment.

To estimate the separate effects of parental employment (D_1) and child-care use (D_2) on child behavior, one needs at least two instruments (Z_1 and Z_2). One way to construct such instruments is from an experiment that examines more than one treatment—for example, an experiment that randomizes sample members to a treatment that is focused on parental employment, to a treatment that is focused on child-

Figure 3.5 A Causal Model for Estimating the Effects of Multiple Mediators on Child Behavior

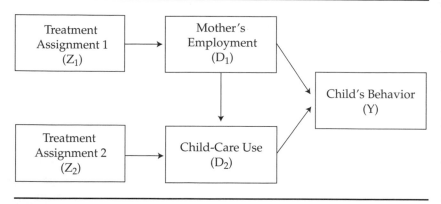

Source: Authors' compilation.

care use, or to a control group that is offered neither treatment. Z_1 would equal 1 for sample members randomized to the first treatment and 0 for all others. Z_2 would equal 1 for sample members randomized to the second treatment and 0 for all others. Because the values of Z_1 and Z_2 for individual sample members are determined randomly, they are completely exogenous, or uncorrelated (in expectation) with all preexisting characteristics of the sample members, making them good candidates as instruments.

An instrumental-variables model of the causal model in figure 3.5 can be specified using the following system of regression equations:[12]

$$D_{1i} = \Pi_{10} + \Pi_{11}Z_{1i} + \Pi_{12}Z_{2i} + \sum_{k>2} \Pi_{1k}X_{ki} + \mu_{1i}$$

(3.15)

$$D_{2i} = \Pi_{20} + \Pi_{21}Z_{1i} + \Pi_{22}Z_{2i} + \sum_{k>2} \Pi_{2k}X_{ki} + \mu_{2i}$$

(3.16)

$$Y_i = B_0 + B_1D_{1i} + B_2D_{2i} + \sum_{k>2} B_kX_{ki} + \varepsilon_i$$

(3.17)

To apply this model, one can first use ordinary least squares to estimate equations 3.15 and 3.16 and create predicted values, $\hat{D}_{1i}$ and $\hat{D}_{2i}$, for the mediators. One can then substitute the predicted values into equation 3.17 and estimate the equation using ordinary least squares. The resulting estimates of B_1 and B_2 represent the effects of parental employment and child-care use, respectively, on child behavior.

Now consider the conditions that must be met for the preceding analysis to yield valid (consistent) and precise causal estimates. The fundamental condition for validity is that no other causal paths exist between treatment assignment and child behavior. If this condition does not hold, the estimation procedure will result in misattribution of the causal effects of additional, unobserved mediators to the two observed mediators. A key condition for precision is that the instruments be strong predictors of the mediators. In an experiment, this implies that the effects of treatment assignment on the mediators are substantial and statistically significant. Another condition for precision is that each instrument have a different and unique relationship to each mediator being estimated. In other words, it must be the case that $\Pi_{11}/\Pi_{12} \neq \Pi_{21}/\Pi_{22}$. One way for this condition to be met in the welfare-to-work program example is for one treatment to affect mainly parental employment and the other to affect mainly child-care use. The more pronounced the difference is between the treatments in their effects on employment as opposed to child-care use, the more information will be available to separate the causal effects of the two mediators from one another.

In theory, one could expand the number of mediators and instruments to account for as many causal paths as exist in a given situation. In practice, however, it is difficult to find enough suitable instruments. To help stimulate creative thinking about how to overcome this limitation in real-world policy experiments, we now describe three approaches to creating multiple instruments from experiments and illustrate each approach with an empirical example drawn from studies of welfare and employment programs.

Using a Multitreatment Experiment: The Effects of Mothers' Employment and Income on Children's School Engagement and Performance

As already mentioned, one approach to creating multiple instruments is to exploit the process of randomization in a multitreatment experiment. In such an experiment, the number of treatments determines the number of instruments that can be created, which in turn determines the maximum number of mediating paths that can be identified. The following analysis based on Pamela Morris and Lisa Gennetian (2003) is an empirical application of this approach to an evaluation of a state welfare-to-work initiative called the Minnesota Family Investment Program (MFIP; for details about the original evaluation, which did not include the analysis presented here, see Miller et al. 2000; Knox, Miller, and Gennetian 2000).

The MFIP evaluation was conducted during the mid-1990s to test two approaches to increasing employment and income among welfare recipients, most of them single mothers, and reducing their reliance on welfare. One approach, known as Full MFIP, combined mandatory employment and training services, sanctions for nonparticipation, and a financial work incentive. The incentive enabled participants to keep more of their welfare payments when they worked than would have been possible under the welfare scheme that existed at the time of the evaluation, namely, Aid for Families with Dependent Children (AFDC). The other approach, known as MFIP Incentives Only, provided the same financial incentive without the mandatory employment services in Full MFIP. Eligible sample members were randomly assigned to one of the two treatment groups or to a control group that received AFDC.

Three years of follow-up data on sample members' quarterly earnings were obtained from state unemployment insurance agency records, which are often used in evaluations of employment and training programs and have been found to be relatively accurate (Kornfeld and Bloom 1999). Data on monthly AFDC and food-stamp payments over the same period were obtained from Minnesota's welfare agency records. The quarterly earnings data were used to construct a measure indicating whether each sample member had been employed at any time during the first year after random assignment. The earnings, AFDC, and food-stamp data were used to measure total income received from all three sources during the year after random assignment. These data indicated that both MFIP programs increased employment and income substantially (Miller et al. 2000) and that whereas the programs' impacts on income were virtually the same, Full MFIP's impacts on employment were much larger than those of MFIP Incentives Only (Miller et al. 2000).[13]

Child outcomes were measured on the basis of a follow-up survey administered to sample members three years after random assignment. The survey asked respondents about their recent experiences and about their "focal" child, that is, the child in their family who had been randomly selected at the beginning of the study to be the focus of the child-related analyses. From these data, it was possible to construct scales measuring school and behavioral outcomes for the focal children, all of whom were between five and twelve years old at the three-year follow-up point. Some of the estimates of program impacts on the child outcomes were statistically significant (Gennetian and Miller 2002), leading the researchers to generate numerous hypotheses about the influences of maternal employment and income on those outcomes.

One of the hypotheses was that increasing a mother's income benefits her children by increasing the material resources available for basic necessities such as food, clothing, shelter, and health care. Two competing hypotheses were formulated regarding employment. On the one hand, it was hypothesized that increasing a mother's likelihood of being employed or the number of hours that she works reduces the time and energy she can devote to her children and thereby undermines their development. On the other hand, it was hypothesized that increasing a mother's likelihood of being employed or the number of hours that she works improves her mental health and thereby enhances her ability to nurture her children and to act as a positive role model.

A purely nonexperimental way to test hypotheses such as these using the experimental data from the MFIP evaluation would be to estimate an ordinary least squares regression model like equation 3.17 with a child outcome as the dependent variable (Y), maternal employment and income as the mediators (D_1 and D_2), and a series of covariates (X_k) representing background characteristics of the mothers or of the focal children that are predicted to affect maternal employment, income, and children's development. As discussed earlier, however, this nonexperimental approach is susceptible to selection bias arising from unobservable correlations between the mediators and the random error in the regression model. The analysis is thus likely to produce biased estimates of the causal effect of the individual mediators, because the mediators may be correlated with other factors that influence child outcomes (for example, parents who are employed may be in better mental health a priori, which could make them more effective parents).

An instrumental-variables solution to this estimation problem begins by constructing two instruments—one for randomization to each MFIP program. These instruments can then be used as independent variables in first-stage regression models like equations 3.15 and 3.16 to predict the values of each mother's employment and income (Morris and Gennetian 2003). The predicted values can then be substituted into a second-stage regression model like equation 3.17. Estimating the second-stage model using ordinary least squares produces consistent estimates of the causal effects of the two mediators, maternal employment and income, on the child outcome, provided that the exclusion restriction is met (in other words, that no other causal paths between treatment assignment and the child outcome exist). The precision of these estimates depends on the strength of and the differences between the covariations among instruments and mediators. Note that, given two mediators and two instruments, the present model is just-identified and that one of the mediators is binary (employed versus unemployed) whereas the other mediator is continuous (total income received).

Table 3.1 presents the estimated relationships between the instruments and mediators obtained from the first-stage regressions. The first column lists the coefficients for employment regressed on the instruments, omitting the coefficients that were estimated for covariates. These findings indicate that randomization to Full MFIP increased the

Table 3.1   First-Stage Regression Estimates for the Minnesota Family
Investment Program: Effects of Treatment Assignment on
Mother's Employment and Income During the Year After
Random Assignment

	Mediator	
Instrument	Employment (Probability)	Income (Thousands of Dollars)
Full MFIP	0.20***	1.40***
	(0.04)	(0.29)
MFIP incentives only	0.09**	1.32***
	(0.04)	(0.29)

Source: Morris and Gennetian (2003). Copyrighted 2003 by the National Council on Family Relations, 3989 Central Ave. NE, Suite 550, Minneapolis, MN 55421. Reprinted by permission.

Notes: The sample includes 879 female single-parent long-term welfare recipients. A mother's employment equals 1 if she was employed at any point and 0 otherwise. A mother's income comprises earnings, welfare payments, and food stamps. Each first-stage regression also includes the following baseline covariates: number of children in the family, earnings in the preceding year, and 0 or 1 indicator variables for mother is black, mother is a member of another racial or ethnic minority, mother was a teen at child's birth, family includes a child aged six or under, mother has no high school diploma or equivalent, mother has never been married, mother has received welfare for at least five years in her lifetime; and a 0 or 1 indicator for which quarter in 1994 the mother was randomly assigned. Standard errors appear in parentheses. Two-tailed statistical significance is indicated as * for the 0.10 level, ** for the 0.05 level, and *** for the 0.01 level.

probability of employment during the first follow-up year by 0.20, whereas randomization to MFIP Incentives Only increased this probability by only 0.09. Both estimates are statistically significant and substantial relative to impacts documented in experimental studies of other welfare-to-work programs (Bloom and Michalopoulos 2001). The second column in the table presents the coefficients for income regressed on the instruments, again omitting the coefficients for covariates. These findings indicate that randomization to Full MFIP increased mean income by $1,400 during the first follow-up year and that randomization to MFIP Incentives Only increased income by $1,320. Both estimates are substantial and statistically significant. Perhaps most important, however, is that the two sets of estimates point to a marked difference in the relationship between each instrument and the mediators, a precondition for identifying and precisely estimating the separate effects of each mediator on the outcome.

Table 3.2 presents estimates of the effects of maternal income and employment on two academic outcomes for children—school achievement and school engagement—using instrumental variables (top panel) and, as a benchmark for comparison, ordinary least squares (bot-

Table 3.2   Second-Stage Regression Estimates for the Minnesota Family Investment Program: Effects of Mother's Income and Employment on Child's School Achievement and Engagement

	Outcome	
Mediator	School Achievement	School Engagement
Instrumental variables		
Income (thousands of dollars)	0.16	0.47*
	(0.14)	(0.27)
Employment (probability)	−0.17	−1.05
	(1.08)	(1.86)
Ordinary least squares		
Income (thousands of dollars)	−0.02	−0.01
	(0.01)	(0.02)
Employment (probability)	−0.02	0.13
	(0.09)	(0.16)

Source: Morris and Gennetian (2003). Copyrighted 2003 by the National Council on Family Relations, 3989 Central Ave. NE, Suite 550, Minneapolis, MN 55421. Reprinted by permission.

Notes: The sample includes 879 children of female single-parent long-term welfare recipients. A mother's employment equals 1 if she was employed at any point and 0 otherwise. A mother's income comprises earnings, welfare payments, and food stamps. Each second-stage regression also includes the following baseline covariates: number of children in the family, earnings in the preceding year, and 0 or 1 indicator variables for mother is black, mother is a member of another racial or ethnic minority, mother was a teen at child's birth, family includes a child aged six or under, mother has no high school degree or equivalent, mother has never been married, mother has received welfare for at least five years in her lifetime; and a 0 or 1 indicator for which quarter in 1994 a mother was randomly assigned. Standard errors appear in parentheses. Two-tailed statistical significance is indicated as *for the 0.10 level, **for the 0.05 level, and ***for the 0.01 level.

tom panel; for the effects on other child outcomes, see Morris and Gennetian 2003). The measure of school achievement reflects sample members' responses to the question: "Based on your knowledge of the child's schoolwork, including report cards, how has he or she been doing in school overall?" Responses could range from a value of 1 ("not well at all") to 5 ("very well"). The mean response for the sample was 4.06, and the standard deviation was 1.10. Student engagement is a scale constructed by summing the responses to four survey questions. Scale values could range from 4 to 12, with higher values indicating greater student engagement. The mean scale value for the sample was 10.10, and the standard deviation was 1.82.

The instrumental-variables findings indicate that whereas the relation between mothers' income and children's school engagement is statistically significant and positive, mothers' employment has no statistically significant effect on either child outcome analyzed here. Thus, although causing welfare recipients to become employed may not by itself affect children's academic outcomes, increasing their income—which raising their likelihood of employment may accomplish—may have positive, albeit modest, effects.[14] Notably, parallel analyses of children's behavioral outcomes reveal that increased income has beneficial effects on children's positive social interactions but no effects on children's problem behavior (results not shown; see Morris and Gennetian 2003). The fact that only some of the instrumental-variables estimates of income on child outcomes are statistically significant, however, makes these findings merely suggestive.

To get a sense of the magnitude of the effect estimates in table 3.2, consider that the statistically significant estimate indicates that a $1,000 increase in maternal income increases average student engagement by 0.47 units. Because the standard deviation for student engagement is 1.82 units, the student engagement result represents an increase of 0.47/1.82, or 0.26, standard deviation for a $1,000 increase in maternal income.

It is worth noting that the instrumental-variables estimates in table 3.2 have much larger standard errors than do their ordinary least squares counterparts. This result, which is usual, reflects the loss of precision incurred by using predicted values of mediators to avoid the bias that can arise from using their actual values. Removing the potentially "contaminated" variation in the mediator reduces the mediator's co-variation with the outcome, and the reduction in covariation lowers the precision of the resulting instrumental-variables coefficient estimate for the mediator. This tradeoff in precision between the ordinary least squares and the instrumental-variables estimates is important. In this example, the ordinary least-squares estimates of the same coefficients tell a very different, and misleading, story. The discrepancy highlights how important it was to examine the hypothesized causal relationships through the lens of instrumental variables.

Using a Multisite Experiment: The Effects of Mothers' Education and Employment on Children's Academic School Readiness

Multitreatment experiments like MFIP are the most straightforward and effective way to produce multiple instruments that are truly exogenous. But it is difficult and expensive to conduct such experiments, and their sample sizes are often prohibitively large. Thus, it is important to explore alternative ways to create multiple instruments.

One way is to exploit natural variation in the implementation of a treatment in a multisite experiment. Consider, for example, an experimental study of an employment program for welfare recipients that is implemented in two sites that, owing to the habits and preferences of the local staff and management, emphasize different program features. One site might emphasize basic education in the belief that a higher level of "human capital" is the shortest, surest path to greater economic self-sufficiency. The other site might emphasize job-search assistance and direct job placement in the belief that the best way to get and advance in a job is to have a job. Eligible sample members in each site are randomized to the treatment group or to a control group.

Given satisfaction of the exclusion restriction and comparability of the effects of the experiments across sites (discussed further below), this situation provides a basis for using the treatment assignment variables for the two sites—that is, the interaction between treatment assignment and site—as instrumental variables to study how two mediators (in the present example, education and employment) affect outcomes for sample members or their families. The first step in this process is to construct three new variables: a site indicator, S, which equals 1 for all sample members from site 1 and 0 for all other sample members; a new instrument, Z_1, which equals 1 for sample members who are randomized to the program at site 1 and 0 for all other sample members; and a new instrument, Z_2, which equals 1 for sample members who are randomized to the program at site 2 and 0 for all other sample members. Substituting the new definitions of Z_1 and Z_2 and adding S to equations 3.15, 3.16, and 3.17, we generate a system of regression equations appropriate for implementing instrumental variables.

Two conditions must hold for these regressions to yield valid estimates of the effects of the mediators on the outcome. First, the exclusion restriction requires that the only way that treatment assignment affects the outcome for either site be through the two mediators. If this condition holds, then no other causal paths are confounded with the mediators. Second, the effects of each mediator on the outcome (the values of B_1 and B_2 in equation 3.17) must be the same for both sites.[15] In the previous section, in which a multitreatment experiment was used to create instruments, the assumption of constant values for B_1 and B_2 across treatment groups held automatically because all sample members were randomized to one of the treatment groups or to the control group from a common pool. Hence, everything about the treatment groups, including their behavioral relationships, was identical (in expectation) at randomization. When groups from different sites are used to construct instruments, the assumption that each mediator has the same effect on the outcome across groups does not hold automatically, although it may be a plausible approximation in many cases.

The necessary conditions for estimating mediator effects from a multisite experiment with adequate precision are the same as those for a multitreatment experiment: the instruments must co-vary strongly with the mediators, and each mediator must exhibit a different pattern of covariation with the instruments. Thus, in the present example, the impact of treatment on education must be larger in one site, and the impact of treatment on employment must be larger in the other site.

Another approach to estimating multiple mediators with instrumental variables is to exploit data from an experimental study that took place in multiple sites and tested multiple treatments in each site. Drawing on Katherine A. Magnuson (2003), we now provide a brief description of a recent study that combines a multisite approach with a multitreatment approach to create multiple instruments. It is based on data from the National Evaluation of Welfare-to-Work Strategies (NEWWS), a large-scale experiment that was conducted during the mid-1990s to study the effects on adults and their children of employment programs for welfare recipients (Hamilton et al. 2001). NEWWS was conducted in seven sites in six states.

Each of three NEWWS sites—Atlanta, Georgia; Grand Rapids, Michigan; and Riverside, California—conducted a multitreatment experiment to compare the effectiveness of the two approaches to helping welfare recipients move into the workforce already briefly described. The labor-force attachment (LFA) approach focused on getting participants into jobs as quickly as possible. The human-capital development (HCD) approach focused first on education and training and then on getting participants employed. Sample members in each site were randomly assigned to one of the two programs or to a control group that received AFDC.

Results from the original evaluation indicated that HCD programs generally had larger effects on education participation and LFA programs generally had larger effects on employment status, with substantial variation in impacts across sites. In addition, some of the programs in some of the sites had appreciable effects on sample members' young children. These findings motivated an instrumental-variables analysis of the effects of parental participation in education and employment on the academic school readiness of young children based on data for female sample members who were single parents at the time of random assignment.

Data on school readiness (the outcome measure, Y) were obtained by administering a cognitive test to each sample member's focal child two years after random assignment.[16] All the children were between five and seven years old when they were tested. The test score used for the analysis was the number of questions answered correctly out of a total of sixty-one, adjusted for the age of each child using a simple regression model. The scores ranged from 0 to 61 points across sample members, and the mean score ranged from 45 to 48 across sites.

Data on maternal participation in education activities (D_1) were obtained from a follow-up survey administered to sample members two years after random assignment. This survey asked respondents to supply timelines for their participation in any of five education activities: high school, adult basic education, vocational training, English as a Second Language, and college or junior college. The total number of months of participation in all these activities was then computed, allowing for more than one month of participation in a given calendar month if a sample member participated in more than one activity during that month. The value of this composite measure ranged from zero to twenty-seven months of participation across sample members, and its mean value ranged from 2.35 to 3.97 months across sites.

Data on the number of quarters that mothers were employed during the two years after random assignment were obtained from the administrative records of state unemployment insurance agencies. Each quarter in which a sample member had earnings of more than zero was counted as a quarter of employment. The value of this measure ranged from 0 to 8 quarters across sample members, and its mean value ranged from 2.0 to 3.5 quarters across sites.

Three site indicators (S_1, S_2, S_3) were created to identify sample members in each experimental site, and six instrumental variables (Z_1 to Z_6) were created by interacting site with treatment assignment.[17] In addition, a series of individual covariates (X_k) were constructed using baseline information about the mothers and children in the sample.

A first-stage regression was then estimated to predict each of the two mediators. Table 3.3 presents the coefficients obtained for each instrument. As the results indicate, the HCD programs in all three sites significantly increased mothers' participation in education activities, and the LFA programs in all three sites significantly increased mothers' employment. Moreover, three of the programs—Atlanta LFA, Grand Rapids LFA, and Riverside HCD—significantly increased both education and employment. Hence, the effects of the six programs are different for the two mediators, satisfying a critical condition for identifying their effects on children's school readiness in the second stage of the analysis.

Table 3.4 presents findings from the second-stage regression of each child's test score on both the predicted employment and education of his or her mother and the covariates and site indicators that were used in the first stage. Corresponding estimates of the relationships using ordinary least squares are included as benchmarks for comparison.

The instrumental-variables results indicate that for each additional month a mother spent in education activities during the two years after random assignment, her child's academic school readiness increased by 0.31 points. This estimate is not only statistically significant but also policy-relevant. Consider its magnitude relative to the standard deviation of test scores for all children in the sample (twelve points). The es-

Table 3.3   **First-Stage Regression Estimates for NEWWS: Effects of Treatment Assignment, by Site, on Mother's Education and Employment During the Two Years After Random Assignment**

	Mediator	
Instrument	Education (Number of Months)	Employment (Number of Quarters)
Atlanta HCD	2.36***	0.25
	(0.34)	(0.17)
Atlanta LFA	0.60*	0.43**
	(0.34)	(0.17)
Grand Rapids HCD	0.96*	0.00
	(0.50)	(0.25)
Grand Rapids LFA	−0.98*	0.96***
	(0.50)	(0.25)
Riverside HCD	2.94***	0.68***
	(0.43)	(0.21)
Riverside LFA	−0.36	1.22***
	(0.44)	(0.22)

Source: Magnuson (2003).
Notes: The sample includes female single-parent long-term welfare recipients from Atlanta (1,422), Riverside (950), and Grand Rapids (646). Each first-stage regression also includes the following baseline covariates: educational attainment, participation in education activities, prior earnings, prior welfare receipt, literacy, numeracy, depressive symptoms, age, race, marital status, number of baseline risk factors, family barriers to employment, number of children, locus of control, sources of social support, child's age, child's gender, and site indicators. Standard errors appear in parentheses. Two-tailed statistical significance is indicated as *for the 0.10 level, **for the 0.05 level, and ***for the 0.01 level.

timate suggests that if a program induced a mother to participate in education activities for ten months, her child's school readiness score would increase by 3.1 units, or 0.26 standard deviation. The instrumental-variables estimate for maternal employment, though positive in sign, is not statistically significant, suggesting that the effects of employment on the school readiness of children are uncertain.

The ordinary least squares results indicate that, for each additional month a mother participates in education activities, her child's academic readiness increases by 0.10 points, or approximately 0.01 standard deviation, which is substantially smaller than the effect estimate obtained using instrumental variables. The discrepancy between the estimates probably stems from selection bias in the ordinary least squares estimate. For example, the sample members who participated the long-

Table 3.4   Second-Stage Regression Results for the National Evaluation of Welfare-to-Work Strategies: Effects of Mother's Education and Employment on Child's Academic School Readiness

Mediator	Instrumental Variables	Ordinary Least Squares
Education (number of months)	0.31*	0.10***
	(0.17)	(0.04)
Employment (number of quarters)	0.67	0.13*
	(0.49)	(0.07)

Source: Magnuson (2003).
Notes: The sample includes female single-parent long-term welfare recipients from Atlanta (1,422), Riverside (950), and Grand Rapids (646). Each second-stage regression also includes the following baseline covariates: education attainment, participation in education activities, prior earnings, prior welfare receipt, literacy, numeracy, depressive symptoms, age, race, marital status, number of baseline risk factors, family barriers to employment, number of children, locus of control, sources of social support, child's age, child's gender, and site indicators. Standard errors appear in parentheses. Two-tailed statistical significance is indicated as *for the 0.10 level, **for the 0.05 level, and ***for the 0.01 level.

est in education activities may have been the most educationally disadvantaged at the outset, making them least equipped to prepare their children for school. If this were true, then examining the school readiness of children as a function of their mothers' participation in education would lead to an underestimate of the effect of maternal education, even when controlling for covariates.

Using Multiple Experiments to Create Multiple Instruments

A third approach to creating multiple instruments is to construct a pooled set of data from two or more experiments. For pooling to be justified, the type and quality of the measures and data sources in each experiment must be comparable. When they are, each experiment can be used to construct a separate instrument or a separate set of instruments. An experiment that tests a single treatment in a single site can provide one instrument. An experiment that tests multiple treatments in a single site, a single treatment in multiple sites, or multiple treatments in multiple sites can be used to construct as many instruments as there are treatments, sites, or treatment-site combinations.

Creating instruments by pooling data across experiments has three main advantages. It can make the analysis more precise by increasing the sample size; it can increase the potential for estimating the effects of multiple mediators by increasing the number of instruments that are available; and it can improve the generalizability of the findings by increasing the diversity of the populations, programs, or environments represented.

A number of conditions must be met, however, for instrumental variables to yield unbiased estimates based on a pooled data set. Notably, all these conditions also pertain to the case of multisite experiments but may be harder to verify in the present case. As in the application of instrumental variables to data from a multisite experiment, here the instruments must covary strongly with the mediators, and each mediator must show a different pattern of covariation with the instruments. In addition, the exclusion restriction (that the only way the treatment affects the outcome is through the modeled mediators) must still hold. In analyses based on multiple experiments in which each program under study is an amalgam of components targeted to affect different outcomes, satisfaction of the exclusion restriction can be even more difficult to verify. Finally, the effect of each mediator on the outcome must be the same in each study or each study-site combination, an assumption that may be especially difficult to test when the experiments take place in very different places and include very different populations.

Even when these conditions are met, extracting comparable information from numerous random-assignment studies is no small feat. In most areas of social and economic policy, no such information is available. Even in fields where numerous randomized experiments have been conducted, such as welfare and employment policy, it could take years before there are enough studies with comparable data to support a productive synthesis. Thanks to the foresight of several private and public funders, a series of large-scale, multisite, and (in some cases) multitreatment welfare-to-work experiments were conducted in the late 1980s and the 1990s that gathered comparable data on a variety of parent, family, and child outcomes.[18] In the remainder of this chapter, we illustrate the approach of using data from multiple experiments to create multiple instruments.

Table 3.5 presents selected preliminary results from first-stage regressions predicting the employment and income of mothers of 11,814 children who were between the ages of two and five at the time of their parents' random assignment in four major welfare-to-work experiments (Morris, Duncan, and Rodrigues 2004): National Evaluation of Welfare-to-Work Strategies (NEWWS; Hamilton et al. 2001), the Los Angeles Jobs-First GAIN program (Freedman et al. 2000), Canada's Self-Sufficiency Project, or SSP (Michalopoulos et al. 2000), and Connecticut's Jobs-First program (Bloom et al. 2000). Because two of the experiments took place in multiple sites and one of these two also encompassed multiple experiments in one site, each regression includes eight

Table 3.5   First-Stage Regression Results Based on Four Welfare-to-Work
Experiments: Effects of Individual Programs on the
Employment and Income of Mothers with Young Children
During the Two Years After Random Assignment

	Mediator	
Instrument	Employment (Percentage of Quarters)	Mean Income Per Year (Dollars)
Work-first programs		
NEWWS, Atlanta LFA	4.7**	340
	(1.9)	(240)
NEWWS, Grand Rapids LFA	10.4***	70
	(2.2)	(380)
NEWWS, Riverside LFA	12.0***	100
	(2.3)	(430)
Los Angeles Jobs-First GAIN	–0.4	–1,050
	(6.2)	(880)
Earnings supplement programs		
SSP, British Columbia	7.6***	1,620***
	(1.9)	(270)
SSP, New Brunswick	13.4***	1,910***
	(1.9)	(220)
SSP-Plus, New Brunswick	11.3***	2,200***
	(4.0)	(370)
Connecticut Jobs First	5.3***	810**
	(2.1)	(360)

Source: Morris, Duncan, and Rodrigues (2004).
Notes: The sample includes 11,814 observations of children's outcomes from 5,806 children (in 5,253 families) who were between the ages of 2 and 5 at random assignment. Each first-stage regression also includes the following baseline covariates: earnings and earnings squared during the preceding year, number of children, age of youngest child, a three-point scale measuring length of prior welfare receipt, and 0 or 1 indicator variables for mother was employed during the preceding year, mother had high school degree or equivalent, mother was under 18 when child was born, mother was never married, mother was separated or divorced, mother was black, mother was white, mother was Latino, length of time to follow-up survey in months, child was between 6 and 9 years old, and child was over 9 years old. Standard errors appear in parentheses. Two-tailed statistical significance is indicated as *for the 0.10 level, **for the 0.05 level, and ***for the 0.01 level.

instruments. Each regression also includes a set of site indicators and covariates, the coefficients of which are not presented.

The two mediators in table 3.5 are based on the labor-market experiences of sample members during the two years after random assignment. Employment was measured as the percentage of quarters in which sample members received earnings of more than zero, which represents the average quarterly employment rate. Income was measured as the average annual dollar amount of earnings plus welfare received (for the programs operated in the United States, welfare included AFDC as well as food-stamp payments).

Although many of the treatments had more than one feature, they are grouped in the table according to which of two program approaches they most closely adhere to: the work-first approach, which aims to increase employment by requiring parents to participate in work-related activities and where income did not change because earned income was a substitute for welfare income; or the earnings-supplement approach, which aims to supplement the amount of earned income that sample members take home while they are employed.

The findings shown in the table suggest that treatment assignment provides good instruments for the two mediators. Many of the impacts of treatment assignment on each mediator are large and statistically significant. For example, four of the eight treatments increased employment rates by ten percentage points or more, and seven of the eight impact estimates for employment are statistically significant. In addition, all four of the estimated impacts of the earnings supplement programs on income are large, with impacts ranging from $810 to $2,200 annually, and are statistically significant. Hence, most of the instruments are strong individually, and they are also strong as a group.

In addition, the effects of the instruments on employment differ from the effects of the instruments on income. The work-first treatment had large and statistically significant impacts on employment but not on income because welfare payments were reduced substantially for each dollar of income earned. The earnings-supplement treatments (many of which also included employment services) increased both employment and income substantially because they supplemented rather than reduced earnings from employment. This range of impacts bodes well for the potential of instrumental variables as a method of disentangling the causal effect of employment from the causal effect of income on child outcomes. It is especially encouraging that the effects of the treatments are consistent with the theories on which they are based. This consistency will lend face validity to future analyses that use these treatment assignments as instruments for the mediators. In other words, such analyses will make theoretical as well as statistical sense.

Conclusion

This chapter has explored an emerging analytic approach that applies a well-known nonexperimental estimation procedure, instrumental variables, to data collected by means of randomized experimentation. This integrative approach promises to help illuminate the black box of how social programs work in three ways.

First, the approach can deal with the conceptual and methodological implications of noncompliance with randomization. It thus allows researchers to measure the impact of being offered a treatment (which can be accomplished within the experimental paradigm) separately from the impact of receiving the treatment (which requires extending the experimental paradigm). For example, it can be used to estimate the effect on high school students' grades of having received special tutorial assistance as compared to having been offered such assistance.

Second, the approach uses randomized treatment assignment to create exogenous variation in a causal agent, or mediator, that can then be used to study the effect of that mediator on outcomes of interest. Thus, the technique makes it possible to answer questions about treatment effects on outcomes in situations where entities or individuals cannot be randomly assigned to the treatment. For example, it allows one to study the effects on children's academic performance of changes in the quality of children's residential neighborhoods induced by their families' random assignment to a housing voucher program.

Third, the approach exploits randomization to multiple treatments, multiple sites, multiple experiments, or combinations thereof to separate the effects of multiple mediators on an outcome. This feature was was illustrated by applying it to pooled data from several experiments in which sample members were randomly assigned to variants of a welfare-to-work program to investigate the effects of low-income parents' employment and income on their children's early academic performance.

In our presentation of the three general approaches to instrumental-variables analysis and the empirical examples thereof, we highlighted the conditions that must be met for these approaches to provide consistent and precise findings. Some of the conditions can be assessed empirically, whereas others must be assessed judgmentally. All the conditions must be carefully considered by researchers who plan to apply the method of instrumental variables in the context of an experimental design.

We expect that as researchers gain more experience with this approach in a wide range of settings and under a wide range of conditions, they will be able to make ever more informed judgments about when and where it is likely to succeed. To take a last example from welfare and employment policy, one intriguing possibility that was not fully explored in this chapter is to use instrumental-variables estimation to gain a better understanding of the effects on family well-being of forms of government assistance that are legally guaranteed to people eligible for them, which is not possible in a purely experimental framework because neither individuals nor families can be randomized not to receive an entitlement. Sometimes referred to as an encouragement design, such a study might be designed to substantially increase take-up on entitlement benefit such as transitional Medicaid. A fraction of people who leave welfare during a certain period could be randomly assigned to a treatment group and targeted by an outreach campaign that provides detailed information about why it is important to obtain transitional medical benefits and how to do so. A simple application of instrumental variables might then yield valuable insights into the effects of this government benefit on family health. We hope that other researchers will take up the challenge of exploring pressing questions that once lay outside the scope of experimental methods by developing similarly innovative applications of the instrumental-variables approach for their own research fields.

Notes

1. This framework also applies to observational data. For details, see Joshua Angrist, Guido Imbens, and Don Rubin (1996), James J. Heckman (1996a, 1996b, 1997), and Charles Manski (1996).
2. Angrist, Imbens and Rubin (1996) called this assumption the exclusion restriction.
3. Because estimates of the average effect of treatment on the treated are a ratio of two sample-based estimates, they are consistent but not unbiased.
4. In order for equation 3.9 to identify the local average treatment effect, the average effect of the program must be the same (or a known multiple) for compliers and defiers or defiers must not exist. Angrist, Imbens, and Rubin (1996) refer to this latter condition as monotonicity.
5. For a description of one of the earliest applications of instrumental-variables estimation, by Philip G. Wright (1928, 1929), see James H. Stock and Francesco Trebbi (2003).
6. Looking into the black box using nonexperimental data is equally, if not more, challenging than doing so within an experimental design. Unlike nonexperimental data, however, experimental data allow one to draw unequivocal links between the effects of an intervention and an outcome.
7. The resulting instrumental variables estimate is asymptotically unbiased. For further discussion of identification and the search for good instruments, see Angrist and Krueger (2001).
8. Estimating the standard error for D_i requires substituting the original values of D_i and Y_i into the estimated version of equation 3.10 and using the resulting residuals (Pindyck and Rubinfeld 1998, 200).
9. The resulting estimator is consistent but not necessarily unbiased.
10. Robert S. Pindyck and Daniel L. Rubinfeld (1998, 194–98) described spec-

ification tests that have been developed to assess whether the condition is met, but these and all other such tests are based on assumptions that are ultimately untestable.

11. Having at least as many instruments as mediators is a necessary but not sufficient condition for identifying an instrumental-variables model. Such models also must meet certain conditions about the correlations among instruments and their patterns of relationships to the mediators.

12. The estimates presented are for the total effect of parental employment on child behavior (including its indirect effect through child-care use) and the total effect of child-care use on child behavior (which has no indirect effects in the present example).

13. Treatment effects on measures of employment and earnings for the full three-year follow-up period were much less pronounced than those for the first follow-up year. The instrumental-variables analysis was therefore based on employment and income data only from the first year, even though one might expect the effects of parents' earnings and income on their children's behavior to accumulate over time.

14. The standard errors were adjusted to account for the two-stage estimation procedure.

15. A weaker, but less practical, variant of this requirement is that the relationships between the impacts of the mediators at the two sites (B_{11}/B_{12} and B_{21}/B_{22}) be known.

16. The test was the Bracken Basic Concept Scale/School Readiness Composite (BBCS/SRC), which assesses children's knowledge of concepts such as colors, letters, numbers, and shapes.

17. Two of the site indicators were included as covariates in the model, which identifies the third site.

18. Together with our colleagues, we are in the early stages of integrating analyses of these studies under the aegis of the Next Generation project. For more information, go to www.mdrc.org/NextGeneration.

References

Angrist, Joshua. 1990. "Lifetime Earnings and the Vietnam Era Draft Lottery: Evidence from Social Security Administrative Records." *American Economic Review* 80(3): 313-35.

Angrist, Joshua, Guido Imbens, and Don Rubin. 1996. "Identification of Causal Effects Using Instrumental Variables." JASA Applications invited paper, with comments and authors' response. *Journal of the American Statistical Association* 91(434): 444–55.

Angrist, Joshua, and Alan Krueger. 2001. "Instrumental Variables and the Search for Identification: From Supply and Demand to Natural Experiments." *Journal of Economic Perspectives* 15(4): 69–85.

Bloom, Dan, Laura Melton, Charles Michalopoulos, Susan Scrivener, and Johanna Walter. 2000. *Jobs First: Implementation and Early Impacts of Connecticut's Welfare Reform Initiative.* New York: MDRC.

Bloom, Dan, and Charles Michalopoulos. 2001. *How Welfare and Work Policies Affect Employment and Income: A Synthesis of Research.* New York: MDRC.

Bloom, Howard. 1984. "Accounting for No-Shows in Experimental Evaluation Designs." *Evaluation Review* 8(2): 225–46.

Bos, Johannes, Susan Scrivener, Jason Snipes, and Gayle Hamilton. 2001. *Improving Basic Skills: The Effects of Adult Education in Welfare-to-Work Programs.* Washington: U.S. Department of Education and U.S. Department of Health and Human Services.

Bound, John, David Jaeger, and Regina M. Baker. 1995. "Problems with Instrumental Variables Estimation When the Correlation Between the Instruments and the Endogenous Explanatory Variables Is Weak." *Journal of the American Statistical Association* 90(430): 443–50.

Cochrane Collaboration. 2002. "Cochrane Controlled Trials Register." Online database. Available at The Cochrane Library: www.cochrane.org (accessed January 3, 2005).

Freedman, Stephen, Jean Knab, Lisa Gennetian, and David Navarro. 2000. *The Los Angeles Jobs-First GAIN Evaluation: Final Report on a Work First Program in a Major Urban Center.* New York: MDRC.

Gennetian, Lisa, and Cynthia Miller. 2002. "Children and Welfare Reform: A View from an Experimental Welfare Program in Minnesota." *Child Development* 73(2): 601–20.

Greenberg, David, and Mark Shroder. 1997. *The Digest of Social Experiments.* Washington: Urban Institute Press.

Hamilton, Gayle, Stephen Freedman, Lisa Gennetian, Charles Michalopoulos, Johanna Walter, Diana Adams-Ciardullo, Anna Gassman-Pines, Sharon McGroder, Martha Zaslow, Jennifer Brooks, and Surjeet Ahluwalia. 2001. *National Evaluation of Welfare-to-Work Strategies: How Effective Are Different Welfare-to-Work Approaches? Five-Year Adult and Child Impacts for Eleven Programs.* Washington: U.S. Department of Health and Human Services and U.S. Department of Education.

Heckman, James J. 1996a. "Randomization as an Instrumental Variable." *Review of Economics and Statistics* 78: 336–41.

———. 1996b. Comment on "Identification of Causal Effects Using Instrumental Variables." *Journal of the American Statistical Association* 91(434): 459–62.

———. 1997. "Instrumental Variables: A Study of Implicit Behavioral Assumptions Used in Making Program Evaluations." *Journal of Human Resources* 32(3): 441–62.

Holland, Paul. 1986. "Statistics and Causal Inference." *Journal of the American Statistical Association* 81: 945–70.

Kling, Jeffrey, and Jeffrey Liebman. 2003. "Causal Effects on Youth Outcomes of Moving Out of High Poverty Neighborhoods in the Moving to Opportunity Experiment." Unpublished paper. Department of Economics, Princeton University.

Knox, Virginia, Cynthia Miller, and Lisa Gennetian. 2000. *Reforming Welfare and Rewarding Work: A Summary of the Final Report on the Minnesota Family Investment Program.* New York: MDRC.

Kornfeld, Robert, and Howard S. Bloom. 1999. "Measuring Program Impacts on Earnings and Employment: Do Unemployment Insurance Wage Reports from Employers Agree with Surveys of Individuals? *Journal of Labor Economics* 17(1): 168–97.

Krueger, Alan, and Pei Zhu. 2003. "Another Look at the New York City School Voucher Experiment." Unpublished paper. Department of Economics, Princeton University.

Magnuson, Katherine A. 2003. "The Effects of Increases in Welfare Mothers' Education on Their Young Children's Academic and Behavioral Outcomes: Evidence from the National Evaluation of Welfare-to-Work Strategies Child Outcomes Study." Institute for Research on Poverty discussion paper 1274-03. Madison: University of Wisconsin.

Manski, Charles. 1996. "Learning About Treatment Effects from Experiments with Random Assignment of Treatments." *Journal of Human Resources* 31(4): 707–33.

Mayer, Daniel P., Paul E. Peterson, David E. Myers, Christina Clark Tuttle, and William G. Howell. 2002. *School Choice in New York City After Three Years: An Evaluation of the School Choice Scholarships Program, Final Report.* Washington, D.C.: Mathematica Policy Research.

Michalopoulos, Charles, David Card, Lisa Gennetian, Kristen Harknett, Philip K. Robins. 2000. *The Self-Sufficiency Project at 36 Months: Effects of a Financial Work Incentive on Employment and Income.* Ottawa: Social Research Demonstration Corporation.

Miller, Cynthia, Virginia Knox, Lisa Gennetian, Martey Dodoo, Johanna Hunter, and Cindy Redcross. 2000. *Reforming Welfare and Rewarding Work: Final Report on the Minnesota Family Investment Program,* volume 1: *Effects on Adults.* New York: MDRC.

Morris, Pamela, Greg Duncan, and Christopher Rodrigues. 2004. "Does Money Really Matter? Estimating the Impacts of Family Income on Children's Achievement with Data from Random Assignment Experiments." Unpublished paper. MDRC, New York.

Morris, Pamela, and Lisa Gennetian. 2003. "Identifying the Effects of Income on Children Using Experimental Data." *Journal of Marriage and the Family* 65(August): 716–29.

Pindyck, Robert S., and Daniel L. Rubinfeld. 1998. *Econometric Models and Economic Forecasts.* 4th edition. Boston: Irwin McGraw-Hill.

Schultz, T. Paul. 2001. "School Subsidies for the Poor: Evaluating the Mexican Progresa Poverty Program." Economic Growth Center discussion paper 834. New Haven: Yale University.

Staiger, Douglas, and James H. Stock. 1993. "Instrumental Variables Regression with Weak Instruments." Cambridge, Mass.: Kennedy School of Government, Harvard University.

Stock, James H., and Francesco Trebbi. 2003. "Retrospectives: Who Invented Instrumental Variables Regression?" *Journal of Economic Perspectives* 17(3): 177–94.

U.S. Department of Education. 2003. "Identifying and Implementing Educational Practices Supported by Rigorous Evidence: A User Friendly Guide." Washington: U.S. Department of Education, Institute of Education Sciences, National Center for Education Evaluation and Regional Assistance.

Wald, Abraham. 1940. "The Fitting of Straight Lines If Both Variables Are Subject to Error." *Annals of Mathematical Statistics* 11(September): 284–300.

Wright, Philip G. 1928. *The Tariff on Animal and Vegetable Oils.* New York: Macmillan.

———. 1929. "Statistical Laws of Demand and Supply." *Journal of the American Statistical Association* 24(166): 207–15.

Chapter 4

Randomizing Groups to Evaluate Place-Based Programs

S OCIAL INTERVENTIONS such as community improvement programs, school reforms, and employer-based efforts to retain workers, whose aim is to change whole communities or organizations,
are often called place-based initiatives. Because such programs are designed to affect the behavior of groups of interrelated people rather
than individuals, it is generally not feasible to measure their effectiveness in an experiment that randomly assigns individuals to the program or to a control group. By randomizing at the level of groups such
as neighborhoods, schools, or companies—also called clusters—researchers can still reap most of the methodological benefits of random
assignment.

Perhaps the earliest application of group, or cluster, randomization
was Harold F. Gosnell's (1927) study of ways to increase voter turnout.
After dividing each of twelve local districts in Chicago into two parts,
he randomly chose one part of each district as a target for a series of
hortatory mailings and used the other part as a control group. This research was conducted a decade before Ronald A. Fisher (1937/1947),
the father of randomized experiments, published his landmark book on
the use of randomization to study cause and effect.[1] Not until about
twenty years ago, in the early 1980s, did evaluators begin to use cluster
randomization with any frequency. Since its application was confined
mostly to research on health, it is no surprise that the only two textbooks on cluster randomization published to date, one by Allan Donner and Neil Klar (2000) and the other by David M. Murray (1998), focus on evaluating health programs.[2]

The use of cluster randomization to study the effects, or impacts, of
social policies is now spreading to many fields (for a review and discussion of the key issues, see Boruch and Foley 2000). Over the past
decade, it has been used to evaluate "whole-school" reforms (Cook,

Hunt, and Murphy 2000), school-based teacher training programs (Blank et al. 2002), community health promotion campaigns (Murray, Hannan et al. 1994), school-based smoking, drinking, and sex prevention programs (Flay 2000), community employment initiatives (Bloom and Riccio 2002), police patrol innovations (Sherman and Weisburd 1995), family-planning programs (Smith et al. 1997), rural health, nutrition, and education initiatives (Teruel and Davis 2000), HIV-prevention programs (Sikkema et al. 2000), and group medical practice interventions (Leviton et al. 1999; Eccles et al. 2001).

To foster more frequent and better-informed use of cluster randomization, this chapter explores the rationale, nature, and consequences of place-based programs; the role, design, and implementation of cluster randomization evaluations of such programs; and the statistical properties and substantive implications of these evaluation designs. Many of the points raised in the chapter have been made by other authors in other settings. By putting these points together in new ways, considering them from new perspectives and contexts, providing new examples, and bringing to bear new empirical information, however, I attempt to advance the state of the art.

Reasons for Place-Based Evaluation

There are five main reasons why a research team might choose to study a program in a place-based design using cluster randomization. The first three depend on features of the program to be evaluated:

1. The effects of the program have the potential to "spill over" to a substantial degree between participants or from participants to nonparticipants.

2. The program's services are delivered most efficiently when targeted at specific locations.

3. The program is designed to address a spatially concentrated problem or situation.

Because such interventions are place-based in nature, it makes sense to evaluate them in a place-based research design.[3] This means conducting random assignment at the level of groups of people who live, work, or receive services in the places being examined. The other two reasons for place-based evaluation relate to the difficulties of implementing random-assignment experiments in real-world settings:

4. Using a place-based design will reduce political opposition to randomization.

5. Maintaining the integrity of the experiment requires the physical separation of program-group members from control-group members.

These situations involve programs that, though not inherently place-based, are studied more readily when random assignment is conducted in a place-based way.

Containing Spillover Effects

For decades, scholars have stressed the importance of tailoring evaluations to the theories underlying the programs to be studied. This emphasis is variously referred to as "theory-driven" evaluation (Chen and Rossi 1983), "theory-based" evaluation (Cook, Hunt, and Murphy 2000), and "theory of change" evaluation (Connell and Kubisch 1998). The primary theoretical reason for place-based evaluation is spillover effects, which occur when the outcomes for some program participants influence those for other participants or for people who are not participating in the program.

Spillover effects (often referred to as system effects) can reflect interdependencies between actors with respect to a single outcome, independencies between outcomes with respect to a single actor, or both. For example, the process of finding a job might spill over in a variety of ways: it might enable one to help friends or family members find jobs too; it might improve one's mental health; it might enable one to help others find jobs, thereby improving one's own and others' mental health. If spillover effects are expected to be an important product or by-product of a program, an evaluation of the program should account for them.

Spillover effects are recognized in many fields. They play a central role in public finance theory, where they are referred to as "externalities" (Musgrave and Musgrave 1973). Externalities occur when a good or service consumed by one individual or group produces benefits or costs for others. For example, education creates direct benefits for its recipients and indirect benefits for society (a positive externality). The use of gasoline to fuel automobiles generates transportation benefits for drivers and passengers and imposes pollution costs on others (a negative externality).

Despite their theoretical and practical importance, spillover effects are difficult to accommodate in a causal model of individual behavior.[4] Thus, when program impacts on individuals are estimated, spillover effects are usually ignored or assumed not to exist. When spillovers do exist, however, one must shift to a higher level of aggregation to accommodate them. This higher level is often defined spatially, that is, with respect to place.

Spillover Effects on a Single Outcome   The first type of spillover occurs when an outcome for one or more people affects the same outcome for other people. Social scientists have developed many causal models to explain how such spillover effects can occur.

Game-theory models seek to explain how one individual's response to a situation influences others' responses. These models have been used to explore the occurrence of transitions in the racial composition of neighborhoods (Schelling 1971).

Network-theory models seek to explain how the flow of information among associated individuals influences their behavior. These models have been used to explain how employment is promoted through family and social connections (Granovetter 1973).

Peer-group models seek to explain how individuals' norms and behaviors are shaped by the norms and behaviors of the people with whom they associate. These models have been used to study how smoking, drinking, drug abuse, and violent behavior spread through a group, a neighborhood, or a school.

Microeconomic models seek to explain how supply-and-demand conditions link consumers' decisions with producers' decisions to determine the quantities and prices of goods, services, capital, and labor. These models have been used to explain how employment programs for one group of people can hurt others' employment prospects by reducing the total number of job vacancies (Garfinkel, Manski, and Michalopoulos 1992).

Macroeconomic models of income determination seek to explain how private investment, production, consumption, and savings decisions when combined with government tax and spending policies cause an increase in one group's income to ripple through an economy in successively larger waves. Such models are used to forecast economic growth (Branson 1972).

Chaos-theory models, which are mathematical representations of nonlinear dynamic systems, provide a general analytic framework for examining unstable equilibria (Kellert 1993), which provides another tool for studying spillover effects.

Embedded within these models and theories are two key features of spillover effects, feedback effects and thresholds. Feedback effects are changes in individual actions caused by previous individual actions. The feedback is positive if, for instance, increased smoking among some adolescents promotes smoking among their peers. The feedback is negative if, for instance, higher employment in one group worsens the job prospects of other groups.

Thresholds represent situations where behaviors change dramatically beyond a certain point (Granovetter 1978). The level at which this occurs is often called a tipping point. Many examples of tipping have been identified, including racial transitions in neighborhoods, outbreaks of crime, and epidemics of disease. The anecdotal evidence for this phenomenon is compelling (Gladwell 2000),[5] but so far only limited statistical evidence for it is available because of methodological difficulties associated with gathering such evidence.[6]

Spillover Effects Between Outcomes   In the second type of spillover, one outcome affects another. According to Gunnar Myrdal's (1944) principle of "cumulation," for example, intense social interactions among members of society make it possible for small changes on one dimension to produce large cumulative changes on other dimensions. He invoked this principle to account for the relationship between white prejudice against nonwhites and the economic circumstances of nonwhites. More recently, William Julius Wilson (1996) posited that high rates of joblessness among adults in a community limit young people's exposure to positive role models and routine modes of living, which in turn increases the likelihood of antisocial and illegal behavior among adolescents in that community.

Although spillover effects across outcomes have been the subject of much theorization, little hard evidence about them exists. For example, the extensive literature examining features of neighborhoods and their effects on children remains inconclusive because of conceptual, measurement, and statistical problems (Tienda 1991; Jencks and Mayer 1990; Brooks-Gunn, Duncan, and Aber 1997; for a randomized experiment on this topic, see Kling, Ludwig, and Katz 2005).

Spillover Effects and Saturation Programs   It is particularly easy to see how the two types of spillover effects just described could occur in the case of programs designed to saturate an area with services targeted at its entire population. A current application of the saturation approach, the Jobs-Plus Community Revitalization Initiative for Public Housing Families (Bloom and Riccio 2002), provides employment and training services, financial incentives to make work pay, and community supports for work to working-age adults in selected public housing developments in six U.S. cities. The program's designers hypothesized that by exposing a high percentage of residents to this rich mix of services and activities, Jobs-Plus would induce a critical mass of participants to become employed, which in turn would motivate others to follow suit. This is an example of a spillover effect on the same dimension (employment) between groups of individuals (between employed and unemployed residents of the Jobs-Plus developments). The designers also hoped that by substantially reducing the local concentration of unemployment, Jobs-Plus would have beneficial effects on the neighborhoods' physical and social environment. This is an example of a spillover effect across dimensions (from employment to outcomes such as crime and the housing vacancy rate), both within the same group and between groups of individuals (among Jobs-Plus participants and between Jobs-Plus participants and other residents of the housing developments). Because producing these spillover effects is an explicit goal of the Jobs-Plus model—hence the "Plus" in its name—the program evaluation was planned to account for them by randomly assigning entire housing developments to the program or to a control group.

Delivering Services Effectively

Another reason for operating programs that focus on groups of people defined by their location instead of a group of dispersed individuals is that place can be an effective platform for service delivery: a program may capitalize on economies of spatial concentration, or it may aim to change the practices and cultures of existing organizations.

Achieving Economies of Spatial Concentration   Spatial concentration of the target-group members benefits place-based initiatives in two major ways, through physical proximity to target-group members and by providing the opportunity to leverage existing channels of communication. Locating a program near its target group may enhance recruitment efforts by raising its profile; may reduce psychological barriers to participation by enabling people to participate in familiar territory; may reduce the time and money costs of transportation to and from the program; and may enable staff to operate the program more effectively by exposing them directly to problems and possibilities in their clients' day-to-day lives.

By concentrating outreach in a few locations instead of dispersing it, some programs can make better use of both formal and informal channels of communication. For example, concentrated outreach can facilitate more comprehensive, coordinated, and frequent use of local media to heighten awareness of a problem being addressed, to publicize how a program will help solve the problem, and to inform target-group members how to participate. Saturating local media with a program's message may also stimulate word-of-mouth communication. In addition, it is easier to make direct personal contact with target-group members when they are located in a small area. When outreach is concentrated spatially, it may be necessary to randomize entire areas—and, by implication, the groups they represent—so as to separate individuals who are supposed to receive the treatment being tested from those who are not. This is why interventions to reduce lifestyle-related health-risk factors that are based on media outreach and information campaigns have been designed and tested as randomized place-based experiments (Murray, Rooney et al. 1994; Murray and Short 1995).

Inducing Organizational Change   Some programs are designed explicitly to change the practices of existing organizations. For example, whole-school reforms are designed to transform the way a primary or secondary school functions by changing the timing, staffing, style, culture, and curriculum of the entire school. It is much easier to evaluate such initiatives by randomly assigning schools to a program rather than individual students within a school to a program. Two examples of this approach are the completed evaluation of the School Development Program (Cook, Hunt, and Murphy 2000) and an ongoing evaluation of the reading program Success for All (Slavin 2002).

Employer-based initiatives aimed at reducing turnover among employees also are designed to change organizations. In attempting to improve procedures for training, supervising, and counseling employees, such programs focus on entire firms, not just on individuals. They may include providing direct services to help employees meet the demands of their jobs more effectively and special training to help supervisors manage their employees better. Random assignment of firms is now being used to evaluate an employer-based program designed to reduce turnover among low-wage workers in the health-care industry (Miller and Bloom 2002).

A third example is programs designed to increase physicians' adoption of clinically proven innovations and to reduce their use of practices that have been shown to have harmful side effects. Although the ultimate goal of such initiatives is to change individual behavior, their focus is on transforming medical practices in entire organizations, such as hospitals and group medical practices. These programs provide education activities, embed audit and feedback procedures in patient information systems, or stimulate other organizational changes to expedite diffusion of improved medical practices. Jeremy M. Grimshaw et al. (2004) presented a systematic review of 100 studies that randomly assigned physician groups or medical practices to evaluate interventions focused on these organizational units.

Tackling Local Problems

In some cases, the nature of the problem being addressed or the test being conducted makes place a natural locus of intervention.

Nature of the Problem: When Locus Is the Focus   Place-based solutions make sense when the focus is on social problems with an uneven spatial distribution. For example, because most crimes are concentrated geographically, crime reduction strategies are often targeted at specific locations. Over three decades, scholars of policing have focused on whether preventative patrol, an inherently place-based activity, can reduce crime (Sherman and Weisburd 1995). The first random-assignment test of this approach was the Kansas City Preventative Patrol Experiment (Kelling et al. 1974). This landmark study randomly assigned fifteen police beats to receive different patrol intensities and compared the subsequent crime rates across beats. The study, which suggested that higher patrol intensities did not produce lower crime rates, had a major effect on police thinking and practice for many years thereafter. In the late 1980s, however, a major study that randomly varied police patrol intensities across one hundred ten "hot spots," small areas of concentrated crime, in Minneapolis found highly targeted intensive police patrol to be effective (Sherman and Weisburd 1995).

Nature of the Test: When Programs Are Evaluated at Scale   The ultimate test of a program, especially if it is one that provides an entitlement intended to benefit everyone eligible for it, is what would happen if it were implemented at full scale. Thus, it is important not only to measure the direct effects of the program on its participants but also to find out what its full-scale implementation would mean with respect to spillover effects, administration, and costs. Doing this requires full implementation of the program in selected locations.

For example, one of the most contentious issues in the debate about vouchers designed to promote school choice is potential system effects. Although researchers have measured the direct effects of school vouchers on small samples of students who were chosen to receive them through lotteries in three U.S. cities (Peterson et al. 2002), it is unclear how they would influence broader outcomes such as racial and economic segregation if they were implemented at full scale. Perhaps the best evidence bearing on this issue is Helen Ladd and Edward B. Fiske's (2000) nonexperimental study of changes that occurred after New Zealand instituted a nationwide school choice program and Chang-Tai Hsieh and Miguel Urquiola's (2003) nonexperimental study of the effects of Chile's nationwide introduction of school choice by providing vouchers to any student wishing to attend a private school.

Possible system effects were also a major concern in a series of studies of housing allowances (a form of rental assistance for low-income people) conducted in the United States during the 1970s (Kennedy 1988). Whereas the direct impacts, administrative feasibility, and costs of housing allowances were assessed in individual-level random assignment studies, their effects on the prices and quantities of low-cost housing were measured by means of nonexperimental analyses of changes in local housing markets after implementation of housing allowance entitlement programs.

The Youth Incentive Entitlement Pilot Projects, an initiative that guaranteed jobs to all interested sixteen-to-nineteen-year-olds in seventeen locations across the United States from 1978 to 1980, likewise included a component to measure system effects (Gueron 1984). The project used a nonexperimental analysis to examine the program's impacts on unemployment and school success among the 76,000 young people who volunteered to participate and also conducted a nonexperimental analysis of what the program's impacts on the youth labor market would be if it were fully implemented in four of the cities in the study.

Although none of these full-scale tests involved randomizing places, it is possible to imagine doing so. The vast scale of such an extensive randomized study, however, means that the practical application of the method is probably limited to a small number of exceptionally important programs.

Facilitating Randomization

Another, very different, reason for testing a program in a place-based experiment is to facilitate political acceptance of randomization by offsetting ethical concerns about "equal treatment of equals."[7] In reality, random assignment treats sample members equally in the sense that each has an equal chance of being offered the program. This fact is often overlooked, however, because, after randomization, program group members have access to the program while control group members do not.

Place-based randomization is generally easier to "sell" than individual randomization in at least three ways. It can assuage the political concerns of policymakers and program managers, who often cannot accept random assignment of individuals within their organizations but might be open to randomization across organizations. It can circumvent legal restrictions that prohibit programs from treating individuals in the same political jurisdiction differently but that do not prohibit them from treating different jurisdictions differently.[8] And it can capitalize on the fact that much program funding is allocated at the level of political jurisdictions, which opens the door to assigning new funding to jurisdictions on a random basis—at least when funds are so limited that not all jurisdictions will receive them.

Avoiding Control-Group Contamination

One of the greatest threats to the methodological integrity of a random-assignment research design is the possibility that some control-group members will be exposed to the program, thus reducing the difference between the group receiving the intervention, or treatment, and the control group. This difference is called the treatment contrast. Such contamination of the control group is especially likely in the case of programs that provide promotional messages and information. For example, if individual students in a school are randomly assigned to a personalized antismoking program, they most likely will share some of the information provided through the program with peers who have been randomly assigned to the control group. This second-hand exposure will attenuate the treatment contrast and make it difficult to interpret impact estimates.

One way to head off this problem is to separate the program group from the control group spatially, by means of place-based randomization. For example, randomly assigning homerooms instead of individual students to an antismoking program or to a control group can limit the extent to which program and control-group members share information. For some types of programs, however, even this degree of separation may not be adequate, and it might be better to randomize larger entities, such as schools (for an example, see Flay et al. 1985).

Similarly, in an experiment testing ways to induce physicians to use proven new medical procedures, randomization of individual physicians might undermine the treatment contrast because physicians often share information in the course of working together in group practices. Thus, it might be preferable to randomize group practices. But if the group practices share privileges at the same hospitals, it might be better yet to randomize hospitals (see Campbell, Mollison, and Grimshaw 2001).

The first major evaluation of the children's television program *Sesame Street* is an illuminating example of control-group contamination and how to avoid it (Bogatz and Ball 1971). In the first year of the evaluation, each eligible household in five U.S. cities was randomly assigned either to a group that was encouraged to watch *Sesame Street* or to a control group that was not. When the data on who had watched the program were analyzed, it was discovered that most control-group members had also watched *Sesame Street* and thus had received the "treatment" being tested. Therefore, in the next phase of the study, which was conducted in two other cities, the program group and the control group were spatially separated. At that time *Sesame Street* was available only through cable in those areas, and the separation was accomplished in one of the additional cities by installing free cable television in all households with eligible young children who lived in groups of street blocks selected randomly from a larger pool. The remaining households, in the control group, did not receive free cable service. All the households were in low-income areas where cable television was prohibitively expensive at the time, so very few households in the control-group blocks were able to watch the program. Thus, place-based randomization greatly reduced the likelihood of control-group contamination.

Statistical Properties of Cluster Randomization

Impact estimates based on cluster random assignment, like those based on individual random assignment, are unbiased (for details, see Raudenbush 1997; Murray 1998; or Donner and Klar 2000). But estimates based on cluster randomization have much less—often much less—statistical precision than those based on individual randomization. The relationship between these two types of randomization is thus analogous to that between cluster sampling and random sampling in survey research (Kish 1965).

Model of Program Impacts

Consider a situation in which there are J clusters of n individual members each. Assuming that a proportion P of these clusters are randomly assigned to the program under study and that the rest (proportion 1 – P) are randomly assigned to a control group, the program's impact on outcome Y can be represented as

$$Y_{ij} = \alpha + B_0 T_{ij} + e_j + \varepsilon_{ij} \tag{4.1}$$

where:

Y_{ij} = the outcome for individual i from cluster j

α = the mean outcome for the control group

β_0 = the true program impact

T_{ij} = 1 for program-group members and 0 for control-group members

e_j = the error component for cluster j

ε_{ij} = the error component for individual i from cluster j

The true program impact, β_0, is the difference between the mean outcome for program-group members and what this mean outcome would have been in the absence of the program. The sample-based estimate of the impact, b_0, is the difference between the mean outcome for the program group and the mean outcome for the control group. The random error for this estimator has two components, e_j for cluster differences and ε_{ij} for individual differences, that are assumed to have independent and identical distributions with means of 0 and variances of τ^2 (for e_j) and σ^2 (for ε_{ij}). Variously referred to as a multilevel, hierarchical, random coefficients, or mixed model, equation 4.1 can be estimated by means of widely available software.[9]

Bias and Precision of Impact Estimators

Because randomization is the basis for the analysis, the expected value of the impact estimator is the true program impact. Because randomization was conducted at the cluster level, the standard error of the impact estimator is the following:[10]

$$SE(b_0)_{CL} = \sqrt{\frac{1}{P(1-P)}} \sqrt{\frac{\tau^2}{J} + \frac{\sigma^2}{nJ}} \qquad (4.2)$$

If, instead of randomizing the J clusters to the program or the control group, one had randomized their nJ members individually, the expected value of the program impact estimator would still be the true impact, but its standard error would be the following:

$$SE(b_0)_{IN} = \sqrt{\frac{1}{P(1-P)}} \sqrt{\frac{\tau^2}{nJ} + \frac{\sigma^2}{nJ}} \qquad (4.3)$$

Thus, unless τ^2 equals 0, the standard error for cluster randomization is larger than its counterpart for individual randomization.

The magnitude of the difference between $SE(b_0)_{CL}$ and $SE(b_0)_{IN}$ depends on the relationship between τ^2 and σ^2 and the size of each cluster. The relationship between τ^2 and σ^2 is usually expressed as an intraclass correlation (Fisher 1925), ρ, which equals the proportion of the total population variance ($\tau^2 + \sigma^2$) across clusters as opposed to within clusters:

$$\rho = \frac{\tau^2}{\tau^2 + \sigma^2} \qquad (4.4)$$

Equations 4.2, 4.3, and 4.4 imply that the ratio between the standard error for cluster randomization and that for individual randomization, given a fixed total number of individual sample members, is a cluster effect multiplier, which can be expressed as:

$$CEM = \sqrt{1 + (n-1)\rho} \qquad (4.5)$$

This cluster effect multiplier is the same as the well-known "design effect" in cluster sampling (Kish 1965).[11]

Equation 4.5 indicates that, for a given total number of individuals, the standard error for cluster randomization increases with the size of the clusters, n, and with the intraclass correlation, ρ. Given that the intraclass correlation reflects the cluster effect (which is what inflates the standard error), it should not be surprising that the standard error increases with it. The cluster size comes into play here too because, for a given total number of individuals, larger clusters imply that there are fewer clusters to be randomized—and thus a larger margin of random error.

Table 4.1 illustrates these relationships. First, note that if the intraclass correlation is 0 (that is, if there is no cluster effect), the cluster effect multiplier is 1, and the standard errors for cluster randomization and individual randomization are the same. Next, note that large clusters (and thus few clusters to be randomized) imply relatively large standard errors, even when the intraclass correlation is small. For example, if ρ equals 0.01, randomizing J clusters of five hundred people each will produce standard errors 2.48 times as large as those produced by separately randomizing 500J individuals. Thus, randomizing public housing developments to evaluate a saturation employment program (Bloom and Riccio 2002) or randomizing communities to evaluate a health-promotion campaign (Murray, Hannan et al. 1994) can produce large standard errors for program impact estimators because it is usually possible to randomize only a small number of such clusters.

Because the intraclass correlation captures the degree to which the outcome is stratified by cluster, its value varies with the type of outcome (for example, academic performance, employment, or health risks) and the type of cluster (for example, schools, communities, or hospitals). The limited empirical literature on this issue suggests that, for numerous outcome measures and policy domains, intraclass correlations generally range between 0.01 and 0.10 and are concentrated between 0.01 and 0.05.[12] Furthermore, it appears that clusters that represent small areas or organizational units (such as census tracts or classrooms) usually have larger intraclass correlations—in other words, are more homogeneous—than are larger clusters (such as municipalities or schools).

For intraclass correlations in the middle of the range that is typically observed, cluster randomization affords much less precision than individual randomization. For example, given an intraclass correlation of 0.05 and clusters of fifty individuals each, the standard error of an impact estimator for cluster randomization is 1.86 times as large as its counterpart for individual randomization.

As table 4.1 underscores, the benefits of cluster randomization can

Table 4.1   The Cluster Effect Multiplier

Intraclass Correlation (ρ)	Cluster Size (n)					
	10	20	50	100	200	500
0.00	1.00	1.00	1.00	1.00	1.00	1.00
0.01	1.04	1.09	1.22	1.41	1.73	2.48
0.02	1.09	1.17	1.41	1.73	2.23	3.31
0.03	1.13	1.25	1.57	1.99	2.64	4.00
0.04	1.17	1.33	1.72	2.23	2.99	4.58
0.05	1.20	1.40	1.86	2.44	3.31	5.09
0.06	1.24	1.46	1.98	2.63	3.60	5.56
0.07	1.28	1.53	2.10	2.82	3.86	5.99
0.08	1.31	1.59	2.22	2.99	4.11	6.40
0.09	1.35	1.65	2.33	3.15	4.35	6.78
0.10	1.38	1.70	2.43	3.30	4.57	7.13
0.20	1.67	2.19	3.29	4.56	6.39	10.04

Source: Computations by the author.
Note: The cluster effect multiplier equals $\sqrt{1 + (n-1)\rho}$.

come at a high cost with regard to the standard errors of impact estimates. The table also illustrates the importance of properly accounting for clustering when computing standard errors. If one computed the standard errors in a cluster randomization design as if individuals had been randomized, the results would understate the true standard errors substantially, thereby giving a false sense of confidence in the impact estimates. As Jerome Cornfield (1978, 101) aptly observed, "Randomization by group accompanied by an analysis appropriate to randomization by individual is an exercise in self-deception."

Implications for Sample Size

Equation 4.2 indicates how five factors determine the standard errors of program impact estimators based on cluster randomization. Two of these factors, τ^2 and σ^2, reflect the underlying variation in the outcome of interest, which must be taken as given. When designing a cluster randomization study, it is thus necessary to obtain information about τ^2 and σ^2, or their relationship as expressed by ρ, by consulting previous research on similar outcomes and groups or by estimating these parameters from existing data. The study by Howard S. Bloom, Johannes M. Bos, and Suk-Won Lee (1999) discussed later in this chapter illustrates how this can be done.

The other three factors—n, J, and P—reflect the size of the evaluation sample and its allocation to the program and control groups, which are research design choices. In this section, I examine the effects of sample size (n and J) on precision.

Using Minimum Detectable Effects to Measure Precision

When examining the statistical precision of an experimental design, it is often helpful to express this property in terms of the smallest program effect that could be detected with confidence. Formally, a minimum detectable effect is the smallest true program effect that has a probability of $1 - \beta$ of producing an impact estimate that is statistically significant at the α level (Bloom 1995). This parameter, which is a multiple of the impact estimator's standard error, depends on the following factors (see the chapter appendix for further discussion):

Whether a one-tailed t-test (for program effects in the predicted direction) or a two-tailed t-test (for any program effects) is to be performed

The level of statistical significance to which the result of this test will be compared (α)

The desired statistical power ($1 - \beta$), the probability of detecting a true effect of a given size or larger

The number of degrees of freedom of the test, which—assuming a two-group experimental design and no covariates—equals the number of clusters minus 2, or $J - 2$

Table 4.2 shows how the minimum detectable effect multiplier (and thus the minimum detectable effect) for one-tailed and two-tailed t-tests varies with the number of clusters to be randomized, assuming use of the conventional statistical significance criterion of .05 and a statistical power level of .80. This pattern reflects how the t distribution varies with the number of degrees of freedom available. This feature of the t distribution, well known for a century, is not pertinent to most studies based on individual randomization because they typically have many degrees of freedom.[13] When small numbers of clusters are randomized and thus very few degrees of freedom are available, however, this pattern has important implications for research design.

The minimum detectable effect is smaller for one-tailed tests than for two-tailed tests because, other things being equal, the statistical power of one-tailed tests is greater than that of two-tailed tests. This, too, is of less concern in studies based on individual randomization because of their much greater statistical power. In cluster randomization, however, the question of whether to use a one-tailed or a two-tailed test often deserves special consideration. And when small numbers of clus-

Table 4.2   The Minimum Detectable Effect Expressed as a Multiple of the
Standard Error

Total Number of Clusters (J)	Multiplier	
	Two-Tailed Test	One-Tailed Test
4	5.36	3.98
6	3.72	3.07
8	3.35	2.85
10	3.19	2.75
12	3.11	2.69
14	3.05	2.65
16	3.01	2.63
18	2.98	2.61
20	2.96	2.60
30	2.90	2.56
40	2.88	2.54
60	2.85	2.52
120	2.82	2.50
Infinite	2.80	2.49

Source: Computations by the author.
Note: The cluster effect multipliers shown here are for the difference between the mean program-group outcome and the mean control-group outcome, assuming equal variances for the groups, a significance level of .05, and a power level of .80.

ters are randomized, the need for statistical power might tip the balance in favor of one-tailed tests. The primary argument for using one-tailed tests in program evaluation is that such analyses are mainly intended to inform decisions about whether or not to support a program. Because it usually makes sense to support a program only if it produces beneficial effects, a one-sided alternative hypothesis—and thus a one-tailed test—is generally indicated. This rationale is different from the standard one in the social sciences, where one-tailed tests are recommended only when there are strong a priori reasons for expecting an effect in one direction and the purpose of statistical inference is to test theories rather than to inform program-related decisions. Nevertheless, the issue of when to use a one-tailed test versus a two-tailed test for a program evaluation remains contentious.

Because program-impact estimates are frequently reported in standardized form as effect sizes, where an effect size equals the impact estimate divided by the control group's standard deviation on the outcome measure,[14] it is useful to express precision as a minimum detectable effect size. A study with a minimum detectable effect size of 0.25, for example, can detect with confidence a true program impact equal to 0.25 standard deviation.

To assess the minimum detectable effect size for a research design, one needs a basis for deciding how much precision is needed. From an economic perspective, this basis might be whether the design can detect the smallest effect that would enable a program to break even in a benefit-cost sense. From a political perspective, it might be whether the design can detect the smallest effect that would be deemed important by the public or by public officials. From a programmatic perspective, it might be whether the study can detect an effect that, judging from the performance of similar programs, is likely to be attainable. Smaller minimum detectable effects imply greater statistical precision.

Although there is no standard basis for assessing the minimum detectable effect size, one widely used classification is that of Jacob Cohen (1977/1988), who proposed that minimum detectable effect sizes of roughly 0.20, 0.50, and 0.80 be considered small, medium, and large, respectively. Mark Lipsey (1990) provided empirical support for this characterization by examining the actual distribution of 102 mean effect size estimates reported in 186 meta-analyses that together represented 6,700 studies with 800,000 sample members. Consistent with Cohen's scheme, the bottom third of this distribution ranges from 0.00 to 0.32, the middle third ranges from 0.33 to 0.55, and the top third ranges from 0.56 to 1.20.

More recently, however, important research has suggested that, at least for education interventions (and perhaps for other types of interventions as well), much smaller effect sizes should be considered substantively important, and thus greater precision might be needed than is suggested by Cohen's categories. Foremost among the findings motivating these new expectations are those from the Tennessee Class Size Experiment, which indicate that reducing elementary school classes from their standard size of 22 to 26 students to 13 to 17 students increases average student performance by about 0.1 to 0.2 standard deviation (Nye, Hedges, and Konstantopoulos 1999). This seminal study of a major education intervention suggests that even big changes in schools result in what by previous benchmarks would have been considered small effects.

Another important piece of related research is that by Thomas J. Kane (2004), who found that, on average nationwide, a full year of elementary school attendance increases students' reading and math achievement by only 0.25 standard deviation. Thus, an education intervention that has a positive effect only half as large as this (0.125 standard deviation) seems still to qualify as a noteworthy success. Further reinforcing these findings are results published by the National Center for Educational Statistics (1997) that indicate that, on average nationwide, a year of high school increases reading achievement by about 0.17 standard deviation and math achievement by about 0.26 standard deviation. Again, the message is clear: program effects on student achievement of as little as 0.1 to 0.2 standard deviation might be highly policy-relevant.

This research serves to highlight the importance in studies of program effects, including studies based on a cluster randomization design, of careful analysis and thought about how much precision is needed to address the key questions.

How Sample Size Affects Minimum Detectable Effects

Now consider how the minimum detectable effect size for cluster randomization, $\text{MDES}(b_0)_{CL}$, varies with the number and size of the clusters randomized, given the intraclass correlation and the proportion of clusters randomly assigned to the program, P. Equation 4.6, which is derived in this chapter's appendix, represents this relationship as follows:

$$\text{MDES}(b_0)_{CL} = \frac{M_{J-2}}{\sqrt{J}} \sqrt{\rho + \frac{1-\rho}{n}} \sqrt{\frac{1}{P(1-P)}}, \qquad (4.6)$$

where M_{J-2} is the minimum detectable effect multiplier in table 4.2.

The number of clusters randomized influences precision through M_{J-2}, (which varies appreciably only for small numbers of clusters) and also as a function of $1/\sqrt{J}$. Hence, for many potential applications, the minimum detectable effect size declines in roughly inverse proportion to the square root of the number of clusters randomized.

The size of the clusters randomized often makes far less difference to the precision of program impact estimators than does the number of clusters, especially given a moderate to high intraclass correlation. This is because the effect of cluster size is proportional to:

$$\sqrt{\rho + \frac{1-\rho}{n}}$$

For example, if ρ were equal to 0.05, the values of this term for randomized clusters of 50, 100, 200, and 500 individuals each would be approximately 0.26, 0.24, 0.23, and 0.23, respectively. Thus, even a tenfold increase in the size of the clusters makes little difference to the precision of program impact estimators.

Table 4.3 lists values for the minimum detectable effect sizes implied by a wide range of sample sizes and intraclass correlations. These find-

Table 4.3   The Minimum Detectable Effect Size for Alternate Sample Sizes and Intraclass Correlations

Total Number of Clusters (J)	Clusters Size (n)					
	10	20	50	100	200	500
When Intraclass Correlation (ρ) = 0.01						
4	1.77	1.31	0.93	0.76	0.66	0.59
6	1.00	0.74	0.52	0.43	0.37	0.33
8	0.78	0.58	0.41	0.33	0.29	0.26
10	0.67	0.49	0.35	0.29	0.25	0.22
20	0.44	0.32	0.23	0.19	0.16	0.15
30	0.35	0.26	0.18	0.15	0.13	0.12
40	0.30	0.22	0.16	0.13	0.11	0.10
60	0.24	0.18	0.13	0.10	0.09	0.08
120	0.17	0.13	0.09	0.07	0.06	0.06
When Intraclass Correlation (ρ) = 0.05						
4	2.04	1.67	1.41	1.31	1.26	1.22
6	1.16	0.95	0.80	0.74	0.71	0.69
8	0.90	0.74	0.62	0.58	0.55	0.54
10	0.77	0.63	0.53	0.49	0.47	0.46
20	0.50	0.41	0.35	0.32	0.31	0.30
30	0.40	0.33	0.28	0.26	0.25	0.24
40	0.35	0.28	0.24	0.22	0.21	0.21
60	0.28	0.23	0.19	0.18	0.17	0.17
120	0.20	0.16	0.14	0.13	0.12	0.12
When Intraclass Correlation (ρ) = 0.10						
4	2.34	2.04	1.84	1.77	1.73	1.71
6	1.32	1.16	1.04	1.00	0.98	0.97
8	1.03	0.90	0.81	0.78	0.77	0.76
10	0.88	0.77	0.69	0.67	0.65	0.64
20	0.58	0.50	0.46	0.44	0.43	0.42
30	0.46	0.40	0.36	0.35	0.34	0.34
40	0.40	0.35	0.31	0.30	0.29	0.29
60	0.32	0.28	0.25	0.24	0.24	0.23
120	0.22	0.20	0.18	0.17	0.17	0.16

Source: Computations by the author.
Note: The minimum detectable effect sizes shown here are for a two-tailed hypothesis test, assuming a significance level of .05, a power level of .80, and randomization of half the clusters to the program.

ings are for experiments where P = .50. Other things being equal, higher intraclass correlations imply larger minimum detectable effect sizes. For example, compare 1.77, 2.04, and 2.34 in the top left corner of each panel of the table (for n = 10 and J = 4); and then compare 0.59, 1.22, and

1.71 in the top right corner of each panel (for n = 500 and J = 4). Moreover, increasing the number of clusters reduces the minimum detectable effect size. For n = 10 and ρ = 0.01, for example, increasing the number of clusters from four to twenty reduces the minimum detectable effect size from 1.77 to 0.44. Scanning the columns within each panel in the table shows that this general result holds independent of the number of clusters and the intraclass correlation.

Finally, for a given total number of sample members, increasing cluster size improves the precision of impact estimates by much less than does increasing the number of clusters. For example, for ρ = 0.01, the minimum detectable effect size for four groups of ten individuals each is 1.77. Whereas doubling the size of each cluster reduces this parameter to 1.31, doubling the number of clusters reduces it to 0.78. In fact, the size of the clusters often has almost no influence on precision. For example, for ρ = 0.05, increasing the size of each cluster from fifty to five hundred individuals reduces the minimum detectable effect size very little; and for ρ = 0.10, the reduction is negligible.

In summary, then, randomizing clusters instead of individuals puts precision at a premium. And randomizing more clusters almost always boosts precision more than does randomizing larger groups.

Implications for Sample Allocation

Sample allocation—the proportion of clusters randomized to the program rather than to the control group—affects the precision of program-impact estimators in a number of ways.

Balanced Versus Unbalanced Allocations

Virtually all research methodology textbooks prescribe a balanced allocation of sample members to the program and control groups (P = 1 – P = .50) because under conditions of homoscedasticity—when the variance of the outcome measure is the same for the program group as it is for the control group—balanced allocation maximizes the statistical precision of impact estimators.[15] Generally overlooked, however, is the fact that precision erodes slowly as sample allocation departs from balance. Hence, there is more latitude than is commonly thought for using unbalanced allocations when the homoscedasticity assumption is a reasonable approximation.[16] This latitude enables researchers to capitalize on such opportunities to increase precision as the availability of public administrative records increases, and these can be used to construct large control groups at low cost. It can also facilitate randomization by allowing for the use of small control groups, which increases the number of individuals who can be given access to a program and thus lowers political resistance to the approach.

Decisions about sample allocation are more complicated under conditions of heteroscedasticity—when the variances of the outcome measure are not the same for the program and control groups. This situation arises when a program produces impacts that vary across individuals or groups.[17] For example, the impacts of whole-school reforms on student achievement may be larger for some types of students or for some types of schools than for others. In such cases, a balanced sample allocation provides greater methodological protection because it is more robust to violations of the assumptions of homoscedasticity.

When the Variances Are Equal

The findings discussed so far in this chapter assume that τ^2 and σ^2 are the same for the program group as for the control group. Equation 4.6 indicates that when this is the case, the minimum detectable effect size is proportional to:

$$\sqrt{\frac{1}{P(1-P)}}$$

This expression is minimized when P equals 0.5, as is the corresponding minimum detectable effect size. The same expression can be used to demonstrate that, given a fixed sample size (n and J), precision hardly changes until one approaches extreme imbalance. To see this, note that:

$$\sqrt{\frac{1}{P(1-P)}}$$

equals 2.00, 2.04, 2.18, 2.50, and 3.33 when P is 0.5, 0.6, 0.7, 0.8, and 0.9, respectively. The pattern is the same when P is 0.5, 0.4, 0.3, 0.2, and 0.1, respectively. And it holds regardless of the number of clusters randomized, the size of the clusters, and the degree of intraclass correlation.

Table 4.4 illustrates the point more concretely. The first column lists sample allocations ranging from P = .10 to P = .90. The next two columns present the minimum detectable effect sizes for each sample allocation, given two hypothetical sets of values of n, J, and ρ. The fourth column displays the ratio between the minimum detectable effect size for each sample allocation and the minimum detectable effect size for a balanced allocation; thus, when P = .50, this ratio is 1.00. As

Table 4.4   The Minimum Detectable Effect Size, by Sample Allocation

Proportion of Clusters Allocated to the Program (P)	Example 1	Example 2	Ratio to Balanced Allocation
.10	0.91	0.29	1.67
.20	0.68	0.22	1.25
.30	0.59	0.19	1.09
.40	0.55	0.18	1.02
.50 (balanced)	0.54	0.17	1.00
.60	0.55	0.18	1.02
.70	0.59	0.19	1.09
.80	0.68	0.22	1.25
.90	0.91	0.29	1.67

Source: Computations by the author.
Notes: Example 1 is for $n = 20$, $J = 10$, $\rho = 0.05$, and a one-tailed hypothesis test. Example 2 is for $n = 80$, $J = 20$, $\rho = 0.01$, and a one-tailed hypothesis test. Both examples assume that the variances are the same for the program group and the control group.

the table illustrates, the minimum detectable effect size changes little until P drops below .20 or exceeds .80.

When the Variances Are Unequal

If a program creates impacts that vary across individuals or clusters, the individual or group variances can increase or decrease relative to those for control-group members. Howard S. Bloom et al. (2001) demonstrated this phenomenon in their evaluation of a whole-school reform called Accelerated Schools, and Anthony S. Bryk and Stephen W. Raudenbush (1988) demonstrated it in their reanalyses of two important education experiments. Consider how the phenomenon might arise in the context of education programs. Some programs may have larger-than-average effects on students who are weaker than average initially. If sufficiently pronounced, this tendency can reduce the individual error variance, σ^2, for members of the program group. The opposite result will occur if programs have larger-than-average effects on students who are initially stronger than average. Similarly, school-level responses to programs might vary, thereby reducing or increasing τ^2 for the program group relative to the control group.

For balanced sample allocations, simulations and analytical proofs have demonstrated that statistical tests that assume equal variances for the program and control groups are valid even if the variances are unequal.[18] This is not true for unbalanced allocations, where the size of the inferential error depends on the relationship between the relative sizes of the program and control groups and the relative sizes of their variances (see Gail et al. 1996 and Kmenta 1971).

As a precaution in unbalanced allocation designs, one can estimate the program-group variance and the control-group variance separately and test the statistical significance of the difference between them. If the difference is statistically significant, the impact analysis can proceed using separate variance estimates. If the difference is not statistically significant, the impact analysis can proceed with a single, pooled variance estimate.

In practice, however, given the small numbers of groups in a typical group randomization design, there are usually very few degrees of freedom with which to derive separate estimates of τ^2. As a result, statistical tests of the significance of the difference in τ^2 tend to have little power. One might therefore opt to skip such tests and simply not assume that τ^2 is the same for the program group as for the control group. Doing away with the homoscedasticity assumption does not circumvent the problem of limited degrees of freedom, however, because the resulting impact estimate is based on two separate estimates of τ^2, each of which uses some of the degrees of freedom in the sample. Furthermore, as the imbalance between the number of program group members and the number of control group members increases, the number of degrees of freedom for the program impact estimator can only be approximated and approaches that for the smaller group. This can greatly reduce precision.[19]

The scarcity of degrees of freedom for estimating variances when homoscedasticity does not hold has received virtually no attention in the literature on randomized experiments, most likely because the vast majority of these experiments call for randomization of individuals rather than clusters. In individual designs, a large number of individuals are typically randomized, and the only variance that must be estimated is σ^2. Thus, there are usually more than enough degrees of freedom to provide separate estimates of σ^2 for the program group and the control group. Researchers using randomized cluster designs do not have this luxury. Furthermore, because little is known about how the impacts of programs vary across types of individuals and settings, it is not clear how problematic heteroscedasticity is likely to be. At this point in the development of randomized cluster studies, it therefore seems prudent to use balanced sample allocations whenever possible. Studies with relatively large numbers of clusters (say, fifty or more) might have greater flexibility in this regard, but even they probably should not depart too much from balance unless the benefits of doing so are compelling.

Implications for Subgroup Analysis

Now consider how to analyze a program's impacts for subgroups defined in terms of program characteristics, cluster characteristics, and individual characteristics. A subgroup analysis addresses two basic questions: What is the impact of the program for each subgroup, and what are the relative impacts of the program across subgroups? Although often honored in the breach, it is proper research protocol to specify in advance the subgroups for which one will report program impact estimates. Doing so limits the extent to which such analyses become "data-mining" exercises that can generate spuriously significant subgroup differences.

Subgroups Defined by Characteristics of the Program

One way to think about sample subgroups is in terms of variants of the program being tested. For example, in a study of a program for reducing the use of X-rays in testing patients for certain medical conditions, one could identify hospitals that implemented the program with high fidelity and hospitals that did not and could split the program group in two on the basis of this distinction. However, it is not possible to estimate program impacts for such subgroups experimentally because there is no way to identify their counterparts in the control group. It might be feasible, however, to randomly assign different groups of hospitals to variants of the program for reducing X-ray use and to experimentally compare the outcomes across variants. Indeed, this approach, often referred to as a multi-arm trial, has been used to test alternative ways of influencing physician practices (Eccles et al. 2001). But because each program variant tested substantially increases the number of clusters to be randomized, the approach is probably only feasible for studying small numbers of program variants.

Subgroups Defined by Cluster Characteristics

Subgroups defined by characteristics of the clusters randomized can provide valid experimental impact estimates. For example, if schools are randomized, one can observe how impact estimates vary by school size, average past performance, and urban versus suburban location. Likewise, if firms are randomized, one can observe how impact estimates vary by firm size, past employee turnover rates, and industry. These impact estimates are experimental because subdividing the program and control groups according to a cluster characteristic that is determined before randomization (and that therefore could have not been influenced by assignment to the program or control group) creates valid "subexperiments." Hence, the difference between the mean program-group outcome and the mean control-group outcome in each subexperiment is an unbiased estimator of the program's net impact for the subgroup in question. Furthermore, the difference between the net impact estimates for two subgroups is an unbiased estimator of the program's differential impact on the subgroups.

Because each subgroup contains only a fraction of the clusters in the full experiment, however, the precision of this type of subgroup analysis is substantially less than that of the full sample analysis. Precision is lost in two ways: the smaller samples of clusters used in subgroup analysis produce larger standard errors and provide fewer degrees of freedom.

To see how this works, consider an experimental sample with two mutually exclusive and jointly exhaustive subgroups, A and B. Assume that n, τ^2, σ^2, and P are the same for both subgroups and for the full sample.[20] Proportion Π_A of the randomized clusters are in subgroup A and proportion $1 - \Pi_A$ are in subgroup B. The ratio between the minimum detectable effect size for subgroup A and that for the full sample is:

$$\frac{MDES(b_{0A})_{CL}}{MDES(b_0)_{CL}} = \frac{M_{\Pi_A J-2}}{M_{J-2}}\sqrt{1/\Pi_A} \qquad (4.7)$$

(See also the chapter appendix.) Equation 4.7 illustrates the two ways in which moving from the full sample to a subgroup increases the minimum detectable effect size. First, it increases the standard error of the impact estimator by decreasing the sample size—from J for the full sample to $\Pi_A J$ for the subgroup. Second, it increases the minimum detectable effect multiplier by decreasing the number of degrees of freedom, from J − 2 for the full sample to $\Pi_A J - 2$ for the subgroup.

To illustrate the likely magnitude of these effects on the minimum detectable effect size, consider a hypothetical example where a subgroup contains half the twenty clusters that were randomized for an experiment. Hence, Π_A equals 0.5, and:

$$\frac{MDES(b_{0A})_{CL}}{MDES(b_0)_{CL}} = \frac{M_8}{M_{18}}\sqrt{1/0.5} = \frac{3.35}{2.99}\sqrt{2} = 1.58$$

In this case, the minimum detectable effect size for subgroup A is 1.58 times that for the full sample.

The implications for differential impacts are more pronounced. The appendix to this chapter demonstrates that the ratio between the minimum detectable effect size of a differential impact estimator for subgroups A and B and that for the net impact estimator for the full sample is:

$$\frac{MDES(b_{0A} - b_{0B})_{CL}}{MDES(b_0)_{CL}} = \frac{M_{J-4}}{M_{J-2}}\sqrt{\frac{1}{\Pi_A(1-\Pi_A)}} \qquad (4.8)$$

Again, precision is reduced through an increase in the minimum detectable effect multiplier, caused by a decrease in the number of degrees of freedom from J − 2 to J − 4,[21] and an increase in the standard error, caused by a decrease in the sample size. But in a differential-impact analysis, the increase in the minimum detectable effect size that occurs as one moves from the full sample to a subgroup reflects two factors: a smaller sample of clusters for each impact estimate and the dual uncertainty produced by taking the difference between the impact estimates for the subgroups. Thus, in the current example, the relative precision of a differential impact estimator is computed as follows:

$$\frac{MDES(b_{0A} - b_{0B})_{CL}}{MDES(b_0)_{CL}} = \frac{M_{16}}{M_{18}} \sqrt{1/((0.5)0.5)} = \frac{3.01}{2.98} \sqrt{4} = 2.01$$

Subgroups Defined by Individual Characteristics

Subgroups defined by the characteristics of individual sample members can also provide valid experimental impact estimates. Thus, even if schools are the unit of randomization, one can measure program impacts experimentally for different types of students, such as boys or girls, whites or nonwhites, and previously high-performing students or previously low-performing students. If at least some students in every school in the sample have the characteristic of interest, one can proceed as if a separate subexperiment had been conducted solely on students in the subgroup. In this case, the only statistical difference between the subexperiment and the full experiment is the number of students per school.

The implications for precision of subgroups defined in this way are entirely different from those already discussed. To see this, recall that the size of clusters has much less influence on precision than does the number of clusters and that, in some cases cluster size hardly matters at all. This phenomenon determines the precision of impact estimates for subgroups of individuals. For example, assuming random assignment of schools, it is possible that the precision of net impact estimates for boys and girls separately will be almost the same as that for boys and girls together. Furthermore, as discussed below, the precision of an estimator for the differential impact on boys as opposed to girls actually can be greater than that of the estimator for the net impact on boys and girls together.

Consider two mutually exclusive and jointly exhaustive subgroups, I and II, defined by an individual characteristic such as gender. Assume that, in each randomized group, a proportion Π_I of the individuals are in subgroup I and proportion $1 - \Pi_I$ are in subgroup II. Also assume that τ^2 and σ^2 are the same for the two subgroups and for the full sample.

The appendix to this chapter demonstrates that for a simple model of subgroup differences the ratio between the minimum detectable effect size for subgroup I and that for the full sample is:

$$\frac{\text{MDES}(b_{0I})_{\text{CL}}}{\text{MDES}(b_0)_{\text{CL}}} = \frac{\sqrt{\rho + \dfrac{1-\rho}{\Pi_I n}}}{\sqrt{\rho + \dfrac{1-\rho}{n}}} \qquad (4.9)$$

Equation 4.9 illustrates how reducing the size of randomized clusters by moving from the full sample to a subgroup defined by an individual characteristic can have little effect on precision. For example, assuming one hundred individuals per cluster in the full sample and an intraclass correlation of 0.05, the minimum detectable effect size for a subgroup net impact when there are fifty individuals in the subgroup per cluster is 1.08 times that for the full sample—a mere 8 percent increase.[22]

The precision for subgroup differential impact estimators can be even greater. As this chapter's appendix demonstrates, for a simplified model of subgroup differences:

$$\frac{\text{MDES}(b_{0I} - b_{0II})_{\text{CL}}}{\text{MDES}(b_0)_{\text{CL}}} = \sqrt{\frac{(1-\rho)}{\Pi_I(1-\Pi_I)(1+(n-1)\rho)}} \qquad (4.10)$$

Thus, with one hundred individuals per cluster in the full sample and fifty individuals per cluster in each subgroup, the minimum detectable effect size for the differential impact estimator is only 80 percent as large as that for the full sample net impact estimator. The greater precision of the differential impact estimator derives from the fact that it "differences away" the cluster error component, e_j, and thereby eliminates τ^2.

Adjusting for Covariates

Adjusting for covariates increases the precision of impact estimates by reducing the amount of unexplained variation in the outcome of interest. This approach is often used for experiments that randomize individuals. But its role can be even more important in experiments that randomize clusters, where precision is more limited and therefore at a higher premium. Furthermore, because the correlations among features of aggregate entities are usually quite high (typically much higher than the correlations among features of individuals), data on cluster characteristics can substantially reduce the unexplained variation in the group error term—the binding constraint on precision in a cluster design.

Aggregate Covariates, Individual Covariates, and Lagged Outcomes

In cluster randomization experiments, the two main types of covariates are aggregate characteristics of the clusters randomized and individual characteristics of the cluster members. Although data on both types of covariates can be obtained in some contexts, it is often possible to collect only aggregate data on cluster characteristics given available resources.

Another important distinction is whether a covariate is a lagged outcome measure, a measure of one of the outcomes of interest before randomization was conducted, or another type of background characteristic. In an experimental study of a new approach to reading instruction, students' reading test scores before being randomly assigned to the program or a control group would be a lagged outcome measure, whereas students' gender and age would be background characteristics. Lagged outcome measures, often called pretests, are usually the most powerful covariates because they reflect the combined result of all the factors that determined the outcome in the past and that therefore are likely to influence it in the future. Put differently, the best predictor of a future outcome is almost always a past measure of the same outcome. Examples include the ability of past earnings to predict future earnings, of past criminal behavior to predict future criminal behavior, of past test scores to predict future test scores, and of past health status to predict future health status.

To provide a framework for this discussion, equation 4.11 adds a single covariate, X_{ij}, to the program impact model in equation 4.1, yielding:

$$Y_{ij} = \alpha + B_0 T_{ij} + B_1 X_{ij} + e^*_j + \varepsilon^*_{ij} \qquad (4.11)$$

Although X_{ij} is defined to have a separate value for every member of the experimental sample, it can represent an individual characteristic or a cluster characteristic. Furthermore, it can represent a lagged outcome measure or another type of background characteristic. Note that equation 4.11 assumes that the variance for the program group and the variance for the control group are equal.

The two error terms in equation 4.11—e^*_j for each cluster and ε^*_{ij} for each individual sample member differ from their counterparts in equation 4.1 because they represent the unexplained variation between and within clusters after controlling for the covariate, X_{ij}. Therefore, the random error terms in equation 4.11 are referred to as conditional errors, and those in equation 4.1 are referred to as unconditional errors.

Effects on Precision

Raudenbush (1997) derived expressions for the standard errors of impact estimators on the basis of cluster randomization given a balanced sample allocation, a single cluster covariate or a single individual covariate, and equal variances for the program and control groups. Equations 4.12 and 4.13 extend his findings to represent balanced or unbalanced allocations (with any value for P):

$$SE(b_{*0})_{CL} = \sqrt{\frac{1}{P(1-P)}} \sqrt{\frac{\tau_*^2}{J} + \frac{\sigma^2}{nJ}} \sqrt{1 + \frac{1}{J-4}} \qquad (4.12)$$

for a single cluster covariate and:

$$SE(b_{*0})_{CL} = \sqrt{\frac{1}{P(1-P)}} \sqrt{\frac{\tau_*^2}{J} + \frac{\sigma_*^2}{nJ}} \sqrt{1 + \frac{1}{nJ-4}} \qquad (4.13)$$

for a single individual covariate.

Comparing these expressions with equation 4.2, which assumes no covariate, reveals several important differences. First, consider:

$$\sqrt{1 + \frac{1}{J-4}}$$

in equation 4.12 and:

$$\sqrt{1 + \frac{1}{nJ-4}}$$

in equation 4.13, which have no counterparts in equation 4.2. The term in equation 4.12 (which is undefined for $J \leq 4$) approaches a value of one as the number of groups randomized increases. At ten groups, the term equals 1.08 and is therefore unimportant for larger samples. Similarly, the term in equation 4.13 (which is undefined for $nJ \leq 4$) approaches a value of one as the number of sample members increases. At ten groups of fifty individuals each, it equals approximately 1.00 and is therefore negligible for most sample sizes that are likely to be used.

More important are the differences between the conditional variances, τ_*^2 and σ_*^2, in equations 4.12 and 4.13 and their unconditional counterparts, τ^2 and σ^2, in equation 4.2.[23] By controlling for some of the unexplained variation between clusters, a cluster characteristic can reduce the cluster variance from τ^2 to τ_*^2. By controlling for some of the unexplained variation both within and between clusters, an individual characteristic can reduce the cluster and individual variances from τ^2 and σ^2 to τ_*^2 and σ_*^2, respectively. In this way, covariates reduce the standard errors of program-impact estimators, sometimes by a significant amount, at a cost of only one degree of freedom per cluster characteristic and of virtually no degrees of freedom per individual characteristic. Hence, the overall effect on precision of adjusting for a single covariate stems almost solely from its effect on standard errors, except in experiments that randomize very few clusters.

An Empirical Example: Randomizing Schools

Bloom, Bos, and Lee (1999) published the first empirical analysis of the extent to which using past test scores as covariates can improve the precision of education program–impact estimates based on randomization of schools. Their analysis used the existing administrative records in twenty-five elementary schools in one urban school district, Rochester, New York, in 1991 and 1992. The authors estimated the between-school and within-school variance components for the standardized math scores and reading scores of third-graders and sixth-graders.

One type of covariate examined was a "student pretest" representing each student's score in the same subject in the preceding grade; thus, individual second-graders' and fifth-graders' scores were used as a student-level pretest to compare with their performance as third- and sixth-graders, respectively. The other type of covariate examined was a "school pretest" representing each school's mean score during the preceding year in the same subject and grade; thus, for example, the mean reading scores of sixth-graders in each school in the preceding year were used as a school-level pretest for current sixth-graders.

Table 4.5 summarizes the variance estimates obtained. The top panel in the table lists estimates without covariates, the middle panel lists estimates with school pretests, and the bottom panel lists estimates with student pretests. The first four columns in the table present results for each subject and grade separately, and the last column presents the mean results. The findings clearly demonstrate the predictive power of pretests.

School pretests reduce the school variance for all subjects and grades from a mean of 18.0 to a mean of 4.4—a dramatic reduction of 76 percent. The corresponding reductions by subject and grade range from 72 to 82 percent. School pretests do not affect the student variance because school pretest scores are the same for all students in a given annual cohort at a given school. (The slight variation in the findings with and without a school-level pretest merely reflects random error in the maximum likelihood estimates of the variance components.)

Student pretests reduce the school variance by roughly the same amount as school pretests, although the pattern is not entirely consis-

Table 4.5   Estimated School and Student Variances for
Standardized-Test Scores

Type of Covariate	Reading		Math		
	Third Grade	Sixth Grade	Third Grade	Sixth Grade	Mean
No covariate					
School variance (τ^2)	19.7	12.9	18.0	21.5	18.0
Student variance (σ^2)	103.7	100.0	82.2	96.6	95.6
School pretest					
School variance (τ_*^2)	5.1	3.6	3.3	5.7	4.4
Student variance (σ^2)	105.5	100.5	83.2	97.4	96.7
Student pretest					
School variance (τ_*^2)	5.4	1.6	13.9	5.2	6.5
Student variance (σ_*^2)	50.1	41.2	56.3	53.6	50.3

Source: Computation by the author using data from Bloom, Bos, and Lee (1999).
Notes: The results shown are based on individual standardized test scores for 3,299 third-graders and 2,517 sixth-graders in twenty-five elementary schools in Rochester, New York, in 1991 and 1992 (Bloom, Bos, and Lee 1999). The student pretest was each student's score in the same subject in the preceding grade. The school pretest was each school's mean score in the same subject and grade in the preceding year.

tent. In addition, student pretests reduce the student variance by 47 percent, from a mean of 95.6 to a mean of 50.3. The corresponding reductions by subject and grade range from 32 to 59 percent. The fact that student pretests reduce the student-level variance by proportionally less than school pretests reduce the school-level variance reflects the fact, already mentioned, that correlations tend to be smaller within individuals than within groups.

Because the school-level variance is the binding constraint on precision when schools are randomized, the ability of student pretests to reduce the student variance does not add much, if anything, to the precision of impact estimators except by reducing the school variance. Hence, the precision of program-impact estimators is roughly the same for the two types of covariates. This point is clearly illustrated in table 4.6, which presents the minimum detectable effect size implied by the estimated variances listed in table 4.5 for a realistic, though hypothetical, education policy example. The example assumes a sample of sixty schools with sixty students per grade. Half the schools are randomly assigned to the program under study, and the other half are randomly assigned to a control group. Without covariates, the minimum detectable effect size ranges from 0.23 to 0.29 and averages 0.27; with school pretests as covariates, it ranges from 0.14 to 0.16 and averages 0.15; and with student pretests as covariates, it ranges from 0.09 to 0.25

Table 4.6   Minimum Detectable Effect Sizes for a Balanced Allocation of Sixty Schools, Each with Sixty Students per Grade

	Reading		Math		
Covariate	Third Grade	Sixth Grade	Third Grade	Sixth Grade	Mean
No covariate	0.27	0.23	0.28	0.29	0.27
School pretest	0.15	0.14	0.14	0.16	0.15
Student pretest	0.15	0.09	0.25	0.15	0.16

Source: Computations by the author using data from Bloom, Bos, and Lee (1999).
Notes: The results shown are based on individual standardized test scores for 3,299 third-graders and 2,517 sixth-graders in twenty-five elementary schools in Rochester, New York, in 1991 and 1992 (Bloom, Bos, and Lee 1999). The student pretest was each student's score in the same subject in the preceding grade. The school pretest was each school's mean score in the same subject and grade in the preceding year.

and averages 0.16. In short, the power of both student and school pretests to improve statistical precision is considerable. Furthermore, school-level aggregate pretests have the advantage of being generally inexpensive to obtain as compared to student-level individual pretests.

One further important property of baseline covariates in a randomized experiment is that missing values for them can be imputed simply without biasing impact estimates. This is because randomization ensures that all baseline covariates are uncorrelated (in expectation) with treatment assignment, which means that their missing values are uncorrelated as well. Therefore, even a simple imputation that sets each missing value of a covariate to its mean for the full experimental sample would make it possible to keep all randomized observations in the impact analysis without creating bias. The only potential cost of not having data on a baseline covariate is a reduction in the precision of the impact estimate due to a reduction in the explanatory power of the covariate.

Blocking and Matching

Baseline covariates can also be used to block, or match, clusters before they are randomized, which means stratifying the clusters to be randomized into blocks defined by specific combinations of baseline characteristics. This is often done to reduce the potential for a "bad draw"—a situation in which the clusters randomly assigned to the program group differ substantially from those randomly assigned to the control group, thus confounding the treatment with other variables. Blocking thus increases the precision of program impact estimators by reducing their standard errors. However, this benefit comes at the cost of increasing the complexity of the impact analysis, which can increase the potential for errors. In addition, blocking reduces the number of degrees of freedom for the impact analysis, which can reduce precision.

Blocking Before Randomization

Each of the clusters in a block is randomly assigned to the program or to the control group. Ordinarily the sample allocation is held constant across blocks; this is called balanced allocation.[24] In a blocked design, blocks are allocated constantly, ensuring that each block is represented in the same proportion in the program and control groups. This in turn guarantees that the program and control groups are identical with respect to the factors that define the blocks. For example, in a study of a reading program being implemented in schools in five different cities, a balanced allocation would involve grouping the schools by city and randomizing half the schools in each city (block) to the program and half the schools in each city to the control group. This procedure would ensure that the program group and the control group each contain the same number of schools from each city.

There are two main criteria for defining blocks within which to randomize: face validity and predictive validity. Face validity is the degree to which characteristics that define blocks appear on their face to be important determinants of the outcome measure being used. Thus, when assessing the face validity provided by blocking on a set of characteristics, it is important to ask: To what extent does ensuring that the program and control groups have the same distributions of these characteristics lend credibility to the evaluation findings? Blocking with respect to individual demographic characteristics such as age, gender, race, and ethnicity or with respect to aggregate group characteristics such as industry, type of organization, and location can boost face validity.

Predictive validity is the degree to which characteristics that define blocks predict and thus can be used to control for random variations in the outcome measure. As noted earlier, the best predictor of future outcomes is usually past outcomes, for both individuals and clusters. Thus, blocking with respect to a baseline measure of past outcomes is usually the best approach.

Given the small numbers of clusters to be randomized in most cases and the large numbers of potential blocking factors, constructing blocks often requires making difficult trade-offs. Probably the most difficult trade-off is that between predictive validity and face validity, which though not necessary in principle is often necessary in practice. For example, the need for predictive validity may call for blocking on past outcomes but the need for face validity may call for blocking on demographic characteristics, even if the latter do not add much predictive power. Unfortunately, blocking on both characteristics usually reduces the quality of the match for each.

If blocking is used, it must be reflected in the corresponding estimates of program impacts and their standard errors. One simple way to take account of blocking is to define a separate 0/1 indicator variable, I_k, for every block but one and to add these variables to the basic impact model in equation 4.1, yielding:[25]

$$Y_{ij} = \alpha + B_0 T_{ij} + \Sigma \gamma_k I_k + e_j^{**} + \varepsilon_{ij}^{**} \tag{4.14}$$

Equation 4.14 specifies the coefficient γ_k for each block as a fixed effect. Doing so removes the outcome differences that exist across blocks from the impact analysis and thereby increases its precision. Statistical inferences (confidence intervals and hypothesis tests) about average impacts obtained from this model thus apply to the specific blocks in the research sample. This approach is most appropriate for samples that have few blocks (and therefore a limited potential for generalization), are chosen opportunistically or in an otherwise idiosyncratic way, or both. To make a broader statistical inference, one could model blocks as random effects, but this strategy adds a new error component to the impact analysis, thereby reducing its precision.

In short, researchers face a vexing trade-off between maintaining the precision of a relatively narrow but well-defined statistical inference (to the set of blocks in their sample) and sacrificing precision to permit a broader statistical inference (to a larger population of blocks). In this author's opinion, for a small sample of blocks (say, fewer than ten) or an idiosyncratic sample of blocks (chosen in ways that make the sample unrepresentative of any readily defined larger population), it is best to use a fixed-effects model to draw statistical inferences and then, using one's judgment, to attempt to broaden these inferences by describing the range of situations reflected by the current sample. In this way, the generalization is made heuristically rather than statistically, which is consistent with the size and nature of the sample of blocks being used.

The indicator variables in equation 4.14 increase the explanatory power, or R^2, of the impact model and thereby reduce the standard error of the impact estimator. But they also reduce the number of degrees of freedom for estimating τ_*^2 and thereby increase the minimum detectable effect. These countervailing forces on precision must be taken into account when the decision is made whether to block and how many blocks to use.

Pairwise Matching Before Randomization

Pairwise matching entails stratifying clusters into pairs before randomizing them; it is an extreme form of blocking. The best way to achieve predictive validity in matching is to rank the clusters from highest to lowest with respect to their values on the baseline characteristic to be used and, starting with the pair with the highest values, to randomly assign one member to the program and the other member to the control group. Alternatively, the ranking can be based on a composite indicator that represents a set of baseline characteristics. Matching ensures that the program and control groups are as similar as possible in terms of the characteristic or characteristics used to identify the pairs.

To estimate program impacts and their standard errors in pairwise matching, indicator variables for all but one pair should be added to the impact model. As observed in the discussion of blocking, there is a trade-off between reducing the standard error and increasing the minimum detectable effect multiplier. Although the indicator variables increase the R^2 of the model and thereby reduce the standard error of the impact estimate, they also reduce the number of degrees of freedom for estimating τ_π^2 and thereby increase the minimum detectable effect multiplier. For example, in a design with ten clusters, there are eight degrees of freedom $(J - 2)$ without matching, but only four degrees of freedom $J/2 - 1$ with matching.

Because limited resources often preclude randomizing more than a small number of clusters, the large loss of degrees of freedom produced by matching clusters can reduce the precision of program impact estimates—unless the predictive power of the matching is high (Martin et al. 1993). For example, consider the following expressions for the minimum detectable effect of an impact estimator given each of three different approaches: pairwise matching with respect to a single group-level baseline characteristic, linear regression adjustment for the same characteristic, and no adjustment. In comparing these expressions, assume a fixed number of clusters and a fixed number of individuals per cluster.

$$MDE(b_{0m})_{CL} = M_{(J/2)-1}\sqrt{1 - R_1^2}\,SE(b_0)_{CL} \qquad (4.15)$$

given pair-wise matching, where R_1^2 is the predictive power;

$$MDE(b_{0r})_{CL} = M_{J-3}\sqrt{1 - R_2^2}\,\sqrt{1 + \frac{1}{J-4}}SE(b_0)_{CL} \qquad (4.16)$$

given regression adjustment, where R_2^2 is the predictive power; and

$$MDE(b_0)_{CL} = M_{J-2}SE(b_0)_{CL} \qquad (4.17)$$

given no adjustment, where $SE(b_0)_{CL}$ is the standard error of the impact estimator with no adjustment.

For no adjustment versus matching, the trade-off is between increasing the minimum detectable effect multiplier from M_{J-2} to $M_{(J/2)-1}$ and reducing the standard error by a factor of $\sqrt{1 - R_1^2}$. One way to capture this trade-off is to compute the minimum predictive power of matching that would offset the increased minimum detectable effect multiplier and thereby increase precision. This expression can be obtained by setting the right side of equation 4.15 (the minimum detectable effect given matching) less than or equal to the right side of equation 4.17 (the minimum detectable effect given no adjustment) and rearranging terms, which results in:

$$R_1^2 \geq 1 - \frac{M_{J-2}^2}{M_{J/2-1}^2} \qquad (4.18)$$

Using this expression, table 4.7 presents the minimum required predictive power of pairwise matching given specific numbers of groups to be randomized. The first column presents results for a two-tailed hypothesis test, and the second column presents results for a one-tailed test.[26] The most striking result is that very high predictive power (R^2_{min}) is required for pairwise matching to be justified, assuming a small sample of randomized groups. For example, for a two-tailed test or a one-tailed test, with six groups to be randomized, matching must predict 52 percent or 40 percent of the variation in the outcome measure, respectively, before it improves the precision of the impact estimator relative to no adjustment for baseline characteristics. This is because in small samples even small differences in the number of degrees of freedom imply large differences in the minimum detectable effect multiplier.

To consider the question of whether to match clusters for a given study more fully, it is also necessary to compare the likely precision of a design that matches clusters according to a baseline characteristic or a composite of such covariates with that of a design that randomizes unmatched clusters and controls for their characteristics through covariates in a regression model. Such an analysis can be done by working through the implications of equations 4.15 and 4.16.

An Empirical Example: Randomizing Firms

Consider how randomization of matched pairs of groups was used to evaluate Achieve, an employer-based program for reducing job turnover rates among low-wage workers in the health-care industry (Miller and Bloom 2002). Achieve offers employees a mix of direct services that include individual job counseling and group informational lunch sessions about job-related issues. It also provides indirect services to employees by training their supervisors to deal more effectively with issues that arise in the workplace. Because the program is being implemented on a firm-wide basis, it was not feasible to randomize individual employees. Therefore, cluster randomization was performed at the

Table 4.7   The Predictive Power Required to Justify Pairwise Matching

Total Number of Clusters J	Required Predictive Power (incremental R^2)	
	Two-Tailed Test	One-Tailed Test
4	0.85	0.73
6	0.52	0.40
8	0.35	0.27
10	0.26	0.20
12	0.21	0.16
14	0.17	0.13
16	0.15	0.11
18	0.13	0.10
20	0.11	0.09
30	0.07	0.05
40	0.05	0.05
60	0.03	0.03
120	0.02	0.01
Infinite	0.00	0.00

Source: Computations by the author.

level of firms. The first round of the program evaluation was implemented by twenty-two health-care firms in Cleveland that volunteered to participate in the study.

Participating firms were recruited in two waves that occurred roughly one month apart, with eight firms in the first wave and fourteen firms in the second wave. To maximize predictive validity, the firms in each wave were ranked according to their reported rates of employee turnover during the previous six months, with one firm in each pair randomized to the program and the other firm randomized to the control group. When it was discovered that the percentage of black employees in the program groups was much different from that for the control group, the original assignment was reversed for one pair in each wave (in opposite directions) to improve the face validity of the evaluation design. (The researchers later realized that such ad hoc adjustments to a random draw can inadvertently bias an experimental design and that a better way to trade off predictive validity against face validity in this situation would have been to randomize the entire matched sample again.)

Cynthia Miller and Howard Bloom (2002) analyzed the relative precision of three research designs—matching firms based on their past turnover rates, linear regression adjustment for past turnover rates, and taking no account of past turnover rates—using data on employee turnover rates during the first month after random assignment (a short-term-outcome measure). As it turned out, the predictive power of matching was sufficient to warrant using that approach, thereby providing a post hoc justification for having done so.

Accounting for Mobility

An inescapable fact for place-based programs is that people move into and out of their places of residence, work, or study, often at a very high rate. A recent analysis of selected public housing developments in four cities indicates that, on average, 29 percent of people who were residents in a given month had moved out two years later (Verma 2003); unpublished calculations indicate that, on average, 43 percent of the employees in the health-care firms participating in the Achieve evaluation left their jobs within a six-month period; and computations by the present author using data from the U.S. Department of Education (2003) indicate that only half of American kindergarteners are still at the same school when they reach the third grade.

Issues Raised by Mobility

Mobility creates important programmatic and evaluation problems both for programs targeted to individuals and for programs targeted to groups or places. From a programmatic standpoint, the main problem is that mobility reduces enrollees' exposure to the treatment because many leave before receiving a full "dose" of the intervention being tested. High rates of mobility can thus undermine a program's chance to make a meaningful difference in the outcomes of interest.

From an evaluation standpoint, mobility creates two main problems. A general problem is that selective mobility can result in subsequent differences between characteristics of the program group and characteristics of the control group, thereby creating selection bias in program-impact estimates. This problem is often referred to as sample "attrition" (for example, see Rossi, Lipsey, and Freeman 2004, 270).

The second problem created by mobility applies only to place-based programs. Two conceptually and substantively different perspectives from which program impacts can be defined and measured need to be clearly distinguished: impacts on people and impacts on places.

Impacts on people reflect how a program changes outcomes for individuals to whom the program is targeted. For example, one might ask whether an education program increases reading achievement levels for students who are exposed to it. Though seemingly precise, this question needs further specification to be meaningful in a context where student mobility is high. In a high-mobility situation, one might ask whether the program raises reading achievement levels for all students who are present in a school when the program is launched (regardless of whether they move away subsequently) or whether it does so for students who remain at the school throughout the analysis period. The policy question addressed in the first case is: What are the impacts of the program on students in general when it is implemented under real-world conditions, which include mobility? The policy question addressed in the second case is: What are the impacts of the program on students who remain in one school long enough to receive a substantial dose of the treatment? Both questions are meaningful and have different priorities in different contexts.

In a cluster randomization study, the most effective way to measure the impacts of programs on people is a longitudinal methodology, one in which outcomes for the same individuals are tracked over time. A longitudinal design to measure the general effects of an education program on students requires following all of them over a fixed period, even after some of them have left the school. Comparing the achievement-related outcomes for students in the program group with those for students in the control group produces valid experimental estimates of the program's impacts on student achievement. Interpretation of the estimates is complicated, however, by the fact that they represent an average response to what is usually a wide range of degrees of exposure to the program being evaluated.

An alternative approach is to conduct a longitudinal analysis only for "stayers," students in the program and control groups who remain in the school throughout the analysis period, so as to reduce variation in exposure to the program. This strategy can produce valid experimental estimates of the impacts of the program assuming that the program does not influence mobility. But if the program affects the types of students who stay in the schools (for example, by improving schools to the extent that families who care more about education are more likely to keep their children in the school than would have been the case otherwise), then stayers in the program schools will differ from stayers in the control schools. Such differences can introduce selection bias into estimates of the program's impacts on student outcomes.

Impacts on places reflect how a program changes aggregate outcomes for locations or organizations targeted by the program. For example, one might ask whether an education program increases reading achievement levels for schools that are exposed to it. The answer may reflect a mixture of two different forces. The first is the effect of the program on the achievement of students who would remain in the same place with or without the program; the second is the effect of the program on student mobility. For example, an education program could raise a school's achievement levels by improving the performance of students who would attend it with or without the program, by attracting and keeping more high-achieving students, or by both.

Impacts on places are best measured in a cluster randomization study using a "repeated cross-section" methodology, in which outcomes are tracked over time for the same places rather than for the same individuals. To obtain valid experimental estimates of the impacts of a program on reading achievement for a group of schools, one might compare the reading test scores of successive annual cohorts (repeated cross-sections) of third-graders in the schools in the program group with those of successive annual cohorts of third-graders in the schools in the control group. To the extent that the program influences student mobility, however, it is not clear how to interpret the resulting impact estimates in the absence of further information.

An Empirical Example: Randomizing Housing Developments

The evaluation of Jobs-Plus mentioned earlier is based on randomization of matched pairs of public housing developments in six U.S. cities and relies on a quasi-experimental method called comparative interrupted time-series analysis to measure the effects of this saturation employment initiative on public housing residents (Bloom and Riccio 2002; for a detailed discussion of interrupted time-series analysis, see Shadish, Cook, and Campbell 2002). The program's core elements are state-of-the-art employment-related activities and services, financial incentives designed to make work financially more worthwhile by reducing the rent increases that would otherwise occur when residents' earnings rise, and a range of activities designed to promote a community environment that is supportive of employment. As already discussed, these elements are intended to create unusually large employment gains that generate spillover effects throughout each participating development.

The Jobs-Plus evaluation assesses impacts on both public housing residents and public housing developments because moves into and out of public housing developments are frequent. The individual-based portion evaluates the impact of Jobs-Plus on the people who were living in the participating developments at a specific point in time, asking: How did Jobs-Plus affect the future experiences of its target population, whether or not they moved away? The analysis focusing on the housing development asks: How did Jobs-Plus affect the conditions in its target environment, given that different people lived there at different times?

**Figure 4.1   A Comparative Interrupted Time-Series Analysis of the
Impacts of Jobs-Plus on Earnings**

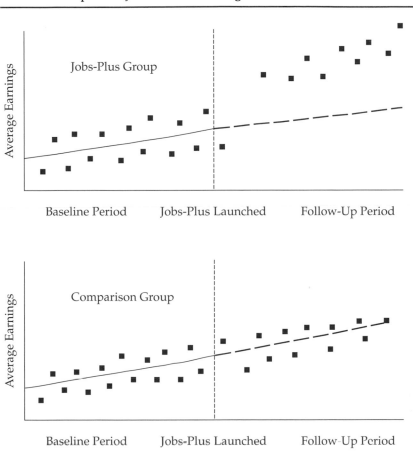

Source: Author's compilation.

Figure 4.1 illustrates the comparative interrupted time-series approach used to estimate the impacts of Jobs-Plus from both perspectives. The graph at the top of the figure illustrates a hypothetical pattern
of average quarterly earnings for residents in a Jobs-Plus development
during the baseline period (before the program was launched) and during the follow-up period (after the program was launched). If Jobs-Plus
increases earnings, the quarterly levels during the follow-up period
should rise above the baseline trend. The analysis focuses on comparing the deviations from the baseline trend in each Jobs-Plus develop-

ment with those in the control-group development with which it was matched before random assignment. The impact of Jobs-Plus on average earnings is estimated as the difference between the two sets of deviations.

To make the analysis operational from the individual perspective, one must identify the people who resided in the developments at the time that Jobs-Plus was launched and follow their earnings levels backward and forward in time, regardless of where they lived before and after the point of the program's launch.[27] To make the analysis from the housing development perspective possible, one must identify the people who resided in the developments during each quarter of the baseline period and after the program's launch and then calculate average earnings in each quarter for the persons who were residents of that quarter. Outcome data for the analyses from both the individual and development perspectives were obtained from public administrative records (Bloom and Riccio 2002).

Summary

This chapter lays out a research strategy that leverages the widely accepted scientific principle of randomization to permit evaluation of place-based social programs. For theoretical or practical reasons, place-based programs are targeted at group-level units such as firms, neighborhoods, and schools rather than at individual-level units such as employees, residents, and students. In place-based programs, it is usually infeasible to randomize individual members of the groups, but it is often possible to randomize the groups or clusters themselves. Because cluster randomization is being used with increasing frequency to measure the impacts of social programs, it is particularly important for researchers to understand its special, and sometimes counterintuitive, properties. The key features of cluster randomization are the following:

Precision is at a premium. Cluster randomization provides estimates of program impacts that are unbiased for the same reason that individual randomization is unbiased. But impact estimates based on randomization of clusters almost always have much less precision than do their counterparts given randomization of the same total number of individuals.

The number of clusters randomized is usually a much more important determinant of precision than is cluster size. In most contexts, resources allow for randomization of only a small number of clusters, putting a strong constraint on the precision of program-impact estimates. Consequently, increasing the number of clusters by a given proportion usually improves precision by a much greater amount than does increasing the number of individuals per cluster by the same proportion.

Covariates can improve the precision of program-impact estimates. Regression adjustments for a baseline covariate, especially if the covariate is a lagged-outcome measure, can substantially increase the precision of program-impact estimates. This finding holds both when the covariate is an aggregate characteristic of the clusters randomized and when it is an individual characteristic of the cluster members.

Subgroup analyses can have counterintuitive properties. Estimates of impacts for subgroups of a cluster randomized sample often have properties that set them apart from those based on randomization of individuals. For example, program-impact estimates offer almost as much precision for some subgroups defined in terms of individual characteristics as do corresponding impact estimates for a full study sample.

To improve precision, the characteristics used in pairwise matching must have considerable predictive power. For an evaluation with a small number of clusters (say, fewer than ten) to be randomized, the gains in precision produced by randomizing matched pairs of clusters may be offset by the loss of degrees of freedom caused by doing so. Thus, unless the predictive power of matching is substantial, it may reduce precision rather than increase it.

Mobility is the Achilles' heel of place-based programs and of cluster randomization experiments. The movement of individuals into and out of randomized clusters tends to erode the connection between people and place. This erosion not only reduces the effectiveness of place-based programs by decreasing the target population's degree of exposure to them but can complicate the design, execution, and interpretation of evaluation findings of such programs.

This chapter has explored in detail the use of cluster-randomized experiments for measuring the impacts of place-based programs. The goal of the chapter was to make clear to readers why the approach has great potential value, when the approach is most appropriate to use, and how to design studies that get the most information possible from it. Given this information it is hoped that future researchers will make more frequent and effective use of cluster randomization to advance the state of the art of evaluation research and thereby improve place-based programs for people.

Appendix: Deriving Expressions for the Minimum Detectable Effect Size for Randomized Cluster Experiments

This appendix derives expressions for the minimum detectable effect size in experiments using cluster randomization. Results for estimates of three types of program impacts are presented—net impacts for the full sample, net impacts for subgroups, and differential impacts for subgroups. Subgroups defined by the characteristics of the clusters randomized and subgroups defined by the characteristics of individual sample members are considered.

Results for the Full Experimental Sample

The net impact, B_0, of a program on an outcome is defined as the difference between the mean outcome in the presence of the program and the mean outcome in the absence of the program. In a cluster randomization design with one program group and one control group, the net impact is estimated as b_0, the difference between the mean outcomes for these two groups. Assume that J clusters of n individuals each are randomly assigned with probability P to the program group and with probability $1 - P$ to the control group. For both the program group and the control group, the between-cluster variance is τ^2, the within-cluster variance is σ^2, and the intraclass correlation is ρ.

Figure 4A.1 illustrates why the minimum detectable effect of a program impact estimator is a multiple M of its standard error (Bloom 1995). The bell-shaped curve on the left represents the t distribution given that the true impact equals 0; this is the null hypothesis. For a positive-impact estimate (presumed for present purposes to reflect a beneficial result) to be statistically significant at the α level for a one-tailed test (or at the $\alpha/2$ level for a two-tailed test), it must fall to the right of the critical t-value, t_α (or $t_{\alpha/2}$), of this distribution. The bell-shaped curve on the right represents the t distribution given that the impact equals the minimum detectable effect; this is the alternative hypothesis. For the impact estimator to detect the minimum detectable effect with probability $1 - \beta$ (that is, to have a statistical power level of $1 - \beta$), the effect must lie a distance of $t_{1-\beta}$ to the right of the critical t-value of the alternative hypothesis and a distance of $t_\alpha + t_{1-\beta}$ (or $t_{\alpha/2} + t_{1-\beta}$) from the null hypothesis. Because t-values are expressed as multiples of the standard error of the impact estimator, the minimum detectable effect is also a multiple of the impact estimator. Thus, for a one-tailed test,

$$M = t_\alpha + t_{1-\beta}, \tag{4A.1}$$

Figure 4A.1   The Minimum Detectable Effect Multiplier

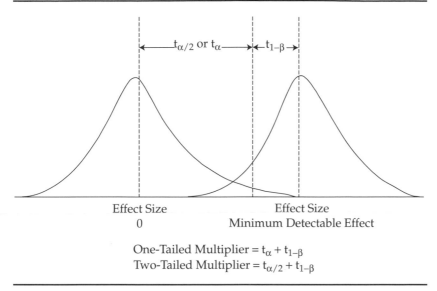

One-Tailed Multiplier = $t_\alpha + t_{1-\beta}$
Two-Tailed Multiplier = $t_{\alpha/2} + t_{1-\beta}$

Source: Illustration by the author.

and for a two-tailed test:

$$M = t_{\alpha/2} + t_{1-\beta} \tag{4A.2}$$

The t-values in these expressions reflect the number of degrees of freedom available for the impact estimator, which for the full sample equals the number of clusters minus two ($J - 2$). The multiplier for the full sample is thus referred to as M_{J-2}. The standard error and minimum detectable effect for the full sample-impact estimator given cluster randomization are referred to as $SE(b_0)_{CL}$ and $MDE(b_0)_{CL}$, respectively. The relationship among these terms is the following:

$$MDE(b_0)_{CL} = M_{J-2}SE(b_0)_{CL} \tag{4A.3}$$

Because the discussion of precision in the chapter is expressed mainly in terms of the metric of effect size—defined as the program impact divided by the standard deviation of the outcome for the target population—this appendix focuses on the minimum detectable effect size, $MDES(b_0)_{CL}$. With cluster randomization, the standard deviation of the outcome for the target population equals $\sqrt{\tau^2 + \sigma^2}$. Hence, the minimum detectable effect size is defined as follows:

$$MDES(b_0)_{CL} = \frac{MDE(b_0)_{CL}}{\sqrt{\tau^2 + \sigma^2}} \qquad (4A.4)$$

Equations 4A.3 and 4A.4 imply:

$$MDES(b_0)_{CL} = \frac{M_{J-2}SE(b_0)_{CL}}{\sqrt{\tau^2 + \sigma^2}} \qquad (4A.5)$$

Recall equation 4.2:

$$SE(b_0)_{CL} = \sqrt{\frac{1}{P(1-P)}} \sqrt{\frac{\tau^2}{J} + \frac{\sigma^2}{nJ}} \qquad (4A.6)$$

Note that the definition of intraclass correlation implies:

$$\tau^2 = \frac{\rho\sigma^2}{1-\rho} \qquad (4A.7)$$

By substituting equation 4A.6 for $SE(b_0)_{CL}$ and equation 4A.7 for τ^2 into equation 4A.5 and simplifying terms, one can express the minimum detectable effect size for the full-sample net impact estimator thus:

$$MDES(b_0)_{CL} = \frac{M_{J-2}}{\sqrt{J}} \sqrt{\rho + \frac{1-\rho}{n}} \sqrt{\frac{1}{P(1-P)}} \qquad (4A.8)$$

Results for Subgroups Defined by Cluster Characteristics

For consistency with the example of subgroup analysis provided in the body of the chapter, consider two mutually exclusive and jointly exhaustive subgroups, A and B, that are defined by the characteristics of clusters. In an experiment where schools are randomly assigned, the subgroups might be urban schools and suburban schools; in an experiment where firms are randomly assigned, the subgroups might be retail firms and food-service firms. Proportion Π_A of the clusters are in subgroup A, and proportion $1 - \Pi_A$ are in subgroup B. For simplicity, it is assumed of each subgroup that P, n, τ^2, and σ^2 (and, by extension, ρ) are equal to their counterparts for the full sample.

The net impact for subgroup A, B_{0A}, is estimated as the difference between the mean outcome for subgroup members who were randomly assigned to the program group and the mean outcome for subgroup members who were randomly assigned to the control group and is denoted b_{0A}. Hence, the minimum detectable effect size for this subgroup can be obtained by substituting the number of clusters that it contains,

$\Pi_A J$ for J, and its multiplier, $M_{\Pi_A J-2}$ for M_{J-2}, into equation 4A.8. The ratio between this result and its counterpart for the full sample is:

$$\frac{\text{MDES}(b_{0A})_{\text{CL}}}{\text{MDES}(b_0)_{\text{CL}}} = \frac{M_{\Pi_A J-2}}{M_{J-2}} \sqrt{1/\Pi_A} \qquad (4A.9)$$

The corresponding ratio for subgroup B can be obtained by replacing Π_A in equation 4A.9 with $1 - \Pi_A$.

The differential impact for the two subgroups, $B_{0A} - B_{0B}$, is estimated as the difference between their net impact estimates, $b_{0A} - b_{0B}$. Because the differential impact reflects the mean outcome estimates for a total of four groups (the program and control groups in each subgroup), it has $J - 4$ degrees of freedom, and the minimum detectable effect multiplier is M_{J-4}.

To calculate the standard error for this impact estimator, first note that equation 4A.6 implies that the variance of the full sample net impact estimator is:

$$\text{VAR}(b_0)_{\text{CL}} = \left[\frac{1}{JP(1-P)}\right]\left[\tau^2 + \frac{\sigma^2}{n}\right] \qquad (4A.10)$$

Replacing J in equation 4A.10 with $\Pi_A J$ or with $(1 - \Pi_A)J$ to represent the number of clusters in subgroup A or B yields:

$$\text{VAR}(b_{0A})_{\text{CL}} = \left[\frac{1}{\Pi_A JP(1-P)}\right]\left[\tau^2 + \frac{\sigma^2}{n}\right] \qquad (4A.11a)$$

$$\text{VAR}(b_{0B})_{\text{CL}} = \left[\frac{1}{(1-\Pi_A)JP(1-P)}\right]\left[\tau^2 + \frac{\sigma^2}{n}\right] \qquad (4A.11b)$$

Note that because subgroups A and B are independent samples, the variance of the difference between their net impact estimates is the sum of their respective variances:

$$\text{VAR}(b_{0A} - b_{0B})_{\text{CL}} = \text{VAR}(b_{0A})_{\text{CL}} + \text{VAR}(b_{0B})_{\text{CL}} \qquad (4A.12)$$

Substituting equation 4A.11a for $\text{VAR}(b_{0A})_{\text{CL}}$ and equation 4A.11b for $\text{VAR}(b_{0B})_{\text{CL}}$ into equation 4A.12 yields:

$$\text{VAR}(b_{0A} - b_{0B})_{\text{CL}} = \left[\frac{1}{\Pi_A JP(1-P)}\right]\left[\tau^2 + \frac{\sigma^2}{n}\right] + \left[\frac{1}{(1-\Pi_A)JP(1-P)}\right]\left[\tau^2 + \frac{\sigma^2}{n}\right]$$

$$= \left[\frac{1}{\Pi_A(1-\Pi_A)JP(1-P)}\right]\left[\tau^2 + \frac{\sigma^2}{n}\right] \qquad (4A.13)$$

Finally, note:

$$\frac{\text{MDES}(b_{0A} - b_{0B})_{CL}}{\text{MDES}(b_0)_{CL}} = \frac{M_{J-4}}{M_{J-2}} \frac{\text{SE}(b_{0A} - b_{0B})_{CL}}{\text{SE}(b_0)_{CL}} \sqrt{\frac{\tau^2 + \sigma^2}{\tau^2 + \sigma^2}}$$

$$= \frac{M_{J-4}}{M_{J-2}} \frac{\text{SE}(b_{0A} - b_{0B})_{CL}}{\text{SE}(b_0)_{CL}} \tag{4A.14}$$

Replacing $\text{SE}(b_0)_{CL}$ and $\text{SE}(b_{0A} - b_{0B})_{CL}$ in equation 4A.14 by the square roots of equations 4A.10 and 4A.11, respectively, and simplifying terms yields:

$$\frac{\text{MDES}(b_{0A} - b_{0B})_{CL}}{\text{MDES}(b_0)_{CL}} = \frac{M_{J-4}}{M_{J-2}} \sqrt{\frac{1}{\Pi_A(1 - \Pi_A)}} \tag{4A.15}$$

Results for Subgroups Defined by Individual Characteristics

Again for consistency with the body of the chapter, consider two mutually exclusive and jointly exhaustive subgroups, I and II, that are defined in terms of individual characteristics. In an experiment where schools are randomly assigned, the subgroups might be boys and girls; in an experiment where firms are randomly assigned, the subgroups might be long-term employees and recent hires. Assume that proportions Π_I and $1 - \Pi_I$ of the individuals in each randomized group belong to subgroups I and II, respectively. Also, assume of each subgroup that P, τ^2, and σ^2 (and, by extension, ρ) are the same as for the full sample.

The net impact for subgroup I, (B_{0I}), is estimated as the difference between the mean outcome for subgroup members who were randomly assigned to the program group and the mean outcome for subgroup members who were randomly assigned to the control group and is denoted b_{0I}. Because the subgroup contains sample members from all J clusters, its net impact estimate has $J - 2$ degrees of freedom, and its minimum detectable effect multiplier is M_{J-2}. Replacing n in equation 4A.8 by $n\Pi_I$ and taking the ratio between this result and its counterpart for the full sample yields:

$$\frac{\text{MDES}(b_{0I})_{CL}}{\text{MDES}(b_0)_{CL}} = \frac{\sqrt{\rho + \dfrac{1 - \rho}{n\Pi_I}}}{\sqrt{\rho + \dfrac{1 - \rho}{n}}} \tag{4A.16}$$

Replacing $n\Pi_I$ in equation 4A.16 with $n(1 - \Pi_I)$ produces the corresponding result for subgroup II.

The differential impact for the two subgroups, $B_{0I} - B_{0II}$, is estimated as the difference between their net impact estimates, $b_{0I} - b_{0II}$. Relative to the minimum detectable effect sizes for the net impact estimators, the minimum detectable effect size for this estimator can be somewhat smaller. This is because in a simple model of subgroup differences, the cluster-level random error, e_j, is "differenced away" when the differential impact is computed, which in turn eliminates τ^2.[28] To demonstrate this finding, note that the net impact estimator for each subgroup is the difference between the mean outcome for its members in the program group and the mean outcome for its members in the control group:

$$b_{0I} = \overline{\overline{Y}}_{PI} - \overline{\overline{Y}}_{CI} \tag{4A.17a}$$

$$b_{0II} = \overline{\overline{Y}}_{PII} - \overline{\overline{Y}}_{CII} \tag{4A.17b}$$

Thus, the differential impact can be expressed not only as a difference between program-control differences within the subgroups but as a difference between subgroup I and subgroup II within the program and control groups:

$$b_{0I} - b_{0II} = \left(\overline{\overline{Y}}_{PI} - \overline{\overline{Y}}_{CI}\right) - \left(\overline{\overline{Y}}_{PII} - \overline{\overline{Y}}_{CII}\right) = \left(\overline{\overline{Y}}_{PI} - \overline{\overline{Y}}_{PII}\right) - \left(\overline{\overline{Y}}_{CI} - \overline{\overline{Y}}_{CII}\right) \tag{4A.18}$$

For each cluster j, the subgroup difference in mean outcomes is $\overline{Y}_{jI} - \overline{Y}_{jII}$, or Δ_j. The variance of this within-cluster subgroup difference for two independent subgroups is:

$$VAR\left(\overline{Y}_{jI} - \overline{Y}_{jII}\right)_{CL} = VAR(\Delta_j)_{CL} = \frac{\sigma^2}{\Pi_I(1-\Pi_I)n} \tag{4A.19}$$

Averaging Δ_j across the PJ clusters in the program or across the $(1 - P)J$ clusters in the control group yields the mean subgroup difference for the program group, $\overline{\overline{\Delta}}_P$, or for the control group, $\overline{\overline{\Delta}}_c$. The variances for these means are:

$$VAR\left(\overline{\overline{\Delta}}_P\right)_{CL} = \frac{\sigma^2}{PJ\Pi_I(1-\Pi_I)n} \tag{4A.20a}$$

and

$$VAR\left(\overline{\overline{\Delta}}_C\right)_{CL} = \frac{\sigma^2}{(1-P)J\Pi_I(1-\Pi_I)n} \tag{4A.20b}$$

Hence, the variance of the difference between the mean subgroup differences for the program and control groups is:

$$VAR\left(\overline{\overline{\Delta}}_P - \overline{\overline{\Delta}}_C\right)_{CL} = VAR(b_{0I} - b_{0II})_{CL} = \frac{\sigma^2}{PJ\Pi_I(1-\Pi_I)n} + \frac{\sigma^2}{(1-P)J\Pi_I(1-\Pi_I)n}$$

$$= \frac{\sigma^2}{P(1-P)J\Pi_I(1-\Pi_I)n} \tag{4A.21}$$

To state the variance of the full-sample net impact estimator in comparable terms, substitute equation 4A.7 for τ^2 into equation 4A.10, and simplify as follows:

$$VAR(b_0)_{CL} = \frac{\dfrac{\rho\sigma^2}{1-\rho} + \dfrac{\sigma^2}{n}}{JP(1-P)} = \frac{\dfrac{n\rho\sigma^2 + (1-\rho)\sigma^2}{n(1-\rho)}}{JP(1-P)} = \frac{\sigma^2(1+(n-1)\rho)}{JP(1-P)n(1-\rho)} \tag{4A.22}$$

Because the differential impact estimator is equivalent to the difference between the program and control groups with respect to their mean subgroup differences, it uses all J clusters and computes two means. Thus, it preserves all $J - 2$ degrees of freedom from the full sample and has a minimum detectable effect multiplier of M_{J-2}. Consequently:

$$\frac{MDES(b_{0I} - b_{0II})_{CL}}{MDES(b_0)_{CL}} = \frac{M_{J-2}\sqrt{\dfrac{\sigma^2}{P(1-P)J\Pi_I(1-\Pi_I)n}}}{M_{J-2}\sqrt{\dfrac{\sigma^2(1+(n-1)\rho)}{JP(1-P)n(1-\rho)}}}$$

$$= \sqrt{\frac{(1-\rho)}{\Pi_I(1-\Pi_I)(1+(n-1)\rho)}} \tag{4A.23}$$

Notes

1. Charles S. Peirce and Joseph Jastrow (1885) put individual randomization to its earliest known use in a study of minimum perceivable differences in the weights of physical objects and in their later studies of mental telepathy (for discussion, see Hacking 1988). Ronald A. Fisher (1926) first wrote about randomization in an article that focused on agricultural experiments.

2. In his textbook on experimental design in psychology and education—one of the first to be published on the subject—E. F. Lindquist (1953) provided an excellent overview of cluster randomization.

3. In the rare instances where the programmatic response to a place-based problem is to induce individuals to move, it is possible to evaluate the program by randomizing individuals. This was done, for example, in the Moving to Opportunity experiment (Kling, Ludwig, and Katz 2005), in which randomly selected residents of public housing projects received rental housing subsidies if they moved to neighborhoods with less concentrated poverty.

4. Donald B. Rubin (1980) referred to the assumed absence of spillover effects as the Stable Unit Treatment Value Assumption. D. R. Cox (1958, 19) referred to the assumed presence of spillover effects as "interference between different units."

5. Malcolm Gladwell (2000) described tipping in a wide range of contexts, including fashion (how Hush Puppy shoes sprang back into vogue), the food and entertainment industries (how restaurants and celebrities fall in and out of favor), criminal behavior (how crime rates plummeted in New York City during the 1990s), and transportation safety (how a few graffiti artists can spark an outbreak of subway crime).

6. In one of the few studies that provide statistical evidence for the existence of the tipping phenomenon, George C. Galster, Robert G. Quercia, and Alvaro Cortes (2000) used U.S. Census data to estimate threshold effects for neighborhood characteristics such as the poverty rate, the unemployment rate, and the school dropout rate.

7. This principle, which is central to the theory of taxation in public finance, is often referred to as "horizontal equity" (Musgrave 1959, 160–61).

8. Graciela Teruel and Benjamin Davis (2000) described such a legal restriction on the PROGRESA program, an initiative designed to improve child health, nutrition, and education in rural Mexico.

9. Among the software packages that can perform this kind of analysis are HLM, SAS Proc Mixed, Stata gllamm6, MLWiN, and VARCL.

10. Equation 4.2 is based on a related expression in Stephen W. Raudenbush (1997, 176).

11. Leslie Kish (1965) defined two design effects, one based on the standard errors of cluster sampling versus random sampling and the other based on the error variances of cluster sampling versus random sampling.

12. This estimated range of intraclass correlations is based on reports by David M. Murray, Brenda L. Rooney et al. (1994) and Ohidul M. Siddiqui et al. (1996) for measures of adolescent smoking clustered by schools; by David Murray and Brian Short (1995) for measures of adolescent drinking clustered by community; by Marion Campbell, Jill Mollison, and Jeremy M. Grimshaw (2001) and Campbell, Grimshaw, and I. N. Steen (2000) for measures of physician practices and patient outcomes clustered by hospitals and by physician groups; and by Obioha C. Ukoumunne et al. (1999) for other kinds of measures.

13. Although William Sealy Gosset established this relationship in a paper published under his pseudonym "Student" (1908), Fisher (1925) first brought it to the attention of empirical researchers.

14. This standardized metric is often used in meta-analyses to synthesize findings across outcomes and studies (Hedges and Olkin 1985).

15. This discussion makes the simplifying assumption that each randomized cluster has the same number of individual members. Similar findings can be obtained when the number of individuals varies across clusters, provided that one uses the harmonic mean of the number of individuals per cluster.

16. Howard S. Bloom (1995) demonstrated this latitude for individual randomization, and Xiaofeng Liu (2003) demonstrated it for cluster randomization.

17. Anthony S. Bryk and Stephen W. Raudenbush (1988) argued that one should expect program impacts to vary across individuals and that this variation provides an opportunity for learning how individuals respond to programs.

18. Mitchell H. Gail et al. (1996) used Monte Carlo simulations to illustrate this fact for parametric t-tests and nonparametric permutation tests. Jan Kmenta's (1971, 254–56) expression for the effect of heteroscedasticity in a bivariate regression can be used to prove the same point.

19. This finding reflects the number of degrees of freedom for a two-sample difference-of-means test given unequal variances and unbalanced samples (Blalock 1972, 226–28).

20. If τ^2 and σ^2 are the same for the subgroups as for the full sample, then the subgroups must have the same mean outcome. When this simplification does not hold, τ^2 and σ^2 are smaller for the subgroups, and equations 4.7 and 4.8 may understate the relative precision of subgroup findings. Nevertheless, because the same reduction in variance can be achieved for the full sample by controlling statistically for subgroup characteristics, this issue can be ignored for the moment.

21. Because the differential impact estimator is a four-group "difference of differences of means" based on all clusters in the full sample, it has $J - 4$ degrees of freedom.

22. The situation is even more favorable if the individual characteristic defining the subgroups is correlated with the outcome measure, as student gender, for example, is correlated with math test scores (boys generally score higher than girls). In this case, part of the individual variance component, σ^2, is related to the subgroup characteristic and does not exist within subgroups. Also, if the subgroup mix varies across clusters and the subgroup characteristic is correlated with the outcome, part of the between-cluster variance, τ^2, is related to the subgroup characteristic and does not exist within subgroups. Because both these improvements can be obtained for the full sample estimator by controlling statistically for subgroup characteristics as a covariate, they are not implications of performing subgroup analysis in cluster randomization experiments per se.

23. Equation 4.12 includes an unconditional rather than conditional individual variance because the cluster covariates are constant within each cluster and thus cannot explain within-cluster variation.

24. Blocked randomization in experiments is analogous to proportionally stratified random sampling in survey research (Kish 1965).

25. As with any set of mutually exclusive, jointly exhaustive categorical variables, one must always have a "left-out" category to estimate a regression with an intercept.

26. Differences between findings for two-tailed tests and one-tailed tests are most pronounced where there are small numbers of clusters to be randomized and therefore few degrees of freedom.

27. At this writing, the final report on Jobs-Plus is being prepared (Bloom, Riccio, and Verma, forthcoming).

28. For simplicity, this section assumes that the cluster-error component is the same for all subgroups in a given cluster. However, the main point of the

section still holds, although with less force, if the cluster-error components for different subgroups of individuals differ but are correlated with each other. In this case, the subgroup differential impact estimator "differences away" part (not all) of the cluster-error component.

References

Blalock, Hubert M., Jr. 1972. *Social Statistics*. New York: McGraw-Hill.

Blank, Rolf K., Diana Nunnaley, Andrew Porter, John Smithson, and Eric Osthoff. 2002. *Experimental Design to Measure Effects of Assisting Teachers in Using Data on Enacted Curriculum to Improve Effectiveness of Instruction in Mathematics and Science Education*. Washington, D.C.: National Science Foundation.

Bloom, Howard S. 1995. "Minimum Detectable Effects: A Simple Way to Report the Statistical Power of Experimental Designs." *Evaluation Review* 19(5): 547–56.

Bloom, Howard S., Johannes M. Bos, and Suk-Won Lee. 1999. "Using Cluster Random Assignment to Measure Program Impacts: Statistical Implications for the Evaluation of Education Programs." *Evaluation Review* 23(4): 445–69.

Bloom, Howard S., and James A. Riccio. 2002. *Using Place-Based Random Assignment and Comparative Interrupted Time-Series Analysis to Evaluate the Jobs-Plus Employment Program for Public Housing Residents*. New York: MDRC.

Bloom, Howard S., James A. Riccio, and Nandita Verma. Forthcoming. *Promoting Work in Public Housing: The Effectiveness of Jobs-Plus*. New York: MDRC.

Bloom, Howard S., JoAnn Rock, Sandra Ham, Laura Melton, and Julieanne O'Brien. 2001. *Evaluating the Accelerated Schools Approach: A Look at Early Implementation and Impacts on Student Achievement in Eight Elementary Schools*. New York: MDRC.

Bogatz, Gerry Ann, and Samuel Ball. 1971. *The Second Year of Sesame Street: A Continuing Evaluation*. Princeton, N.J.: Educational Testing Service.

Boruch, Robert F., and Ellen Foley. 2000. "The Honestly Experimental Society: Sites and Other Entities as the Units of Allocation and Analysis in Randomized Trials." In *Validity and Social Experimentation: Donald Campbell's Legacy*, edited by Leonard Bickman. Volume 1. Thousand Oaks, Calif.: Sage Publications.

Branson, William H. 1972. *Macroeconomic Theory and Policy*. New York: Harper & Row.

Brooks-Gunn, Jeanne, Greg J. Duncan, and J. Lawrence Aber, eds. 1997. *Neighborhood Poverty: Context and Consequences for Children*. New York: Russell Sage Foundation.

Bryk, Anthony S., and Stephen W. Raudenbush. 1988. "Heterogeneity of Variance in Experimental Studies: A Challenge to Conventional Interpretations." *Psychological Bulletin* 104(3): 396–404.

Campbell, Marion K., Jeremy M. Grimshaw, and I. N. Steen. 2000. "Sample Size Calculations for Group Randomised Trials." *Journal of Health Services and Policy Research* 5: 12–16.

Campbell, Marion K., Jill Mollison, and Jeremy M. Grimshaw. 2001. "Group Trials in Implementation Research: Estimation of Intragroup Correlation Coefficients and Sample Size." *Statistics in Medicine* 20: 391–99.

Chen, Huey-tsyh, and Peter H. Rossi. 1983. "Evaluating with Sense: The Theory-Driven Approach." *Evaluation Review* 7(3): 283–302.

Cohen, Jacob. 1977/1988. *Statistical Power Analysis for the Behavioral Sciences.* New York: Academic Press.

Connell, James P., and Anne C. Kubisch. 1998. "Applying a Theory of Change Approach to the Evaluation of Comprehensive Community Initiatives: Progress, Prospects, and Problems." In *New Approaches to Evaluating Community Initiatives,* volume 2: *Theory, Measurement, and Analysis,* edited by Karen Fulbright-Anderson, Anne C. Kubisch, and James P. Connell. Washington, D.C.: Aspen Institute.

Cook, Thomas H., David Hunt, and Robert F. Murphy. 2000. "Comer's School Development Program in Chicago: A Theory-Based Evaluation." *American Educational Research Journal* (Summer).

Cornfield, Jerome. 1978. "Randomization by Group: A Formal Analysis." *American Journal of Epidemiology* 108(2): 100–102.

Cox, David R. 1958. *Planning of Experiments.* New York: John Wiley.

Donner, Allan, and Neil Klar. 2000. *Design and Analysis of Group Randomization Trials in Health Research.* London: Arnold.

Eccles, Martin P., I. Nick Steen, Jeremy M. Grimshaw, Lois Thomas, Paul McNamee, Jennifer Souter, John Wilsdon, Lloyd Matowe, Gillian Needham, Fiona Gilbert, and Senga Bond. 2001. "Effect of Audit and Feedback and Reminder Messages on Primary-Care Referrals: A Randomized Trial." *The Lancet* 357: 1406–9.

Fisher, Ronald A. 1925. *Statistical Methods for Research Workers.* Edinburgh: Oliver & Boyd.

———. 1926. "The Arrangement of Field Experiments." *Journal of Agriculture* 33: 503–13.

———. 1937/1947. *The Design of Experiments.* Edinburgh: Oliver & Boyd.

Flay, Brian R. 2000. "Approaches to Substance Use Prevention Utilizing School Curriculum Plus Social Environment Change." *Addictive Behaviors* 25(6): 861–85.

Flay, Brian R., Katherine B. Ryan, J. Allan Best, Stephen Brown, Mary W. Kersell, Josie R. d'Avernas and Mark P. Zanna. 1985. "Are Social-Psychological Smoking Prevention Programs Effective? The Waterloo Study." *Journal of Behavioral Medicine* 8(1): 37–59.

Gail, Mitchell H., Steven D. Mark, Raymond J. Carroll, Sylvan B. Green, and David Pee. 1996. "On Design Considerations and Randomization-Based Inference for Community Intervention Trials." *Statistics in Medicine* 15: 1069–92.

Galster, George C., Roberto G. Quercia, and Alvaro Cortes. 2000. "Identifying Neighborhood Thresholds: An Empirical Exploration." *Housing Policy Debate* 11(3): 701–32.

Garfinkel, Irwin, Charles F. Manski, and Charles Michalopoulos. 1992. "Micro Experiments and Macro Effects." In *Evaluating Welfare and Training Programs,* edited by Charles F. Manski and Irwin Garfinkel. Cambridge, Mass.: Harvard University Press.

Gladwell, Malcolm. 2000. *The Tipping Point: How Little Things Can Make a Big Difference.* Boston: Little, Brown.

Gosnell, Harold F. 1927. *Getting Out the Vote: An Experiment in the Stimulation of Voting.* Chicago: University of Chicago Press.

Gosset, William Sealy ["Student," pseud.]. 1908. "The Probable Error of a Mean." *Biometrika* 6: 1–25.

Granovetter, Mark. 1973. "The Strength of Weak Ties." *American Journal of Sociology* 78(6): 1360–80.

———. 1978. "Threshold Models of Collective Behavior." *American Journal of Sociology* 83(6): 1420–43.

Grimshaw, Jeremy M., Ruth E. Thomas, Graeme MacLennan, Cynthia Fraser, Craig Ramsay, Luke Vale, Paula Whitty, Martin P. Eccles, Lloyd Matowe, L. Shirran, Michel Wensing, Rob Dijkstra, and C. Donaldson. 2004. "Effectiveness and Efficiency of Guideline Dissemination and Implementation Strategies." *Health Technology Assessment.*

Gueron, Judith M. 1984. *Lessons from a Job Guarantee: The Youth Incentive Entitlement Pilot Projects.* New York: MDRC.

Hacking, Ian. 1988. "Telepathy: Origins of Randomization in Experimental Design." *Isis* 79: 427–51.

Hedges, Larry V., and Ingram Olkin. 1985. *Statistical Methods for Meta-Analysis.* Boston: Academic Press.

Hsieh, Chang-Tai, and Miguel Urquiola. 2003. "When Schools Compete, How Do They Compete? An Assessment of Chile's Nationwide School Voucher Program." Working paper w10008. Washington: National Bureau of Economic Research. Available at: www.nber.org/papers/w10008 (accessed January 5, 2005).

Jencks, Christopher, and Susan E. Mayer. 1990. "The Social Consequences of Growing Up in a Poor Neighborhood." In *Inner-City Poverty in the United States,* edited by Laurence E. Lynn, Jr., and M. McGeary. Washington, D.C.: National Academy Press.

Kane, Thomas J. 2004. "The Impact of After-School Programs: Interpreting the Results of Four Recent Evaluations." New York: W. T. Grant Foundation.

Kellert, Stephen H. 1993. *In the Wake of Chaos: Unpredictable Order in Dynamical Systems.* Chicago: University of Chicago Press.

Kelling, George, A. M. Pate, D. Dieckman, and C. Brown. 1974. *The Kansas City Preventative Patrol Experiment: Technical Report.* Washington, D.C.: Police Foundation.

Kennedy, Stephen D. 1988. "Direct Cash Low-Income Housing Assistance," in *Lessons From Selected Program and Policy Areas,* edited by Howard S. Bloom, David S. Cordray, and Richard J. Light. San Francisco: Jossey-Bass.

Kish, Leslie. 1965. *Survey Sampling.* New York: John Wiley.

Kling, Jeffrey R., Jens Ludwig, and Lawrence F. Katz. 2005. "Neighborhood Effects on Crime for Female and Male Youth: Evidence from a Randomized Housing Voucher Experiment." *Quarterly Journal of Economics* 120(1): n.p.

Kmenta, Jan. 1971. *Elements of Econometrics.* New York: Macmillan.

Ladd, Helen F., and Edward B. Fiske. 2000. *When Schools Compete: A Cautionary Tale.* Washington, D.C.: Brookings Institution Press.

Leviton, Laura C., Robert L. Goldenberger, C. Suzanne Baker, and M. C. Freda. 1999. "Randomized Controlled Trial of Methods to Encourage the Use of Antenatal Corticosteroid Therapy for Fetal Maturation." *Journal of the American Medical Association* 281(1): 46–52.

Lindquist, Everet Franklin. 1953. *Design and Analysis of Experiments in Psychology and Education.* Boston: Houghton Mifflin.

Lipsey, Mark W. 1990. *Design Sensitivity: Statistical Power for Experimental Research.* Newbury Park, Calif.: Sage.

Liu, Xiaofeng. 2003. "Statistical Power and Optimum Sample Allocation Ratio for Treatment and Control Having Unequal Costs per Unit of Randomization." *Journal of Educational and Behavioral Statistics* 28(3): 231–48.

Martin, Donald C., Paula Diehr, Edward B. Perrin, and Thomas D. Koepsell. 1993. "The Effect of Matching on the Power of Randomized Community Intervention Studies." *Statistics in Medicine* 12: 329–38.

Miller, Cynthia, and Howard Bloom. 2002. "Random Assignment in Cleveland—Round One." Internal memorandum. New York: MDRC.

Murray, David M. 1998. *Design and Analysis of Group-Randomized Trials.* New York: Oxford University Press.

Murray, David M., Peter J. Hannan, David R. Jacobs, Paul J. McGovern, Linda Schmid, William L. Baker, and Clifton Gray. 1994. "Assessing Intervention Effects in the Minnesota Heart Health Program." *American Journal of Epidemiology* 139(1): 91–103.

Murray, David M., Brenda L. Rooney, Peter J. Hannan, Arthur V. Peterson, Dennis V. Ary, Anthony Biglan, Gilbert J. Botvin, Richard I. Evans, Brian R. Flay, Robert Futterman, J. Greg Getz, Pat M. Marek, Mario Orlandi, MaryAnn Pentz, Cheryl L. Perry, and Steven P. Schinke. 1994. "Intraclass Correlation Among Common Measures of Adolescent Smoking: Estimates, Correlates and Applications in Smoking Prevention Studies." *American Journal of Epidemiology* 140(11): 1038–50.

Murray, David M., and Brian Short. 1995. "Intraclass Correlation Among Measures Related to Alcohol Use by Young Adults: Estimates, Correlates and Applications in Intervention Studies." *Journal of Studies on Alcohol* 56(6): 681–94.

Musgrave, Richard A. 1959. *The Theory of Public Finance.* New York: McGraw-Hill.

Musgrave, Richard A., and Peggy B. Musgrave. 1973. *Public Finance in Theory and Practice.* New York: McGraw-Hill.

Myrdal, Gunnar. 1944. *An American Dilemma.* New York: Harper & Row.

National Center for Educational Statistics. 1997. "Reading and Mathematics Achievement Growth in High School." Issue brief 98–038. Washington: U.S. Department of Education.

Nye, Barbara, Larry V. Hedges, and Spyros Konstantopoulos. 1999. "The Long-Term Effects of Small Classes: A Five-Year Follow-up of the Tennessee Class Size Experiment." *Educational Evaluation and Policy Analysis* 21(2):127–42.

Peirce, Charles S., and Joseph Jastrow. 1885. "On Small Differences of Sensation." *Memoirs of the National Academy of Sciences for 1884* 3: 75–83.

Peterson, Paul E., Patrick J. Wolf, William G. Howell, and David E. Campbell. 2002. "School Vouchers: Results from Randomized Experiments." Unpublished paper. Kennedy School of Government, Harvard University.

Raudenbush, Stephen W. 1997. "Statistical Analysis and Optimal Design for Group Randomized Trials." *Psychological Methods* 2(2): 173–85.

Rossi, Peter H., Mark W. Lipsey, and Howard W. Freeman. 2004. *Evaluation: A Systematic Approach.* 7th edition. Thousand Oaks, Calif.: Sage Publications.

Rubin, Donald B. 1980. "Discussion of 'Randomization Analysis of Experimental Data: The Fisher Randomization Test Comment,' by D. Basu." *Journal of the American Statistical Association* 75(371): 591–93.

Schelling, Thomas. 1971. "Dynamic Models of Segregation." *Journal of Mathematical Sociology* 1: 143–86.

Shadish, William R., Thomas D. Cook, and Donald T. Campbell. 2002. *Experimental and Quasi-Experimental Designs for Generalized Causal Inference.* Boston: Houghton Mifflin.

Sherman, Lawrence W., and David Weisburd. 1995. "General Deterrent Effects of Police Patrol in Crime 'Hot Spots': A Randomized Controlled Trial." *Justice Quarterly* 12(4): 625–48.

Siddiqui, Ohidul, Donald Hedeker, Brian R. Flay, and Frank B. Hu. 1996. "Intra-Class Correlation Estimates in a School-based Smoking Prevention Study: Outcome and Mediating Variables by Gender and Ethnicity." *American Journal of Epidemiology* 144(4): 425–33.

Sikkema, Kathleen J., Jeffrey A. Kelly, Richard A. Winett, Laura J. Solomon, V. A. Cargill, R. A. Roffman, T. L. McAuliffe, T. G. Heckman, E. A. Anderson, D. A. Wagstaff, A. D. Norman, M. J. Perry, D. A. Crumble, and M. B. Mercer. 2000. "Outcomes of a Randomized Community-Level HIV Prevention Intervention for Women Living in 18 Low-Income Housing Developments." *American Journal of Public Health* 90(1): 57–63.

Slavin, Robert E. 2002. "Evidence-Based Education Policies: Transforming Educational Practice and Research." *Educational Researcher* 31(7): 15–21.

Smith, Herbert L., Tu Ping, M. Giovanna Merli, and Mark Hereward. 1997. "Implementation of a Demographic and Contraceptive Surveillance System in Four Counties in North China." *Population Research and Policy Review* 16(4): 289–314.

Teruel, Graciela M., and Benjamin Davis. 2000. *Final Report: An Evaluation of the Impact of PROGRESA Cash Payments on Private Inter-Household Transfers.* Washington, D.C.: International Food Policy Research Institute.

Tienda, Marta. 1991. "Poor People and Poor Places: Deciphering Neighborhood Effects on Poverty Outcomes." In *Macro-Micro Linkages in Sociology,* edited by Joan Huber. Newbury Park, Calif.: Sage Publications.

Ukoumunne, Obioha C., Martin C. Gulliford, Susan Chinn, Jonathan A. C. Sterne, and Peter G. J. Burney. 1999. "Methods for Evaluating Area-Wide and Organisation-Based Interventions in Health and Health Care: A Systematic Review." *Health Technology Assessment* 3(5): entire issue.

U.S. Department of Education. 2003. *Early Childhood Longitudinal Study, Kinder-*

garten Class of 1998–99 (ECLS-K). Washington: National Center for Education Statistics. Available at: nces.ed.gov/ecls (accessed January 5, 2005).

Verma, Nandita. 2003. *Staying or Leaving: Lessons from Jobs-Plus About the Mobility of Public Housing Residents and the Implications for Place-Based Initiatives*. New York: MDRC.

Wilson, William Julius. 1996. *When Work Disappears: The World of the New Urban Poor*. New York: Alfred A. Knopf.

Chapter 5

Using Experiments to Assess Nonexperimental Comparison-Group Methods for Measuring Program Effects

T HE PAST three decades have seen an explosion in the number of social program evaluations funded by government and nonprofit organizations. These evaluations span a wide range of policy areas, including education, employment, welfare, health, criminal justice, housing, transportation, and the environment. Properly evaluating a social program requires answering three fundamental questions: How was the program implemented? What were its effects? How did its effects compare with its costs?

Perhaps the hardest part of the evaluation process is obtaining credible estimates of a program's impacts. The impacts of a program are defined as the changes experienced by people exposed to the program that would not have occurred in its absence. Therefore, measuring the impact of a program or a treatment requires comparing the outcomes for people in the program group (for example, the reading test scores of participants in an adult literacy program) with an estimate of what these outcomes would have been had the people not been in the program. Constructing the latter set of outcomes, called the counterfactual, can be extremely difficult.

One way to construct a counterfactual is to randomly assign each eligible individual or group of individuals to either the program group or a control group that is neither subject to the program's requirements nor eligible for its services. Considered by many to be the methodological gold standard in evaluation research, this lotterylike process helps ensure that the two groups do not differ systematically in any respect at the outset of the study and that any subsequent differences between them can be attributed to the differences in treatment assignment. In keeping with the convention used throughout this volume, we refer to an evaluation in which people are randomly assigned to a program group or a control group as a randomized experiment, or simply an experiment.

In practice, there are many situations in which it is impossible or unethical to use random assignment. A widely used alternative way to establish a counterfactual is to select or construct a nonexperimental group of people who did not have access to the program under study, and this is called a comparison group.[1] While a control group is denied access to the program under study by chance, a comparison group does not have access to the program for other reasons. For example, they might not meet the program's eligibility requirements. The differences between the observed outcomes for the program group and those for the comparison group provide nonexperimental estimates of the program's effects. This approach is highly problematic, however, owing to the difficulty of finding a comparison group that is identical to the program group in every respect except program access. Because the credibility of comparison-group methods depends on the degree of faith that researchers place in the usually untestable assumptions on which they rest, their perceived value has fluctuated over time, and their findings rarely have led to consensus.

In an effort to find a nonexperimental approach that could serve as an acceptable alternative to random assignment, some researchers have assessed the effectiveness of comparison-group methods by comparing experimental and nonexperimental findings. In this chapter, we use this benchmarking approach to examine two related questions:

1. *Which comparison-group methods yield the best estimates of program impacts, and under what conditions do they do so?* This question is of particular interest to the statisticians, econometricians, and evaluation researchers who develop, assess, and apply program evaluation methods.

2. *Under what conditions, if any, do the best comparison-group methods produce estimates of program impacts valid enough to stand in for estimates based on a randomized experiment?* This question is most relevant to the program funders, policymakers, and administrators who rely on evidence from program evaluations to help inform their policy decisions.

Research on these questions has focused mainly on social and education programs in which people volunteer to participate. In this chapter, in contrast, we explore the questions in the context of welfare-to-work initiatives designed to promote work among low-income people—programs in which participation is mandatory. Although the conclusions presented are consistent with much corresponding research on voluntary programs, they are most directly generalizable to mandatory programs.

The Fundamental Problem and Approaches to Addressing It

Figure 5.1 presents a simplified causal model of the relationships underlying a comparison-group analysis. The model specifies that the values of the outcome, Y, are jointly determined by sample members' program status (whether they are in the program group or in the comparison group), P; a baseline causal factor, X; and a random-error term, e. Note that X can be an observable characteristic such as education level, gender, or race; an unobservable (or difficult-to-observe) characteristic such as motivation or ability; or some combination of these two types of characteristics.

The effect of the program on the outcome is represented in the figure by an arrow from P to Y; its size and sign are represented by β_0. The effect of the baseline characteristic on the outcome is represented in the figure by an arrow from X to Y; its size and sign are represented by β_1. The difference between the mean value of the baseline characteristic for the program group and that for the comparison group is represented by δ.

Consider the implications of the model in figure 5.1 for estimating program impacts. In the simplest comparison group analysis, the impact of P on Y is estimated as the difference between the mean value of

Figure 5.1   Selection Bias in a Comparison-Group Design

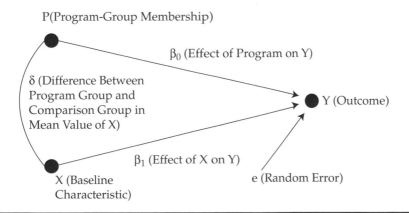

P(Program-Group Membership)

β_0 (Effect of Program on Y)

δ (Difference Between Program Group and Comparison Group in Mean Value of X)

Y (Outcome)

β_1 (Effect of X on Y)

X (Baseline Characteristic)

e (Random Error)

Source: Authors' compilation.

the outcome for the program group and the mean value of the outcome for the comparison group. As shown in the figure, however, this difference actually reflects two relationships: a direct, causal relationship between P and Y and an indirect, spurious relationship between P and Y through baseline characteristic X. Because the observed relationship between P and Y represents more than the impact of the program, it gives a biased impact estimate unless the effect of X can be taken into account. Because the bias arises from how the program and comparison groups were selected, it is known as selection bias.

This situation can be represented algebraically using the notation in figure 5.1. The true impact of the program equals β_0, whereas the expected value of the difference in mean outcomes for the program and comparison groups equals $\beta_0 + \beta_1\delta$ (the true impact plus the difference in Y that is due to the difference between the groups in the mean value of X). Hence, the selection bias equals $\beta_1\delta$.

To put the problem of selection bias in concrete terms, suppose you are examining how an employment program affects people's earnings. Given that Y is average annual earnings and X is the number of years of prior formal education, assume that, for β_0, the true program impact is $500; for β_1, each year of prior formal education increases average annual earnings by $400; and, for δ, program-group members had an average of two more years of formal education at the beginning of the study than did comparison-group members. These values imply that the difference between the average earnings of the program and comparison groups that you observe will be not $500 (the true program impact) but $1,300—that is, the true program impact plus $400 times 2. In this example, the selection bias ($800) is large both in absolute terms and relative to the true impact, seriously compromising the quality of your results. Recall that selection bias may result from failing to control for not only an observable characteristic, as in this example, but also an unobservable characteristic, or some combination of the two.

In a nonexperimental study, the program group and the comparison group may differ systematically with respect to many factors that are related to the outcomes of interest. The nature of the differences depends on how program- and comparison-group members are selected for inclusion in a study. For example, in self-selection, individuals select themselves by learning about, applying for, and deciding whether to participate in a program; in staff selection, program staff recruit and screen potential study members; and in geographic selection, families and individuals become potential study members because of where they work or live. Unless the selection method is random, a researcher who estimates a program impact as a simple difference between the program group's and the comparison group's mean outcomes risks confounding the true impact of the program with the effects of other factors that are unequally distributed between the two groups.

The following are the main strategies researchers have used to eliminate the possibility that selection bias may create spurious relationships between program status and observed outcomes (for a more extensive discussion of the strategies, see Winship and Morgan 1999).

1. *Use random assignment to eliminate all systematic differences between the program and comparison groups.* A randomized experiment eliminates selection bias by severing the relationship between sample members' every characteristic—whether observed or unobserved—and their program status. This well-known property of randomization ensures that the expected value of the difference between the program group and the control group is 0 with respect to every characteristic. Thus, although the actual difference may be positive or negative in any given experiment, the possible differences are equally likely to occur by chance and offset each other across many experiments. In addition, the larger an experimental sample is, the closer to 0 the actual difference is likely to be. It is important to note that the confidence one places in the findings of a specific experiment derives from the statistical properties of the process used to select its program and control groups, not from the particular groups chosen for that experiment.

2. *Perform statistical balancing to eliminate differences between the program and comparison groups with respect to observed characteristics.* One way to deal with selection bias in nonexperimental studies is to match, or balance, the program and comparison groups with respect to as many observed characteristics as possible.[2] The balanced characteristics, each of which will have the same mean in both groups, can be ruled out as a source of selection bias. When many characteristics need balancing, it is often easier to represent them by a composite index and to balance the groups with respect to the index than to balance the characteristics individually. There are a number of matching estimators that use indexes, but perhaps the most widely used in recent years has been the propensity score, which was developed by Paul R. Rosenbaum and Donald B. Rubin (1983). This index expresses the probability (propensity) of being in the program group as opposed to the comparison group as a function of the observed characteristics of sample members. The first step is to estimate the relationship between each characteristic in the balancing index and the probability of being the program group using data for the full sample of program- and comparison-group members. Next, a propensity score is estimated for each sample member by applying his or her values for the characteristics to the index equation. Finally, the estimated propensity scores of the program and comparison groups are balanced by means of one of several methods described later in this chapter.

As acknowledged by Rosenbaum and Rubin (1983), all propensity-score balancing or matching methods have the limitation that they can balance only measured characteristics. If all relevant characteristics are measured and included in the estimated propensity score, then balancing the program and comparison groups with respect to this score eliminates selection bias. But if some important characteristics are not measured—perhaps because they cannot be—selection bias might remain. Thus, the quality of program impact estimates obtained from propensity-score balancing methods depends on how well the comparison group matches the program group before matching and on the nature and the quality of the data available to measure (and thus further balance) sample members' characteristics. As for any impact estimation procedure, the result is only as good as the research design that produced it.

3. *Estimate a regression model of the characteristics associated with the outcome, and use the model to predict what the program group's outcomes would have been if it had not been assigned to the program.* An alternative strategy for reducing selection bias in nonexperimental impact estimation is to predict the counterfactual by modeling the relationships between the outcome measure and sample members' observable characteristics. The simplest and most widely used version of this approach is ordinary least-squares (OLS) regression analysis. The goal of the approach is to model the systematic variation in the outcome so as to account for all the variation related to selection.

With respect to most outcomes of interest, past behavior is usually the best predictor of future behavior. This is because past behavior reflects many factors that affect the outcome, including factors that are not directly measurable. Thus, including a measure of past outcomes is often the best way to use a regression-modeling approach to measure program impacts. The ability of models that include a measure of the past to produce impact estimates that are free of selection bias depends, however, on how well they account for the systematic determinants of future outcomes. And, in practice, there is no way to know when this goal has been achieved except to compare the nonexperimental impact estimate with an estimate of the same impact based on a randomized experiment.

4. *Control for unobserved characteristics by making assumptions about how the program and comparison groups were selected.* Still another approach to improving comparison-group estimates of program impacts is to control for unobserved characteristics using selection models, models that are based on assumptions about the relationships between unobserved characteristics and program status.

One common selection model applies when researchers can identify and measure exogenous variables, variables that are related to selection but unrelated to unobserved determinants of the outcome (Maddala and Lee 1976). If exogenous variables can be found that are sufficiently powerful correlates of selection, then selection modeling can produce impact estimates that are valid and reliable. This approach is a variant of the econometric estimation method called instrumental variables (discussed at length in chapter 3 in this volume). Unfortunately, it is generally very difficult to identify exogenous correlates of selection. An alternative way to address selection with respect to unobservable characteristics is to make specific assumptions about the functional forms of the error terms in impact and selection models (Gronau 1974; Heckman 1976, 1978). The results from such models, however, are highly sensitive to the underlying assumptions (Vella 1998). Both approaches are clearly explained by Burt S. Barnow, Glen G. Cain, and Arthur S. Goldberger (1980).

To get a more concrete sense of how selection models work, imagine that you are evaluating the effects on earnings of a local employment program for low-income people. You know both that people who live near the program are more likely than others to participate in it and that distance from the program is unrelated to future earnings. Because you have selected a random sample of local low-income residents as a comparison group, you can estimate a person's probability of being in the program group as a function of the distance between his residence and the program site and use this function to correct for selection bias.

5. *Use longitudinal baseline data and follow-up data to subtract out any preexisting differences between the program and comparison groups.* Another way to deal with unobserved characteristics is to "difference them away" using longitudinal outcome data and assumptions about how the outcome measure does or does not change over time. Two popular versions of this method are often referred to as fixed-effects models (known as difference-in-difference models when program and comparison groups are being compared) and random-growth models.[3] Fixed-effects models assume that unobserved individual differences related to the outcome do not change during the study period; random-growth models assume that these differences change at a constant rate during the study period. As described later in the chapter, these assumptions allow the effects of characteristics that cannot be observed directly to be subtracted from impact estimates by comparing how program-group outcomes change over time with how comparison-group outcomes change over time.

6. *Use structural-equation methods to adjust for random error in measurements of underlying constructs that predict key outcomes and that differ, on average, between the program and comparison groups.* Random-measurement error in a background characteristic usually causes OLS regressions to produce biased results.[4] In principle, this problem can be solved by

using structural-equation models of causal relationships, which include measurement models for key underlying constructs or latent variables (Joreskog and Sorbom 1988; Muthén 1994; Muthén and Muthén 1998). These measurement models provide assumptions for estimating and removing random measurement error in the characteristics being modeled. When these models are used to estimate program effects, they can adjust for measurement error in key characteristics of the program and comparison groups being used and thereby improve statistical control for differences in these characteristics.

Because structural-equation models can control only for characteristics that have been measured, however, they have the same limitation as all comparison-group approaches. As a result, and because these models have not been used widely in evaluation research or in studies of comparison-group methods, they are not included in the present analysis.

Past Assessments of Comparison-Group Methods

Nonexperimental comparison-group methods typically have been assessed in one of two ways: by means of within-study comparisons that test the methods' ability to replicate impact findings from specific experiments or by means of cross-study comparisons that compare the estimated effects of a set of experimental studies with the estimated effects of a set of nonexperimental studies.

Within-Study Comparisons of Impact Estimates for Employment and Training Programs

In the past two decades, the ability of nonexperimental comparison-group estimators to emulate experimental results has been assessed using data from four major random-assignment studies, or demonstrations, that tested employment and training programs. (For a formal meta-analysis of the studies described as well as of several others, see Steven Glazerman, Dan M. Levy, and David Myers 2003.)

Conducted in the mid-1970s in twelve sites across the United States, the National Supported Work Demonstration used random assignment to evaluate voluntary training and assisted work programs targeted at four groups of individuals with serious barriers to employment: long-term recipients of Aid to Families with Dependent Children (AFDC), which was the federal cash welfare program until 1996; former drug addicts; former criminal offenders; and young school dropouts.[5] Data from the demonstration formed the basis of an extensive series of investigations of nonexperimental methods that used comparison groups drawn from two national surveys: the Current Population Survey and the Panel Study of Income Dynamics (LaLonde 1986; Fraker and Maynard 1987; Heckman and Hotz 1989; Dehejia and Wahba 1999; and Smith and Todd 2005).

In the early to mid-1980s, state welfare-to-work demonstrations were conducted in several sites to evaluate mandatory employment, training, and education programs for welfare recipients. Data from four of these randomized experiments were used to test nonexperimental impact estimation methods based on comparison groups drawn from three sources: earlier cohorts of welfare recipients from the same local welfare offices, welfare recipients from other local offices in the same state, and welfare recipients from other states (Friedlander and Robins 1995). The four experiments were the Arkansas WORK Program, the Baltimore Options Program, the San Diego Saturation Work Initiative Model, and the Virginia Employment Services Program.

The AFDC Homemaker–Home Health Aide Demonstrations used random assignment to evaluate voluntary training and subsidized work programs for welfare recipients in seven states (Arkansas, Kentucky, New Jersey, New York, Ohio, South Carolina, and Texas) in the mid- to late 1980s. Data from these experiments were used to test nonexperimental impact estimation methods based on comparison groups composed of applicants who did not participate in the program because they withdrew before completing the program intake process (labeled "withdrawals"), were judged by intake staff to be unsuitable for the program ("screen-outs"), or were selected for the program but did not show up ("no-shows"; Bell et al. 1995).

In the National Job Training Partnership Act (JTPA) Study, random assignment was used to test a nationwide voluntary employment and training program created by federal legislation in 1982 for economically disadvantaged adults and youth (Bloom et al. 1997). In four of the sixteen study sites—Corpus Christi, Texas; Fort Wayne, Indiana; Jersey City, New Jersey; and Providence, Rhode Island—there was a nonexperimental research component in which data were collected for a comparison group of people who lived in the area served by the program and met its eligibility requirements but did not participate in it. This information formed the foundation of a detailed exploration of comparison-group methods by James J. Heckman and colleagues (see, for example, Heckman, Ichimura, and Todd 1997, 1998; Heckman et al. 1998).

Though limited to employment and training programs, the methodological research that has grown out of these four experiments is based on data spanning a lengthy time period (from the 1970s to the 1990s); many geographic areas representing different labor markets; voluntary as well as mandatory programs (the characteristics of whose participants probably reflect considerably different selection processes); a wide variety of comparison groups, including national survey samples, out-of-state welfare populations, in-state welfare populations, people who were eligible for the program but did not participate (most of whom did not even apply), and program applicants who ended up not participating; and a vast array of statistical and econometric methods for estimating program effects using comparison groups. As discussed below, the evidence on the effectiveness of such methods is at best mixed.

The National Supported Work Demonstration   The main conclusions from the benchmarking research based on the National Supported Work Demonstration are expressed here in terms of two points and counter-points.

Point 1: Nonexperimental methods can produce impact estimates that are ambiguous or misleading. The first two investigations of nonexperimental methods using data from the National Supported Work Demonstration highlighted the large biases that can arise from matching and modeling using comparison groups from a national survey, which was common practice at the time:

> This comparison shows that many of the econometric procedures do not replicate the experimentally determined results, and it suggests that researchers should be aware of the potential for specification errors in other nonexperimental evaluations. (LaLonde 1986, 604)

> The results indicate that nonexperimental designs cannot be relied on to estimate the effectiveness of employment programs. Impact estimates tend to be sensitive both to the comparison group construction methodology and to the analytic model used. (Fraker and Maynard 1987, 194)

This bleak prognosis was reinforced by the inconsistent findings obtained around the same time from nonexperimental evaluations of the federal employment and training program funded under the Comprehensive Employment and Training Act of 1973. Though conducted by different researchers, these evaluations addressed the same impact questions and used the same data sources. Unfortunately, the answers obtained depended crucially on the methods used. As Barnow (1987, 190) concluded in a review of the nonexperimental studies, "Experiments appear to be the only method available at this time to overcome the limitations of nonexperimental evaluations."

Coupled with the disconcerting methodological results obtained by Robert J. LaLonde (1986) and Thomas M. Fraker and Rebecca A. Maynard (1987), these ambiguous evaluation findings led a special advisory panel appointed by the U.S. Department of Labor to recommend that the evaluation of JTPA, which was still in the planning stage, be conducted using random assignment and include a component designed to develop and test nonexperimental methods (Stromsdorfer et al. 1985). These recommendations shaped the design of the National Job Training Partnership Act Study (Bloom et al. 1997).

Another factor that contributed to this decision was an influential report issued by the National Academy of Sciences decrying the lack of knowledge about the effectiveness of youth employment programs despite the investment of millions of dollars in nonexperimental studies of them (Commission on Behavioral and Social Sciences and Education 1985). The general lack of conclusive evidence about employment and training programs had been recognized much earlier by, for example, Jon Goldstein (1972): "The robust expenditures for research and evaluation of training programs ($179.4 million from fiscal 1962 through 1972) are a disturbing contrast to the anemic set of conclusive and reliable findings" (14). The dearth of evidence—numerous nonexperimental evaluations notwithstanding—prompted Orley Ashenfelter (1974), among others, to call for experimental evaluations of employment and training programs: "Still, there will never be a substitute for a carefully designed study using experimental methods, and there is no reason why this could not still be carried out" (12).

Counterpoint 1: Accurate nonexperimental impact estimates are possible, provided one is careful to separate the wheat from the chaff. In response to the preceding negative assessments, Heckman and V. Joseph Hotz (1989) argued that systematic tests of the assumptions underlying nonexperimental methods, known as *specification tests*, can help invalidate methods that are likely to be affected by selection bias and help validate methods that are not. Their goal was to use such tests to reduce the range of nonexperimental impact estimates worthy of serious consideration to those based on methods shown to have successfully approximated experimental findings. In the area of employment and training programs, most of these specification tests use baseline earnings data to assess how well a nonexperimental method balances program-group members' and comparison-group members' earnings before the study began. Although this approach had been proposed more than a decade earlier by Ashenfelter (1974), Heckman and Hotz's (1989) use of it was more comprehensive, systematic, and formal than any previous application (for example, LaLonde 1986; Fraker and Maynard 1987). Based on their empirical analyses, the authors concluded:

> A reanalysis of the National Supported Work Demonstration data previously analyzed by proponents of social experiments reveals that a simple testing procedure eliminates the range of nonexperimental estimators at variance with the experimental estimates of program impact. . . . Our evidence tempers the recent pessimism about nonexperimental evaluation

procedures that has become common in the evaluation community. (Heckman and Hotz 1989, 862, 863)

An important limitation of the specification test approach is its inability to account for changes in personal circumstances that can affect outcomes after the study begins. Thus, in a later analysis (discussed below) of data from the National JTPA Study, Heckman, Hidehiko Ichimura, and Petra Todd (1997, 629) concluded, "It is, therefore, not a safe strategy to use pre-programme tests about mean selection bias to make inferences about post-programme selection bias, as proposed by Heckman and Hotz (1989)."

The other types of specification tests proposed by Heckman and Hotz (1989) can be used if the amount of data available exceeds that needed to estimate the parameters of a model. In that case, the model can be estimated in several different ways to find out how sensitive the estimates are to which data are used (for example, to test whether the estimates change when an additional year of earnings history is added). Because there are seldom enough data "left over" for specification tests, however, this approach often cannot be applied.

The limitations of specification tests notwithstanding, when performing a nonexperimental analysis, one generally ought to test the sensitivity of the results to the specification of the method and the validity of the assumptions underlying the method. In this sense, specification tests set necessary (but not sufficient) conditions for establishing the validity of empirical findings.

Point 2: When longitudinal baseline outcome data are available, propensity score balancing might offer a ray of hope. Rajeev H. Dehejia and Sadek Wahba (1999) suggested that propensity-score balancing methods developed by Rosenbaum and Rubin (1983) are sometimes more effective than parametric models at controlling for observed differences between the program group and the comparison group, at least when more than one year of baseline outcome data are available. The authors supported these suggestions with an empirical analysis focusing on a subset of LaLonde's (1986) sample of adult men for whom earnings data pertaining to the two years before the study began are available. Using propensity-score methods to balance the program and comparison groups with respect to these earnings measures and a number of other covariates, Dehejia and Wahba obtained impact estimates close to the experimental benchmark:

> We apply propensity score methods to this composite dataset and demonstrate that, relative to the estimators that LaLonde evaluates, propensity score estimates of the treatment impact are much closer to the experimental benchmark. . . . This illustrates the importance of a suffi-

ciently lengthy preintervention earnings history for training programs. . . .
We conclude that when the treatment and comparison groups overlap,
and when the variables determining assignment to treatment are observed, these methods provide a means to estimate the treatment impact.
(Dehejia and Wahba 1999, 1053, 1061, 1062)

These encouraging findings and the authors' plausible explanations
for them have drawn widespread attention among social scientists and
evaluation researchers. This interest, which has inspired many new ex-
plorations and applications of propensity-score methods, including
further study by Dehejia and Wahba (2002), was a principal motivation
for the present analysis.

*Counterpoint 2: High expectations of propensity-score methods may rest on
a fragile empirical foundation.* Based on a reanalysis of the data used by
Dehejia and Wahba (1999) to assess the sensitivity of their findings, Jeffrey Smith and Petra Todd (2005) argue that the favorable performance
of propensity-score methods documented by Dehejia and Wahba is an
artifact of the sample used:

> We find that the low bias estimates obtained by [Dehejia and Wahba] us-
> ing various cross-sectional matching estimators are highly sensitive to
> their choice of a particular subsample of LaLonde's (1986) data for their
> analysis. We also find that changing the set of variables used to estimate
> the propensity scores strongly affects the estimated bias in LaLonde's
> original sample. . . . More generally, our findings make it clear that
> propensity score matching does not represent a "magic bullet" that
> solves the selection problem in every context. . . . The optimal nonexper-
> imental evaluation strategy in a given context depends critically on the
> available data and on the institutions governing selection into the pro-
> gram. (Smith and Todd 2005, 306, 307)

To understand Smith and Todd's argument, consider the samples
at issue. Originally, LaLonde's (1986) adult male sample included 297
program-group members and 425 control-group members. Only one
year of baseline earnings data were available for everyone in this sample. To restrict their analysis to men with at least two years of baseline
earnings data, Dehejia and Wahba (1999) applied two criteria, obtaining a sample composed of 185 program-group members and 260
control-group members. Because of their concerns about one of these
criteria, Smith and Todd (2005) used a simpler approach, obtaining
a sample of 108 program-group members and 142 control-group
members. Smith and Todd then tested a broad range of new and existing propensity-score methods on all three samples and found that only
for Dehejia and Wahba's (1999) subsample do the findings from
propensity-score methods emulate the experimental findings. This sen-

sitivity to the specific sample analyzed casts doubt on the generalizability of the earlier results.

Recall that all these findings are based on comparison groups drawn from national survey samples. Despite their ready availability and low cost, such comparison groups pose serious challenges owing to program-comparison mismatches with respect to geography (and thus macroenvironmental conditions), sociodemographics (and thus individual differences in background, motivation, ability, and so on), and data sources and measures. The other three studies reviewed in this section focus on comparison groups drawn from sources that are closer to home.

State Welfare-to-Work Demonstrations   Daniel Friedlander and Philip K. Robins (1995) benchmarked nonexperimental methods using data from a series of large-scale random-assignment studies of mandatory welfare-to-work programs in four states. To avoid comparing earnings across areas with different costs of living, the authors focused on employment rates (instead of earnings) during the third quarter and the sixth through the ninth quarters after random assignment. Their basic analytic strategy was to estimate the programs' impacts on employment rates using the (randomly selected) control group in one location or time period as a nonexperimental comparison group for program groups in other locations or time periods. They assessed the quality of the impact estimates using not propensity-score matching but rather OLS regressions and a matching procedure called Mahalanobis matching, whereby individuals are matched directly on the basis of their characteristics rather than their propensity scores.

Friedlander and Robins's (1995) focus on welfare recipients is directly relevant to a large, active field of evaluation research. Furthermore, their approach to choosing comparison groups closely follows evaluation designs that have been used in the past and are candidates for use in the future. The evaluation problem they addressed may be easier than others to tackle, however, for two reasons. First, mandatory programs eliminate the role of client self-selection and, by extension, the need to model this factor. Second, because welfare recipients are a fairly homogeneous group relative to participants in other employment-related services, they may be easier to match.

Each comparison group used by Friedlander and Robins (1995) was drawn from one of three sources: earlier cohorts of welfare recipients from the same welfare offices, welfare recipients from other offices in the same state, and welfare recipients from other states. The estimated effect for each comparison group was compared with its experimental counterpart. Although the authors acknowledged the inherent limitations of specification tests, they used tests of the type proposed by Heckman and Hotz (1989) to assess each method's ability to remove baseline employment differences between the program and comparison groups.

Friedlander and Robins (1995) found that in-state comparison groups worked better than did out-of-state comparison groups, although both were problematic. Furthermore, they found that the specification tests did not adequately distinguish between good and bad estimators. They concluded:

> The results of our study illustrate the risks involved in comparing the behavior of individuals residing in two different geographic areas. Comparisons across state lines are particularly problematic . . . . When we switched the comparison from across states to within a state we did note some improvement, but inaccuracies still remained . . . . Overall, the specification test was more effective in eliminating wildly inaccurate "outlier" estimates than in pinpointing the most accurate nonexperimental estimates. (Friedlander and Robins 1995, 935)

The AFDC Homemaker–Home Health Aide Demonstrations   Another way to construct comparison groups is to select individuals who applied for a program but did not participate in it. This strategy facilitates matching of program- and comparison-group members with respect to geography and individual characteristics. It also helps ensure that comparable data on the same outcomes are available.

Stephen H. Bell et al. (1995) tested this approach using data from the AFDC Homemaker–Home Health Aide Demonstrations. Specifically, they compared experimental estimates of program effects with estimates obtained from OLS regressions (without matching) based on comparison groups composed of one of three types of program applicants: withdrawals, screen-outs, or no-shows. Program effects on average earnings in each of the six years after random assignment were estimated for each comparison group, permitting an assessment of selection bias for a lengthy follow-up period. In addition, data were collected on staff assessments of applicants' (and participants') suitability for the program. Because the suitability index was used to screen out potential participants, it provided a way to model participant selection and thus to reduce selection bias.

The authors found that, relative to experimentally derived impact estimates, the estimates based on the no-show comparison group were the most accurate, those based on the screen-out comparison group were the next most accurate, and those based on the withdrawal comparison group were the least accurate. Moreover, the accuracy of the estimates based on screen-outs improved over time, from being only slightly better than those for withdrawals at the beginning of the follow-up period to being almost as good as those for no-shows at the end.

To ground the interpretation of the findings in the framework of public policymaking, the authors addressed the question of how close nonexperimental impact estimates have to be to experimental estimates for their use in government program evaluations to be justified. Applying this framework to their findings, they concluded:

> On the basis of the evidence presented here, none of the applicant groups yielded estimates close enough to the experimental benchmark to justify the claim that it provides an adequate substitute for an experimental control group. . . . Nevertheless, there are several reasons for believing that the screen-out and no-show groups could potentially provide a nonexperimental method for evaluating training programs that yields reliable and unbiased impact estimates. . . . We conclude that further tests of the methodology should be undertaken, using other experimental data sets. (Bell et al. 1995, 109)

The National Job Training Partnership Act Study   Heckman and colleagues conducted the most comprehensive, detailed, and technically sophisticated assessment of nonexperimental comparison-group methods for measuring program effects. Based on a special data set constructed for the National Job Training Partnership Act Study, their results are reported for each of four target groups of voluntary JTPA participants: male adults, female adults, male youth, and female youth (for details, see Heckman, Ichimura, and Todd 1997, 1998; Heckman et al. 1998).

Heckman and colleagues extensively tested a broad range of propensity-score methods and econometric models. They assessed both the ability of the methods to emulate experimental findings and the validity of their underlying assumptions. They developed and tested extensions of several statistical procedures: kernel-based matching and local linear matching. These methods compare outcomes for control-group members with a weighted average of the outcomes for comparison-group members; the weights are set according to the similarity between the two groups' propensity scores. They also used various combinations of matching with econometric models, including a matched fixed-effects estimator.

The analytic approach to benchmarking used by Heckman and colleagues differs from but is consistent with that used by other researchers. Rather than comparing program impact estimates based on nonexperimental comparison groups with estimates based on experimental control groups, as had been done previously, they compared outcomes for each comparison group with those for its control-group counterpart. Doing so enabled them to observe directly how closely the nonexperimental comparison group approximates the experimental counterfactual using different statistical and econometric methods.

Applying this strategy, the authors decomposed selection bias, as conventionally defined, into three fundamentally different and intuitively meaningful components: bias owing to the inclusion of control-group members who have no counterparts with similar observable characteristics in the comparison group and of comparison-group members who have no counterparts with similar observable characteristics in the control group (in other words, comparing the wrong people), bias owing to differential representation of observationally similar people in the two groups (comparing the right people in the wrong proportions), and bias owing to unobserved differences between people with similar observable characteristics (the most difficult component of selection bias to eliminate). Although the three components had been recognized by other researchers (for example, LaLonde 1986; Dehejia and Wahba 1999), Heckman and colleagues were the first to produce separate estimates of their effects.

Heckman and colleagues based their analyses on data from the four sites in the National JTPA Study. Neighborhood surveys were fielded to collect baseline and follow-up information on samples of local residents who met the JTPA eligibility criteria but were not in the program. The benefits of using these eligible nonparticipants for comparison groups are that they match the experimental sample with respect to geography and program eligibility and that the data and measures collected for them and for comparison-group members are comparable.

Although eligible nonparticipants were the primary source of comparison groups, Heckman and colleagues also examined comparison groups drawn from a national survey (the Survey of Income and Program Participation) and from the sample of no-shows in the four JTPA sites. In their benchmarking analyses, the outcome measure used to compare nonexperimental and experimental estimators was average earnings during the eighteen months after random assignment.

Heckman and colleagues' main findings and conclusions, which generally reinforce those of previous researchers, are the following (for details, see Heckman, Ichimura, and Todd 1997):

- For the samples examined, most of the selection bias was attributable to comparing the wrong people and comparing the right people in the wrong proportions. Only a small fraction was attributable to unobserved individual differences, although such differences can be problematic.

- Choosing a comparison group from the same local labor market and for which comparable measures from a common data source are available markedly improves program impact estimates.

- Baseline data on recent labor market experiences are important.

- For the samples examined, the method that performed best overall was a fixed-effects estimator conditioned on matched propensity scores.

- For nonexperimental impact estimates to be valid, both high-quality data and rigorous methods are required. In Heckman, Ichimura, and Todd's (1997, 607) words: "This paper emphasizes the interplay between data and method. Both matter in evaluating the impact of training on earnings. . . . The effectiveness of any econometric estimator is limited by the quality of the data to which it is applied, and no programme evaluation method 'works' in all settings."

Within-Study Comparisons of Impact Estimates for Education Programs

To expand the base of substantive knowledge about whether nonexperimental comparison-group methods can replicate experimental findings, two recent benchmarking studies explored the ability of comparison-group methods to replicate experimental estimates of the impacts of voluntary education programs. One study (Agodini and Dynarski 2004), based on a multisite experimental evaluation of school dropout programs, focused on the ability of comparison-group methods to replicate experimental estimates of program effects on dropout rates and hypothesized antecedents thereof (such as self-esteem, education aspirations, and absenteeism) for students in middle school and high school. The other study (Wilde and Hollister 2002), based on an experimental study of class size conducted in Tennessee, focused on the ability of comparison-group methods to replicate experimental estimates of program impacts on achievement outcomes for students in the early grades of elementary school. Both studies yielded conclusions similar to those from employment and training experiments.

The School Dropout Prevention Experiment   Roberto Agodini and Mark Dynarski (2004) compared experimental estimates of impacts for dropout prevention programs in eight middle schools and eight high schools with alternative nonexperimental estimates. Comparison groups were drawn from the National Educational Longitudinal Study and from comparison schools in locations other than those examined in the experiment. Using extensive baseline data, the authors tested propensity-score matching methods, standard OLS regression models, and fixed-effects models. They also performed specification tests of the propensity-score matches to determine which of them produced acceptable comparison groups. Through these analyses, Agodini and Dynarski (2004) found:

- Most of the comparison groups did not pass the specification test: "We could only identify a well-matched comparison group for six of the sixteen treatment groups" (188).

- Even the comparison groups that passed the specification test did not reliably replicate the experimental impact estimates: "Among the programs for which we could identify a comparison group that is well matched to its treatment group, there are only scattered instances in which the experimental and propensity-score impacts are similar" (180).

- OLS regression methods performed no better (or worse) than propensity score methods: "We also find that impacts based on regression methods . . . are not any more capable of replicating experimental impacts in this setting than are propensity score methods" (192).

The Tennessee Class-Size Experiment   Elizabeth Ty Wilde and Robinson Hollister (2002) compared experimental and nonexperimental estimates of the impacts on student achievement of reducing class size from the standard range of twenty-two to twenty-five students to a range of thirteen to seventeen students. The analysis was based on data for the eleven of the seventy-nine schools in the experiment that had at least one hundred kindergarten students. Each school had randomly assigned individual students and teachers to classes of reduced size (the program group) or to classes of standard size (the control group). To create a nonexperimental comparison group for each of the eleven schools, Wilde and Hollister (2002) used propensity-score methods to find matches for the school's program-group students in the pooled sample of control-group students in the other ten schools. The authors also compared experimental impact estimates with nonexperimental estimates obtained from OLS regression methods without propensity-score matching. Having considered several alternative frameworks for assessing how close is close enough in comparisons of experimental and nonexperimental impact estimates, the authors found:

- Propensity-score methods did not reliably replicate the experimental findings: "We found that in most cases, the propensity-score estimate of the impact differed substantially from the 'true impact' estimated by the experiment" (32).

- The policy implications of the propensity-score findings often conflicted with those of the experimental findings: "We found that in 35 to 45 percent of the 11 cases where we had used propensity score matching for the nonexperimental estimate, it would have led to the 'wrong decision,' i.e., a decision about whether to invest which was different from the decision based on the experimental estimates" (32).

- Standard regression methods performed about as well as propensity-score matching: "Somewhat to our surprise, the propensity-score matched estimator did not perform notably better than the multiple-regression-corrected estimators for most of the 11 cases" (33).

Cross-Study Comparisons of Impact Estimates Using Meta-Analysis

An alternative to conducting within-study comparisons of experimental and nonexperimental impact estimates is to summarize and contrast findings from experimental and nonexperimental studies. This cross-study approach to benchmarking grows out of the field of meta-analysis, a term coined by Gene V. Glass (1976) to refer to a systematic, quantitative method of synthesizing results from multiple studies on the same topic. A central concern for meta-analysis is the quality of the studies being synthesized, and an important criterion of quality is whether random assignment was used. Hence, a number of meta-analyses, beginning with Mary Lee Smith, Glass, and Thomas I. Miller (1980), have compared summaries of findings based on experimental studies with summaries based on nonexperimental studies, yielding mixed results (Heinsman and Shadish 1996, 155).

The most extensive such comparison was a meta-analysis of meta-analyses in which Mark W. Lipsey and David B. Wilson (1993) synthesized earlier research on the effectiveness of psychological, education, and behavior treatments. In part of their analysis, they compared the means and standard deviations of experimental and nonexperimental impact estimates from seventy-four meta-analyses for which findings from both types of studies were available. Representing hundreds of primary studies, this comparison revealed little difference between the mean effect estimated on the basis of experimental studies and that estimated on the basis of nonexperimental studies: the estimated mean effect size, a standardized measure of treatment impact, was 0.46 for experimental studies and 0.41 for nonexperimental studies. The standard deviation of the impact estimates was somewhat larger for nonexperimental studies (0.36) than for experimental ones (0.28; Lipsey and Wilson 1993, table 2). In addition, some of the meta-analyses found a large difference between the average experimental and nonexperimental impact estimates for a given type of treatment. Because these differences were as often positive as negative, they canceled out across the seventy-four meta-analyses. Lipsey and Wilson (1993, 1193) concluded:

These various comparisons do not indicate that it makes no difference to the validity of treatment effect estimates if a primary study uses random versus nonrandom assignment. What these comparisons do indicate is that there is no strong pattern or bias in the direction of the difference made by lower quality methods. . . . In some treatment areas, therefore, nonrandom designs (relative to random) tend to strongly underestimate effects, and in others, they tend to strongly overestimate effects.

Implications

By highlighting important issues, the findings in the foregoing literature review served to guide both the selection of and the approach to assessing the nonexperimental methods used in this chapter.

With respect to selecting nonexperimental methods to assess, the methods that are most likely to successfully replicate an experiment should be chosen. The most successful methods generally have the following ingredients: local comparison groups of individuals from the same economic or institutional settings (Bell et al. 1995; Friedlander and Robins 1995; Heckman, Ichimura, and Todd 1997); comparable outcome measures from a common data source (Heckman, Ichimura, and Todd 1997); longitudinal data on baseline outcomes (Heckman, Ichimura, and Todd 1997; Dehejia and Wahba 1999); and a nonparametric way to choose comparison-group members who are observationally similar to program-group members and to eliminate those who are not (Heckman, Ichimura, and Todd 1997; Dehejia and Wahba 1999).

Taken together, the assessments of nonexperimental methods reviewed here suggest the following guidelines:

- *Replicate the assessment for as many samples and situations as possible.* Only a small number of randomized experiments have been used to assess nonexperimental methods for evaluating employment and training programs, and most of these studies are based on the experiences of a few hundred people in a single experiment conducted almost three decades ago (the National Supported Work Demonstration). In addition, only two random-assignment studies have been used to assess nonexperimental methods for evaluating education programs. Thus, a broader foundation of evidence is needed.

- *Conduct the assessment for as long a follow-up period as possible.* Because employment and training programs and education programs represent a substantial investment in human capital, it is important to measure their returns over a sufficiently long period. The same is undoubtedly true of other social policies. The policy relevance of doing so is reflected in the strong interest in reports of long-term follow-up findings from several major experiments (Couch 1992; Hotz, Imbens, and Klerman 2000; and Hamilton et al. 2001).

- *Consider a broad range of matching and modeling procedures.* Statisticians, econometricians, and evaluation methodologists have developed many different approaches to measuring program effects, and debates about these approaches are heated and complex. Any further analysis should fully address the many points at issue.

- *Use a summary measure that accounts for the possibility that large biases in individual studies may cancel out across studies.* The meta-analyses described indicate that although biases can be problematic for a given evaluation, they may cancel out across evaluations. Thus, to assess nonexperimental methods, it is important to use a summary statistic, such as the mean absolute bias, that does not mask substantial biases through averaging.

A New Look at Comparison-Group Methods

The remainder of the chapter measures the selection bias resulting from nonexperimental comparison-group methods by benchmarking them against the randomized experiments that made up the National Evaluation of Welfare-to-Work Strategies (NEWWS), a six-state, seven-site evaluation that investigated different program approaches to moving welfare recipients to work. It collected extensive, detailed baseline information and outcome data for several large samples of research subjects over an unusually long follow-up period (five years). Random assignment was performed separately in each of the seven sites, and the program approaches under study varied from site to site.

In the present analysis, a nonexperimental comparison group was constructed for each site by drawing on control-group members from within the same site or from other sites. Applying this strategy (used by Friedlander and Robins 1995) to the NEWWS data allowed us to assess a wide range of nonexperimental impact estimators for different comparison-group sources, analytic methods, baseline data configurations, and follow-up periods. As already noted, there are two equivalent approaches to assessing these estimators.

In one approach, the nonexperimental impact estimate for a given program group is compared with the experimental impact estimate obtained using the control group. This comparison captures the extent to which the nonexperimental impact estimate deviates from the experimental impact estimate. In the other approach, the outcome for the comparison group—estimated using whatever statistical methods would have been applied for the program impact estimate—is compared with the observed outcome for the experimental control group. This comparison captures the extent to which the counterfactual used in the nonexperimental approach deviates from the experimental counterfactual.

Because the experimental impact estimate is simply the difference between the observed outcome for the program group and that for the control group (the counterfactual), the difference between the experimental and nonexperimental impact estimates amounts to the difference between their estimates of the counterfactual. To see why, consider that the experimental impact estimate equals the difference between the mean outcome for the program group and that for the control group $(\overline{Y}_p - \overline{Y}_{cx})$. The nonexperimental impact estimate equals the difference between the mean outcome for the program group and that for the comparison group $(\overline{Y}_p - \overline{Y}_{cnx})$. The difference between these two estimates, $(\overline{Y}_p - \overline{Y}_{cnx}) - (\overline{Y}_p - \overline{Y}_{cx})$, simplifies to $(\overline{Y}_{cx} - \overline{Y}_{cnx})$, which is the difference between the experimental and nonexperimental estimates of the counterfactual.

To simplify the analysis, we assess the ability of nonexperimental comparison-group methods to emulate experimental counterfactuals rather than experimental impact estimates. Thus, we compare nonexperimental comparison-group outcomes with their control-group counterparts, as did Heckman and colleagues.

It is important to keep in mind that the present benchmarking analysis focuses on a program in which people were obliged to participate (like that examined by Friedlander and Robins 1995). The selection processes for mandatory programs differ in important ways from those for programs that are voluntary. Indeed, it could be argued that because self-selection plays no role in mandatory programs (unlike in voluntary programs), selection bias is easier to address and eliminate in studies of mandatory programs. Nevertheless, as we show, selection bias appears to be a problem for nonexperimental comparison-group methods even in this favorable context.

Program Setting

The programs whose control groups we examined operated under the rules of the Job Opportunity and Basic Skills (JOBS) program created by the Family Support Act of 1988. Under JOBS, all single-parent recipients of cash welfare whose youngest child was three or older (or one or older, at the state's discretion) were required to participate in a welfare-to-work program. JOBS was designed to help states reach hard-to-serve people, some of whom had fallen through the cracks of earlier programs.

NEWWS tested eleven mandatory welfare-to-work programs that were created or adapted to fit the provisions of JOBS. The programs were operated in seven metropolitan sites: Atlanta; Columbus, Ohio;

Detroit; Grand Rapids; Oklahoma City; Portland, Oregon; and Riverside, California. In four sites two different programs were run. In Atlanta, Grand Rapids, and Riverside, the two were a job-search-first program that emphasized getting people connected to jobs quickly and an education-first program that emphasized providing basic education and training before job search. In Columbus, two types of case management, traditional and integrated, were tested. In the traditional approach, some staff members took charge of checking eligibility for benefits, while others managed program participation. In the integrated approach, the same welfare case manager performed both functions for a given individual (Hamilton and Brock 1994; Hamilton et al. 2001).

The program in Portland assigned a large proportion of participants to look for work and a large proportion of others to get further education or training. The programs in Detroit and Oklahoma City, like the education-first programs in Atlanta, Grand Rapids, and Riverside, prioritized providing education services over job-search assistance.

In the four sites that operated two programs, people were randomly assigned to one of the two program groups or to a control group that remained in AFDC, the traditional welfare program at the time. In the other three sites, people were randomly assigned to the program group or to a control group. NEWWS included a total of 41,715 cash welfare recipients and applicants, about 95 percent of them women.

Columbus was the only site not included in our analysis because the requisite two years of baseline earnings data were not available. In five of the six sites analyzed, random assignment took place at the JOBS program orientation. In Oklahoma City, random assignment occurred when individuals applied for welfare; thus, some Oklahoma City sample members never attended a JOBS orientation, and some never received welfare payments (Hamilton et al. 2001).

Analysis Sample

Two factors, gender and program status, were used to determine which NEWWS sample members would be included in the present analysis. Instead of conducting separate analyses for men and women, as is standard practice in labor economics, we analyzed data only for women because they represent the overwhelming majority of the sample and because there were too few men to allow us to conduct a separate analysis for them. Regarding program status, only control-group members—13,729 in NEWWS, excluding Columbus—were included in the analysis for the reasons already discussed. Although restricting the sample to control-group members was straightforward, it makes references to control groups potentially ambiguous because everyone included is a control-group member. We therefore reserve the term "control group" for the benchmark group for each comparison and refer to the group used to emulate the counterfactual for the benchmark group as its comparison group. The results of two types of comparisons between control and comparison groups are reported: in-state comparisons, those with control-group members drawn from local welfare offices in the same site or the same state, and out-of-state comparisons and multistate comparisons, those with control-group members drawn from different states.

In-State Comparison Groups   The first part of our analysis examines control groups and comparison groups drawn from different welfare-to-work offices in the same state, usually in the same county or in neighboring counties. Local comparison groups were considered promising for two reasons. First, previous research suggests that they are more likely than other groups to face similar job markets (see, for example, Friedlander and Robins 1995; Heckman, Ichimura, and Todd 1997, 1998). Second, it may be easier for evaluators to collect data from the same or a nearby location.

In the four NEWWS sites with multiple local offices (Detroit, Oklahoma City, Portland, and Riverside), the offices were aggregated into one control group and one comparison group per site on the basis of geographic proximity. This process allowed for four analyses of in-state comparison groups. A fifth analysis compared the only two sites located in the same state, Grand Rapids and Detroit. Table 5.1 lists the offices and the sample sizes involved.

Additional in-state analyses could have been produced by using different combinations of local offices in each site or by redefining each site's control group as its comparison group and each site's comparison group as its control group. We restricted our in-state analysis to the five comparisons in table 5.1 to produce replications that were independent, except for the use of Detroit's Hamtramck office in two comparisons. The in-state comparison groups were geographically close to their control-group counterparts, but some of them probably faced different labor markets and thus could have reflected different site effects, for which it is difficult to control.

Out-of-State and Multistate Comparison Groups   Although previous research suggests that local comparison groups produce the least selection bias, comparison groups from another state or a national survey sample may be more feasible or less costly for some evaluations. We examined two types of such comparison groups.

To construct out-of-state comparison groups, we used the entire control group in one site as a comparison group for the entire control group in another site. Fourteen such comparisons were possible. For each pair

Table 5.1   In-State Control and Comparison Groups

In-State Comparison	Control Group Offices	Control Group Sample Size	Comparison Group Offices	Comparison Group Sample Size
Oklahoma City	Cleveland Pottawatomie	831	Southwest City Southeast City Central City	3,184
Detroit	Fullerton	955	Hamtramck	1,187
Riverside	Riverside	1,459	Hemet, Rancho, Elsinore	1,501
Michigan	Grand Rapids	1,390	Detroit (Fullerton and Hamtramck)	2,142
Portland, Ore.	West Office	328	East Office North Office	1,019

Source: Calculations by the authors from National Evaluation of Welfare-to-Work Strategies data.

of sites, only one of the two permutations was used. (For example, in the comparison of Riverside and Portland, Riverside was used as the control group and Portland was used as the comparison group, but not vice versa.) This is because estimates of bias for statistical methods that do not use propensity scores—that is, difference of means, OLS regressions, fixed-effects models, and random-growth models—are identical for the two permutations except with respect to their sign. Estimates of bias for all other statistical methods may differ in magnitude for each site pair but should yield similar results.

The first step in defining the out-of-state comparisons was to choose one site at random (Riverside) as the first control group. Each of the remaining five sites was then used as a nonexperimental comparison group for Riverside. The next step was to choose one of the remaining sites at random (Portland) as the second comparison group. Each of the four remaining sites was then used as a nonexperimental comparison group for Portland. This process was repeated until the final out-of-state comparison, Atlanta versus Oklahoma City, was chosen.

The multistate analysis consisted of six separate subanalyses. To construct multistate comparison groups, each of the subanalyses used one site as a control group and the other five sites as a composite comparison group for that analysis. This approach pools information about clients across states, which may be particularly useful for some nonexperimental methods.

Data Used

Data came from two sources: the unemployment insurance system in each state and information collected by welfare staff before and at random assignment.

Earnings and Employment   State unemployment insurance records provide information on quarterly earnings and employment for each sample member. Quarterly earnings data are available for a five-year period following the calendar quarter of random assignment. These data are also available for a pre-random-assignment baseline period of at least two years for all sample members; for many sample members, three years of baseline data are available. Quarterly earnings were converted into 1996 dollars using the Consumer Price Index for All Urban Consumers (U.S. Department of Labor, Bureau of Labor Statistics 2002).

The top portion of table 5.2, "Earnings and employment," summarizes the baseline earnings and employment experiences of the in-state control and comparison groups. Table 5.3 provides the same information for the out-of-state groups. The tables also list average annual earnings in the short run (during the two years after random assignment) and the medium run (during the third, fourth, and fifth years after random assignment).

Demographic Characteristics   Data on clients' background characteristics were provided by welfare caseworkers at the time of random assignment. This information included, among other characteristics, their education level, the number and ages of their children, and their race and ethnicity. The bottom portions of tables 5.2 and 5.3, "Baseline characteristics," summarize these data, which are included as covariates in the regression models described later in the chapter, for the control groups and the comparison groups separately.

Methods Tested

Our first step in assessing nonexperimental comparison-group methods was to calculate a simple difference in mean outcomes for each in-state, out-of-state, and multistate control-comparison group pair. This difference represents the raw bias that would exist if no statistical adjustment were made.

Bias estimates were then made for each control-comparison group pair using selected combinations of the statistical adjustment methods that have been the most frequently used in previous research on nonexperimental methods: OLS regression, propensity-score balancing using subclassification and one-to-one matching (balancing strategies will be

Table 5.2   Selected Sample Characteristics for In-State Comparison Groups

Outcome or Characteristic	Oklahoma City		Detroit	
	Control	Comparison	Control	Comparison
Earnings and employment				
Mean annual earnings in the two years before random assignment (1996 dollars)	1,314	1,707	1,074	972
Mean number of quarters employed in the two years before random assignment	1.78	2.13	1.41	1.40
Mean annual earnings in the two years after random assignment (1996 dollars)	1,742	1,888	2,080	2,008
Mean annual earnings in the third, fourth, and fifth years after random assignment (1996 dollars)	3,164	3,081	5,042	5,631
Baseline characteristics				
Average age (in years)	28.3	27.6	29.2	30.3
Race or ethnicity (percentage)				
White, non-Hispanic	77.2	52.6	0.7	18.0
Black, non-Hispanic	8.0	35.8	98.1	80.1
Hispanic	2.2	5.3	0.9	0.8
Other	12.7	6.3	0.2	1.1
Percentage with high school diploma or GED	55.5	54.0	58.8	54.4
Percentage never married	22.6	39.9	74.8	64.8
Number of children (percentage)				
One child	47.2	51.8	46.2	40.9
Two children	34.0	29.2	30.0	29.9
Three or more children	18.9	19.0	23.8	29.2
Percentage with a child younger than five years old	65.4	66.7	68.0	63.0
Sample size	831	3,184	955	1,187

Source: Authors' calculations from information collected by welfare staff and earnings reported to state unemployment insurance systems.

Riverside		Michigan		Portland	
Control	Comparison	Control	Comparison	Control	Comparison
2,849	2,470	2,085	1,017	1,909	1,515
2.15	2.16	2.57	1.40	2.25	1.85
2,289	2,382	2,484	2,040	3,096	2,331
4,100	3,526	5,392	5,369	5,538	4,876
31.2	31.6	27.9	29.8	29.7	29.9
46.0	56.3	48.1	10.2	87.4	66.8
22.9	11.1	40.9	88.2	1.8	23.8
27.0	29.6	8.1	0.9	7.1	2.5
4.1	3.1	2.9	0.7	3.7	7.0
65.9	61.6	59.3	56.4	68.3	60.7
37.0	31.3	58.3	69.2	42.4	53.1
39.6	38.1	45.6	43.2	39.1	35.2
31.2	33.8	35.8	30.0	29.4	34.8
29.2	28.1	18.6	26.8	31.5	30.1
58.5	57.7	69.2	65.2	72.2	70.5
1,459	1,501	1,390	2,142	328	1,019

described in detail), fixed-effects models, random-growth models, and least-squares regression weighted by a function of propensity scores. We also report findings for several methods that combine propensity score balancing with fixed effects and random growth models. Although we also estimated selection models that adjust OLS regressions for assumed differences in unobserved characteristics (Gronau 1974; Heckman 1976; 1978), the results are not presented because identification of the models was extremely weak (Bloom et al. 2002, appendix C).

Ordinary Least-Squares Regression   OLS regressions specify the outcome measure as a function of program status and a series of characteristics, or covariates. It is an approach that Heckman and Hotz (1989) called a linear control function. Nonlinearities can be specified through higher-order terms (squares, cubes, and so on), and interactions can be specified through cross-products of covariates. When baseline measures of the outcome are included as covariates, the regression specification is often referred to as an autoregressive model (Ashenfelter 1978). Our OLS regressions had the following specification:

$$Y_i = \alpha + \lambda C_i + \sum_j \beta_j Z_{ij} + \sum_j \gamma_j W_{ij} + \sum_m \delta_m X_{im} + \varepsilon_i, \qquad (5.1)$$

where:

Y_i = earnings for sample member i after random assignment

C_i = 1 if sample member i is in the control group and 0 if sample member i is in the comparison group

Z_{ij} = earnings for sample member i in the jth quarter before random assignment

W_{ij} = 1 if sample member i was employed in the jth quarter before random assignment and 0 otherwise

X_{im} = the mth background characteristic for sample member i

The parameter λ provides an estimate of the selection bias.

Propensity-Score Balancing   Two types of propensity-score balancing methods were used, subclassification and one-to-one matching with replacement. These methods eliminate comparison-group members who are very different from control-group members. Other versions of propensity-score matching were not explored because recent research suggests that the results do not depend strongly on the specific version used (Zhao 2004).[6] Methods of matching that do not use propensity scores were not tested for the same reason.

Table 5.3 Selected Sample Characteristics for Out-of-State Comparison Groups

Outcome or Characteristic	Oklahoma City	Detroit	Riverside	Grand Rapids	Portland	Atlanta
Earnings and employment						
Mean annual earnings in the two years before random assignment (1996 dollars)	1,626	1,017	2,657	2,085	1,611	2,063
Mean number of quarters employed in the two years before random assignment	2.05	1.40	2.15	2.57	1.95	1.98
Mean annual earnings in the two years after random assignment (1996 dollars)	1,858	2,040	2,336	2,484	2,517	2,680
Mean annual earnings in the third, fourth, and fifth years after random assignment (1996 dollars)	3,098	5,369	3,809	5,392	5,037	4,895
Baseline characteristics						
Age (in years)	27.7	29.8	31.4	27.9	29.9	32.5

(Table continues on p. 204.)

Table 5.3 *Continued*

Outcome or Characteristic	Oklahoma City	Detroit	Riverside	Grand Rapids	Portland	Atlanta
Race or ethnicity (percentage)						
White, non-Hispanic	57.7	10.2	51.2	48.1	71.8	4.1
Black, non-Hispanic	30.1	88.2	16.9	40.9	18.4	94.5
Hispanic	4.7	0.9	28.3	8.1	3.6	0.7
Other	7.6	0.7	3.6	2.9	6.2	0.7
Percentage with high school diploma or GED	54.3	56.4	63.8	59.3	62.6	61.2
Percentage never married	36.3	69.2	34.1	58.3	50.5	60.7
Number of children (percentage)						
One child	50.8	43.2	38.8	45.6	36.1	36.0
Two children	30.2	30.0	32.6	35.8	33.4	33.8
Three or more children	18.9	26.8	28.6	18.6	30.4	30.3
Percentage with a child younger than five years old	66.5	65.2	58.1	69.2	70.9	43.2
Sample size	4,015	2,142	2,960	1,390	1,347	1,875

Source: Authors' calculations from information collected by welfare staff and earnings reported to state unemployment insurance systems.
Note: Characteristics are shown only for sample members for whom at least two years of earnings data before random assignment are available.

Subclassification   In the subclassification approach, each sample member is placed in a subclass of sample members with similar propensity scores. The bias within each subclass is estimated as the difference between the control-group outcomes and the comparison-group outcomes for that subclass, and the bias for the full sample is estimated as a weighted average of the subclass biases.

The intuition underlying the subclassification approach is as follows. Because propensity scores are more similar within subclasses than within the full sample, covariates tend to be better balanced within subclasses. Thus, when estimates are computed for each subclass, the individuals being compared are more similar to each other than they would be if the entire control group and the entire comparison group were compared.

The subclassification process involved four basic steps: a propensity score was computed for each sample member; subclasses were formed based on the quintile distribution of the control group's propensity scores; each comparison-group member was placed in the appropriate subclass; and the subclasses were checked for balance. If balance was achieved, then the selection bias was estimated. If balance was not achieved, a series of supplementary steps was taken to attempt to balance the subclasses. We now describe in detail the four basic steps, the supplementary steps, and how selection bias was estimated.

The first step in the subclassification process was to estimate a logistic regression of the factors predicting membership in the control group (as opposed to membership in the comparison group) from the pooled sample for the two groups.[7] This model was used to convert each sample member's individual characteristics into a propensity score.

The second step was to create subclasses of sample members with similar propensity scores, which began with the creation of five subclasses based on the quintile distribution of the control group's propensity scores. In the third step, comparison-group members whose propensity scores lay outside this range were dropped from further analysis, and the rest were placed in the appropriate subclass. All control-group members were kept in the analysis.

In the fourth step, the following regression model was estimated for each subclass to determine whether the background characteristics of its control-group members and comparison-group members were balanced:

$$C_i = \alpha + \sum_j \beta_j Z_{ij} + \sum_j \gamma_j W_{ij} + \sum_m \delta_m X_{im} + \varepsilon_i, \tag{5.2}$$

where the variables are defined as in equation 5.1.

The parameter β_j indicates how earnings in the jth quarter before random assignment predict control-group membership; the parameter γ_j indicates how employment status in the jth quarter before random assignment predicts control-group membership; and the parameter δ_m indicates how the mth demographic characteristic predicts control-group membership. The overall F-test for the model tests the joint null hypothesis that all its parameters except the intercept equal 0 and thus that none of the background characteristics in the model have any predictive power. In this context, nonrejection of the null hypothesis is desirable because it implies that the mean values of all the variables in the model are similar for the control and comparison groups, that is, that the two groups are balanced.

If one or more of the five subclasses was not balanced, we performed a series of supplementary steps in an attempt to achieve balance, beginning with subdividing the unbalanced subclasses and testing for balance again. For example, if the bottom quintile was unbalanced, it was split into two parts. Splitting a subclass in this way had one of two results: either both parts were balanced, in which case the selection bias was estimated; or at least one part was not balanced, in which case the unbalanced part or parts were split again. The subsequent round of splitting had one of two results: either all parts were balanced, in which case the selection bias was estimated; or at least one part included fewer than ten control-group members or fewer than ten comparison-group members, in which case no further attempt was made to balance the subclasses using the set of covariates in the original estimated model.

If the second round of splitting failed to achieve balance, the logistic regression was reestimated (using data for the full sample) after adding higher-order terms, interactions, or both in an attempt to find a model specification that would result in balance. The t-statistics of the coefficient estimates for the unbalanced subclass regressions guided the choice of terms to add. If only one variable had a large t-statistic, its square was added to the logistic regression. If two or more variables had large t-statistics, their squares, interactions, or both were added.

Using results from this reestimated model, the entire subclassification process was repeated, starting with the four basic steps. When necessary, the model specification process was repeated several times until balance was achieved. If balance could not be achieved for a given pair of control and comparison groups, no attempt was made to estimate its bias, because it did not pass the specification test required to use the propensity-score estimator.

In general, balance was much easier to achieve for the in-state comparisons than for the out-of-state comparisons. For in-state comparisons, splitting the sample into five to seven subclasses resulted in balance for all but one group (Detroit), to which two interaction terms were also added. For the out-of-state and multistate comparisons, dividing the sample into six to eight subclasses usually resulted in balance. One comparison required eleven subclasses to achieve balance. For fewer than half the comparisons, the addition of a few higher-order terms or interaction terms were needed to achieve balance (age-squared was one of the most effective terms). For some out-of-state and multistate comparisons, balance could not be achieved.

If the specification tests indicated that all subclasses were balanced—specifically, if the overall F-test for the model parameters in each subclass was not statistically significant at the 0.10 level—the selection bias was estimated for each subclass by regressing earnings for each sample member on the covariates used in the original estimated model (plus an age-squared covariate) and an indicator variable denoting whether she was in the control group or the comparison group. The mean selection bias for the full sample was estimated as a weighted average of the estimated coefficient of the control-group indicator variable for each subclass. Subclass weights were set equal to the proportion of all control-group members in the subclass. That is, the estimated bias was:

$$\sum_{k=1}^{K} w_k \lambda_k,$$

where K is the number of subclasses, w_k is the proportion of control-group members in subclass k, and λ_k is the estimated bias for that subclass.

One-to-One Matching   One-to-one matching (also referred to in the literature as single nearest neighbor matching) entails choosing for each control-group member the comparison-group member with the closest estimated propensity score. In other words, each control-group member defines a subclass that consists of a matched pair of sample members. The average bias is estimated as the mean difference in outcomes across matched pairs. The matching procedure for a given comparison started with the propensity scores computed from the final logistic regression used to balance the subclasses. Each control-group member was paired with the comparison-group member who had the closest estimated propensity score. If several comparison-group members matched a given control-group member equally well, one of them was chosen randomly to form a pair with the control-group member. (An alternative method, which was not used, is one-to-many matching, which allows more than one comparison-group member to be matched with each control-group member.) If a given comparison-group member was the best match for more than one control-group member, she was paired with all control-group members whose propensity scores she matched. In other words, matching was done with replacement. If a comparison-group member was not a best match for any control-group member, she was dropped from the analysis. Thus, some comparison-group members were paired more than once, and others were not paired at all. Every control-group member, however, was paired with a comparison-group member.

Matching with replacement may result in less precision than matching without replacement because dropping some comparison-group members reduces the sample size. The advantage of matching with replacement is that it offers a better potential match and thus less bias. In practice, the difference between the two approaches is often small (Zhao 2004).

Once matching was complete, the resulting bias was estimated using only matched sample members in a way similar to that expressed in equation 5.1. To account for the fact that each comparison-group member was included in the regression as many times as she was used for a match, the variance of the bias estimate was computed as:

$$se^2 * \left[\left(1 + \frac{1}{n} \sum_{j=1}^{m} k_j^2 \right) / 2 \right],$$

where k_j is the number of times that the jth comparison-group member was matched to a control-group member, m is the number of comparison-group members in the analysis, and se is the standard error of the estimated bias from the regression (see Bloom et al. 2002, appendix A). Note that if k equals 1 for all comparison-group members (that is, if no comparison-group member is used more than once), the variance reduces to se^2.

Fixed-Effects Models   Fixed-effects models use observed past behavior to control for unobserved individual differences that do not change during the analysis period (see, for example, Bassi 1984; Hsiao 1990). This strategy removes unobserved fixed effects by computing changes in sample members' values on the outcome measure from the baseline period to the follow-up period. Bias is estimated as the difference between the mean change in the outcome for the control group and the mean change in the outcome for the comparison group, as shown in equation 5.3:

$$Y_{it} - Y_{is} = \alpha + \lambda C_i + \sum_j \gamma_j W_{ij} + \sum_m \delta_m X_{im} + \varepsilon_i, \tag{5.3}$$

where t is a follow-up period and s is a baseline period. Earnings in both periods were measured as annual averages.

People who enroll in job-training or welfare programs often experience a temporary decline in earnings before enrolling in the program, which Ashenfelter (1978) called a "pre-program dip." Thus, it might not be appropriate to control for earnings on the basis of the period immediately before random assignment. We therefore estimated two fixed-effects models. In the first model, Y_{is} was set equal to sample members' annual earnings averaged over the two years before random assignment. In the second model, Y_{is} was set equal to their earnings in the second year before random assignment. Because the two estimates were similar, we report only those that were based on baseline earnings data for the two years before random assignment.

We present findings for three applications of fixed-effects models. The first application includes all sample members who were part of a control group or its comparison group. The second and third applications use fixed-effects estimation (with $Y_{it} - Y_{is}$ as the dependent variable) for a sample that was balanced using propensity score subclassification and one-to-one matching, respectively (as recommended by Heckman, Ichimura, and Todd 1997; and Smith and Todd 2005).

Random-Growth Models   Random-growth models take fixed-effects models a step further by accounting for unobserved individual differences that change at a fixed rate during the analysis period. To this end, the models specify a separate time trajectory for each sample member's outcome, the simplest being a line with individual-specific intercepts and slopes (see, for example, Bloom and McLaughlin 1982; Ashenfelter and Card 1985; Heckman and Hotz 1989). More complex random-growth models, such as hierarchical linear modeling (Raudenbush and Bryk 2002), have become increasingly popular with the advent of software for estimating them and the increased availability of longitudinal datasets to support them.

At least two baseline observations and one follow-up observation with respect to the outcome measure are required to estimate a linear random growth model. This information makes it possible to control for each sample member's random growth path by estimating the difference between the control group and the comparison group with respect to changes in the outcome's rate of change over time. The following is a random growth model:

$$Y_{it} = \phi_{1i} + \phi_{2i}t + \lambda_t C_i + \sum_j \gamma_j W_{it} + \sum_m \delta_m X_{im} + \varepsilon_{it}, \qquad (5.4)$$

where ϕ_{1i} and ϕ_{2i} are the intercept and slope, respectively, of sample member i's underlying earnings trend.[8] Estimating this model requires computing changes from the baseline period to the follow-up period in the outcome's rate of change. (For a derivation of the random-growth specification that was used, see Bloom et al. 2002, appendix A.)

Propensity Score–Weighted Least-Squares Regression In propensity score–weighted least-squares regression, each control-group member receives a weight of 1 and each comparison-group member receives a weight of $p/(1-p)$, where p is the estimated propensity score (Hirano, Imbens, and Ridder 2003). The difference between the weighted mean outcome for the control group and the weighted mean outcome for the comparison group provides an estimate of the bias produced by this method.

The procedure realigns the comparison group to make its weighted distribution of propensity scores equal to that for the control group, which in turn equalizes their weighted distributions of covariates. This can be done only for ranges of propensity scores that exist in both groups, that is, in regions of "overlapping support." Consider, for example, a subgroup of sample members who share a given set of characteristics. Suppose that 90 percent of these people are in the control group, that is, that the subgroup's overall propensity score is 0.9. Each control-group member in the subgroup receives a weight of 1, and each comparison-group member receives a weight of $0.9/(1-0.9)$, or 9. This procedure ensures that the subgroup's weight in the control group is equal to its weight in the comparison group.

Research Protocol

A potential threat to the validity of tests of nonexperimental methods is that the researchers know the right answers—that is, the experimental counterfactual and the experimental impact estimate—in advance. Whatever benchmarking approach one takes, it is possible to continue testing nonexperimental estimators until one finds an estimator that closely mimics the experimental estimators. Doing this would expose one to the risk of basing findings on chance relationships in the data for a specific sample. To help guard against this possibility, we conducted our analysis according to a research protocol with three main features:

1. *Prespecification of the methods to be tested and ways to test them.* At the outset of the project, we specified as carefully and completely as possible the nonexperimental methods to be tested, the manner in

which they would be tested, and the criteria for gauging their success. Although some changes were made subsequently, most steps were specified in advance.

2. *Ongoing peer review.* An advisory panel of experts representing widely varying experiences with and expectations of nonexperimental comparison-group methods guided the design of our research, the conduct of our analysis, and the interpretation of our findings.[9] The panel finalized the project design and analysis plan, reviewed the first round of analyses, helped finalize the plan for the second round, and reviewed a draft report.

3. *Replication of the analysis using additional samples and outcome measures.* The first round of our analysis was based on short-run outcomes for a subset of the sites in the analysis. The second round was expanded to include medium-run outcomes and the remainder of the sites. Thus, embedded in the second round was a replication of the first.

Although no research protocol is foolproof, we believe that these procedures provided substantial protection against researcher bias.

Findings and Conclusions

Our findings and conclusions, which are presented in more detail in Bloom et al. (2002, chapter 3) and Charles Michalopoulos, Howard Bloom, and Carolyn J. Hill (2004), are organized here with respect to the two research questions that this benchmarking analysis was designed to answer: Which comparison-group methods yield the best estimates of program impacts, and under what conditions do they do so? Under what conditions, if any, do the best comparison-group methods produce estimates of program impacts valid enough to stand in for estimates based on a randomized experiment?

Which Methods Work Best?

As already described, selection biases were estimated as the differences between the counterfactuals from a series of experiments (the control-group outcomes) and the counterfactuals constructed from nonexperimental comparison groups. These differences represent the biases that would have resulted had the nonexperimental comparison-group methods been used instead of experimental control-group methods to estimate program impacts. Biases were estimated for both a short-run follow-up period (the two years after random assignment) and a medium-run follow-up period (the third, fourth, and fifth years after random assignment).

The results indicate that biases attributable to the use of nonexperimental methods are positive in some of the in-state, out-of-state, and multistate comparisons and negative in other comparisons and that the sign of the bias in a given comparison cannot be predicted in advance. Although the biases tend to cancel out when averaged across many impact estimates, they can be quite large for any given one. This discussion of findings therefore focuses on the mean absolute bias—the magnitude of the bias for a given estimate—that each of the nonexperimental methods can be expected to produce.

Table 5.4 summarizes the mean absolute bias of the nonexperimental estimators for the comparisons for which baseline balance was achieved using propensity-score methods as a specification test.[10] It is expressed both in dollars (top panel) and as a percentage of the control group's mean earnings (bottom panel). In addition, the number of bias estimates that were statistically different from 0 at the 0.10 level according to a two-tailed significance test are listed in parentheses after the mean absolute bias for each estimation procedure and each comparison-group source. The findings in the table thus represent the likely bias produced by impact estimates when propensity-score methods are used to screen out inappropriate comparison groups.

We found that when a simple difference of mean outcomes is used to estimate program impacts with, for example, an in-state comparison group, the mean absolute bias is $304 (see the figure at the top of the far-left column in table 5.4), and two of the five in-state comparison groups for which the difference of means was computed yield statistically significant biases. Expressed as a percentage of the control group's mean earnings for the comparison on which it is based, the mean absolute percentage bias for a difference of means estimator with in-state comparison groups is 12 percent (see the top figure in the far-left column in the table's bottom portion).

Whereas all the in-state comparison groups achieved balance on the basis of the propensity-score specification test, only eight of the fourteen out-of-state comparisons and four of the six multistate comparisons did so. Table 5.5 therefore presents bias estimates separately for comparisons that achieved balance and for comparisons that did not achieve balance (the latter were computed by means of estimation approaches that do not check for balance). The first column for each time period and each type of comparison represented in the table lists the findings for comparisons where balance was achieved, and the second column lists the corresponding findings for comparisons where balance was not achieved.

Table 5.4 Mean Absolute Bias Estimates for Balanced Comparisons

	Short Run			Medium Run		
Nonexperimental Method	In-State Comparisons (n = 5)	Out-of-State Comparisons (n = 8)	Multistate Comparisons (n = 4)	In-State Comparisons (n = 5)	Out-of-State Comparisons (n = 8)	Multistate Comparisons (n = 4)
Mean absolute bias estimates in 1996 dollars (number of statistically significant estimates)						
Difference of means	304 (2)	285 (4)	337 (4)	387 (2)	845 (5)	1,027 (4)
OLS regression	238 (2)	400 (5)	374 (4)	671 (2)	1,350 (6)	1,066 (4)
Propensity-score subclassification	235 (2)	449 (4)	350 (4)	628 (4)	1,239 (6)	1,027 (3)
Propensity-score one-to-one matching	234 (0)	409 (2)	327 (2)	689 (2)	1,242 (3)	974 (3)
Fixed effects	272 (2)	568 (4)	446 (4)	623 (3)	1,573 (6)	1,147 (3)
Random growth	390 (2)	792 (6)	754 (2)	1,180 (2)	1,594 (4)	1,739 (3)
Fixed effects with subclassification	268 (2)	339 (2)	374 (4)	565 (2)	1,381 (4)	1,072 (3)
Fixed effects with one-to-one matching	201 (0)	287 (1)	348 (2)	679 (2)	1,249 (4)	993 (3)
Propensity score–weighted regression	239 (2)	325 (6)	360 (4)	592 (3)	1,179 (8)	1,048 (4)

Table 5.4 *Continued*

Nonexperimental Method	Short Run			Medium Run		
	In-State Comparisons (n = 5)	Out-of-State Comparisons (n = 8)	Multistate Comparisons (n = 4)	In-State Comparisons (n = 5)	Out-of-State Comparisons (n = 8)	Multistate Comparisons (n = 4)
Mean absolute bias estimates in percentages						
Difference of means	12	12	14	8	21	20
OLS regression	9	17	15	14	33	20
Propensity score subclassification	9	19	14	13	30	20
Propensity score one-to-one matching	10	17	13	15	30	19
Fixed effects	11	24	18	13	39	22
Random growth	15	34	30	24	40	34
Fixed effects with subclassification	10	14	15	12	33	21
Fixed effects with one-to-one matching	8	12	14	15	30	20
Propensity score–weighted regression	9	14	15	12	29	20

Source: Authors' calculations.

Notes: The short run is defined as the two years after random assignment. The medium run is defined as the third through the fifth years after random assignment. The estimates are calculated for the comparisons for which balance could be achieved (see Bloom et al. 2002, chapter 3). Statistical significance was assessed at the 0.10 level for a two-tailed test.

Table 5.5 Mean Absolute Bias Estimates for Balanced and Unbalanced Comparisons

	Short Run				Medium Run			
	Out-of-State Comparisons		Multistate Comparisons		Out-of-State Comparisons		Multistate Comparisons	
	Balanced (n = 8)	Unbalanced (n = 6)	Balanced (n = 4)	Unbalanced (n = 2)	Balanced (n = 8)	Unbalanced (n = 6)	Balanced (n = 4)	Unbalanced (n = 2)
Mean absolute bias estimates in 1996 dollars (number of statistically significant estimates)								
Difference of means	285 (4)	494 (5)	337 (4)	330 (1)	845 (5)	1,585 (6)	1,027 (4)	1,127 (2)
OLS regression	400 (5)	636 (6)	374 (4)	425 (2)	1,350 (6)	1,601 (5)	1,066 (4)	1,326 (2)
Fixed effects	568 (4)	572 (6)	446 (4)	543 (2)	1,573 (6)	1,507 (4)	1,147 (3)	1,434 (2)
Random growth	792 (6)	1,694 (6)	754 (2)	821 (2)	1,594 (4)	4,008 (6)	1,739 (3)	2,021 (2)
Mean absolute bias estimates in percentages								
Difference of means	12	20	14	17	21	31	20	35
OLS regression	17	26	15	22	33	31	20	40
Fixed effects	24	24	18	26	39	29	22	42
Random growth	34	69	30	42	40	79	34	63

Source: Authors' calculations.
Notes: The short run is defined as the two years after random assignment. The medium run is defined as the third through the fifth years after random assignment. Because this table shows the mean absolute bias estimates for unbalanced as well as for balanced comparisons, methods based on propensity scores (which required balance to estimate the selection bias) are not shown. Statistical significance was assessed at the 0.10 level for a two-tailed test.

Three conclusions emerge from the findings shown in tables 5.4 and 5.5:

1. *The biases when nonexperimental comparison groups were used were consistently larger for medium-run impact estimates than for short-run impact estimates.* For every combination of a comparison group and an estimation method, the mean absolute bias was larger in the medium run than in the short run. In many cases, the medium-run bias was several times the size of its short-run counterpart. Thus, it was easier to predict a counterfactual that was close to the point of random assignment than one that was distant from the point of random assignment. This finding is consistent with the fact that it is usually easier to predict something that is close in time than it is to predict something in the distant future.

2. *In-state comparison groups produced the smallest mean absolute biases.* For estimates of medium-run impacts, in-state comparison groups generally produced biases about one third to one half the size of those for out-of-state and multistate comparison groups. This finding accords with results from previous research (Friedlander and Robins 1995; Bell et al. 1995; Heckman, Ichimura, and Todd 1997). For estimates of short-run impacts, the differences in the biases produced by in-state comparisons versus out-of-state and multistate comparisons were similar but less pronounced and less consistent across nonexperimental methods.

3. *None of the statistical adjustment methods used to refine nonexperimental comparison-group approaches reduced biases substantially or consistently. Propensity-score methods, however, provided a specification check that tended to eliminate larger-than-average biases.*

Looking across the full range of nonexperimental impact estimation methods considered, a simple difference of means generally performed about as well as the approaches involving statistical adjustment. OLS regression, especially when used for groups that could be balanced by means of propensity scores, also performed well compared with the more complex methods. Furthermore, using a fixed-effects model, with or without propensity-score balancing, did not consistently improve the results. And using a random-growth model often increased the bias, in some cases substantially. These findings, which hold regardless of the comparison group used or the time period encompassed by the analysis, run counter to findings from numerous benchmarking studies (LaLonde 1986; Fraker and Maynard 1987; Heckman and Hotz 1989; Heckman, Ichimura, and Todd 1997; Dehejia and Wahba 1999), although Wilde and Hollister (2002) also found that OLS regression performed as well as propensity-score methods.

In short, it appears that a local comparison group produces the best results in the contexts examined here and that for local comparison groups, a simple difference between means or OLS regression may perform as well or better than more complex comparison group approaches. For less proximate comparison groups, propensity-score balancing methods may provide a useful specification check by eliminating especially problematic comparison groups from consideration. If such groups are eliminated, a simple difference of means or OLS regression can perform as well as more complex estimators.

Do the Best Methods Work Well Enough?

In light of the fact that OLS regression with an in-state comparison group, referred to hereafter as the nonexperimental estimator, performed as well as or better than more complex methods, is the approach good enough to substitute for a randomized design in evaluations of mandatory welfare-to-work programs? (We use OLS regression instead of a simple difference of means—which, as already noted, performs as well or better than OLS regression—because, in practice, some adjustment procedure would likely be used if possible.)

Nonexperimental Mismatch Error   Bloom et al. (2002) presented five short-run estimates (–$30, –$65, –$275, –$168, and $652) and five medium-run estimates ($280, –$913, $367, –$1,164, and $634) of the bias produced by OLS regression with an in-state comparison group. For both time periods, the mean value of the five bias estimates was close to 0 ($23, or 1 percent, and –$159, or –3 percent, respectively), although the variation around the mean was substantial. This negligible mean bias is consistent with the fact that the sign of the bias for any given application is arbitrary and, in many cases, would be reversed if the roles of the comparison and control groups were reversed.

Because the mean bias is small, it is appropriate in the present context to view the theoretical sampling distribution of nonexperimental mismatch error across applications as having a grand mean or expected value of 0. In this regard, the error is not really a bias (which implies an expected value other than 0) but rather an additional random-error component. In large part, this error component reflects unobserved site effects, which have proved very difficult to control for in past research (Hollister and Hill 1995). The standard error of the sampling distribution of mismatch error can be inferred from the standard deviation of the five bias estimates for a given follow-up period and from information about the sampling errors and sample sizes of these estimates (see the appendix to this chapter).

Equipped with the mean and standard error of the mismatch error, one can assess the use of nonexperimental comparison groups by comparing their estimated sampling distribution with that of their experimental counterpart in NEWWS. Both sampling distributions are centered on the true impact for a given analysis. Because the experimental estimator has one source of random error—the error attributable to sampling a finite number of welfare recipients—its standard error reflects a single component. The nonexperimental estimator, in contrast, has two sources of random error: the same sampling error to which an experiment is subject and the nonexperimental mismatch error. Reflecting both components, the standard error of the nonexperimental estimator is thus necessarily larger than that of its corresponding experimental estimator if the nonexperimental comparison group is the same size as the experimental control group. Although the effect of random sampling error on a single application can be reduced by increasing the sample size, the effect of nonexperimental mismatch error cannot be reduced in this way (see the appendix). The mismatch error component can be reduced only by averaging findings across a series of applications.

The primary effect of mismatch error in the present context is to reduce the statistical power of nonexperimental estimators. Comparing such estimators with their experimental counterparts requires comparing their ability to detect a specific program impact. Figure 5.2 illustrates such a comparison by showing the sampling distributions of experimental and nonexperimental impact estimators for a hypothetical true impact of $1,000. Near the true impact, the experimental distribution is higher than the nonexperimental distribution, implying that the experiment is more likely to produce an accurate estimate. Far from the true impact, the nonexperimental distribution is much higher than the experimental distribution, implying that the nonexperimental estimator is more likely to produce a highly inaccurate estimate (for example, $0 or $2,000).

The types of comparisons shown in figure 5.2 are possible only in methodological studies that, like the present one, directly compare experimental estimates with nonexperimental estimates of the same impacts. In contexts where nonexperimental estimators are used on their own, it is impossible to estimate mismatch error or to account for it in the standard errors of nonexperimental impact estimates. Having established the basic relationship between the sampling distributions for corresponding experimental and nonexperimental impact estimators, we can now compare their implications for specific conclusions from NEWWS. Our approach is in a similar spirit to, but a different form from, that developed by Bell et al. (1995).

Figure 5.2   Sampling Distributions of Impact Estimators for a
Hypothetical Program

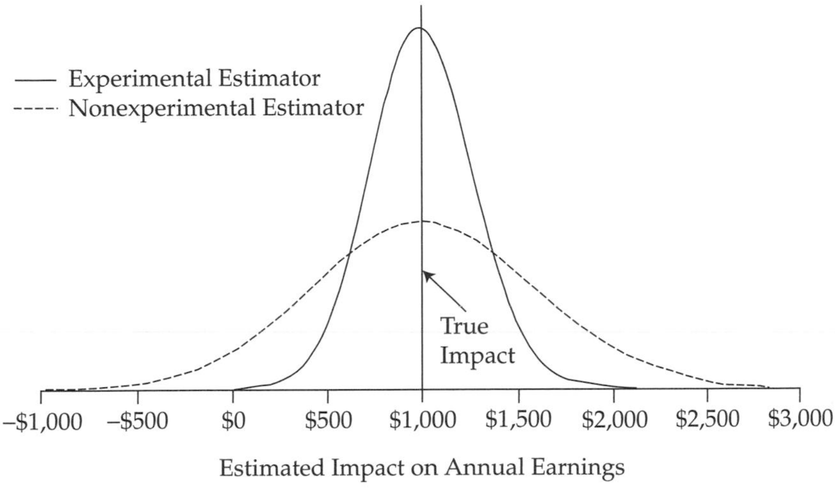

Source: Authors' illustration.

Replicating the Findings Experimentally and Nonexperimentally   NEWWS
was designed to estimate the impacts of several welfare-to-work strategies that had been the subject of widespread debate among policymakers, program administrators, and researchers for many years. The study
examined both the net impacts of each program approach (its impacts
relative to no mandatory welfare-to-work services) and the differential
impacts of each program approach (its impacts relative to the other program approaches).

The impact findings for NEWWS were reported for four categories
of programs (Hamilton et al. 2001): the program in Portland, which was
unique among the NEWWS programs in using a mix of job-search and
education services; job-search-first programs, in Atlanta, Grand Rapids,
and Riverside, which focused on helping clients find jobs quickly; high-
enforcement education-first programs, in Atlanta, Grand Rapids,
Riverside, and Columbus, which focused on providing education services first and reduced the welfare benefits of clients who did not meet
the program's participation requirements (in Columbus, as already described, both traditional and integrated case management programs
were operated); and low-enforcement education-first programs, in Detroit and Oklahoma City, which focused on providing education ser-

vices first and were less vigorous than the high enforcement programs in getting clients to participate.

One way to assess the importance of nonexperimental mismatch error is to examine its implications for replicating the basic conclusions from NEWWS for these four types of programs. Table 5.6 summarizes this assessment with respect to net impacts on total earnings during the five years after random assignment. This summary measure reflects the overall influence of estimation bias in the short run and in the medium run.

The first row in table 5.6 presents the experimental point estimate and statistical significance level (p-value) for each net program impact.[11] The impact on total five-year earnings equals $5,034 for Portland, which is statistically significant at the 0.001 level. The other categories of programs have impacts of $2,138, $1,503, and $770, respectively, all of which are statistically significant at the 0.10 level. The experimental point estimate and its estimated standard error for each program impact provide estimates of the corresponding expected value and standard error of the sampling distribution for each estimator.

For the corresponding nonexperimental estimator, the sampling distribution has the same expected value, but its standard error includes the additional component reflecting mismatch error. One way to assess the implications of the mismatch error is to compare the likelihoods that the experimental and nonexperimental estimators would generate an impact estimate in a replication that is positive and statistically significant at the 0.05 level. This procedure amounts to comparing the likelihoods that the two estimators would lead to the same conclusion about whether the program approach is effective.

For the Portland program, the experimental estimator, with its large expected value and small standard error, has a 98 percent chance of producing a statistically significant positive impact estimate. In contrast, the nonexperimental estimator, with the same expected value and a much larger standard error, has only a 53 percent chance of finding a statistically significant positive impact estimate.

For the next two categories of programs, there are even larger discrepancies between the experimental and nonexperimental estimators. In both cases, the experimental estimator is almost certain to produce a statistically significant positive finding, despite the fact that its expected values are only a fraction of Portland's. This is because the sample sizes for these categories are much larger than the sample size for Portland (each includes several programs), and their experimental standard errors are correspondingly smaller. Nevertheless, the corresponding nonexperimental estimators have a relatively small chance of yielding the statistically significant positive impact found in NEWWS (39 percent and 30 percent, respectively). This is because of the large nonexperimental mismatch error, the variance of which does not de-

Table 5.6 Estimation Error for Net Impacts on Earnings over Five Years

		NEWWS Program Category		
	Portland	Job-Search-First	High-Enforcement Education-First	Low-Enforcement Education-First
Experimental point estimate of impact[a]	$5,034 (p < 0.001)	$2,138 (p < 0.001)	$1,503 (p < 0.001)	$ 770 (p = 0.075)
Likelihood of replicating a statistically significant positive impact				
Experimental replication[b]	98%	~100%	99%	56%
Nonexperimental replication[c]	53%	39%	30%	11%

Source: Authors' calculations.

[a]Impacts are expressed in 1996 dollars. The numbers of program- and control-group members are, respectively, 3,529 and 499 (Portland), 5,382 and 6,292 (job-search-first), 9,716 and 8,803 (high-enforcement education-first), and 6,535 and 6,591 (low-enforcement education-first).

[b]The experimental standard errors are $1,327 (Portland), $455 (job-search-first), $385 (high-enforcement education-first), and $432 (low-enforcement education-first; for details on the calculation of these standard errors, see the appendix to this chapter).

[c]The nonexperimental standard errors are $2,967 (Portland), $1,598 (job-search-first), $1,356 (high-enforcement education-first), and $1,926 (low-enforcement education-first; for details on the calculation of these standard errors, see the appendix to this chapter).

cline with increases in the sample size in each site. The variance does decline, however, with increases in the number of sites included for each type of program—a factor that was accounted for in our analysis (see the appendix).

For the fourth program category in the table, the experimental estimator, which is statistically significant at the 0.10 level, has only a 56 percent chance of producing a statistically significant positive impact—but its nonexperimental counterpart has an even smaller chance of doing so (11 percent).

Now consider the findings for the differential impact estimates summarized in table 5.7. A differential impact estimate for two programs is simply the difference between their net impact estimates, and the standard error of this difference for independent samples is the square root of the sum of the error variances for each net impact estimate. For overlapping samples, an additional covariance term is included.

The top panel in table 5.7 presents the point estimates and p-values obtained for each differential impact. These estimates equal the differences between the net impact estimates for the programs identified in the corresponding columns and rows. Thus, for example, the net impact estimate for Portland was $2,896 larger than that for the job-search-first programs, $3,531 larger than that for the high-enforcement education-first programs, and $4,264 larger than that for the low-enforcement education-first programs. The three differential impact estimates are statistically significant at the 0.05, 0.01, and 0.01 levels, respectively. The only other statistically significant positive differential impact estimate is that for the job-search-first programs versus the low- enforcement education-first programs.

The second panel in table 5.7 presents the likelihood that a given experimental impact estimator would also produce a statistically significant positive impact estimate at the 0.05 level. Thus, for the four differential impact estimates that are positive and statistically significant, this panel indicates the likelihood that an experimental replication would produce a statistically significant differential impact. The third panel in the table shows the likelihood that a given nonexperimental estimator would produce a positive statistically significant impact.

In sum, in terms of replicating both the statistically significant positive net impact of the four categories of programs and the statistically significant positive differential impacts of program categories in NEWWS, even the best nonexperimental estimator in this analysis is not a good substitute for an experimental estimator.

Summary

We have assessed the ability of nonexperimental comparison group methods to measure the impacts of mandatory welfare-to-work pro-

Table 5.7 Estimation Error for Differential Impacts on Earnings over Five Years

	NEWWS Program Category			
	Portland	Job-Search-First	High-Enforcement Education-First	Low-Enforcement Education-First
Experimental point estimate of differential impact[a]				
Portland	—			
Job-search-first	$2,896 (p = 0.039)	—		
High-enforcement education-first	$3,531 (p = 0.011)	$634 (p = 0.575)	—	
Low-enforcement education-first	$4,264 (p = 0.002)	$1,368 (p = 0.029)	$733 (p = 0.205)	—
Likelihood of replicating a statistically significant positive impact				
Experimental replication[b]				
Portland	—			
Job-search-first	66%	—		
High-enforcement education-first	82%	14%	—	
Low-enforcement education-first	92%	70%	35%	—
Nonexperimental replication[c]				
Portland	—			
Job-search-first	22%	—		
High-enforcement education-first	29%	7%	—	
Low-enforcement education-first	33%	14%	9%	—

Source: Authors' calculations.

[a] Impacts are expressed in 1996 dollars. The numbers of program- and control-group members are, respectively, 3,529 and 499 (Portland), 5,382 and 6,292 (job-search-first), 9,716 and 8,803 (high-enforcement education-first), and 6,535 and 6,591 (low-enforcement education-first).

[b] The experimental standard errors are $1,327 (Portland), $455 (job-search-first), $385 (high-enforcement education-first), and $432 (low-enforcement education-first; for details on the calculation of these standard errors, see the appendix to this chapter).

[c] The nonexperimental standard errors are $2,967 (Portland), $1,598 (job-search-first), $1,356 (high-enforcement education-first), and $1,926 (low-enforcement education-first; for details on the calculation of these standard errors, see the appendix to this chapter).

grams by comparing their results with those from a series of randomized experiments. The approaches tested included two propensity-score balancing methods (subclassification and one-to-one matching), three statistical modeling methods (OLS regression, fixed-effects models, and random-growth models), and several combinations of these methods.

Our tests of the approaches were based on detailed, consistent data on sample members' background characteristics, including up to three years of quarterly baseline earnings and employment data and extensive socioeconomic information. Furthermore, the population used as the basis for testing, sample members in experimental studies of mandatory welfare-to-work programs, is relatively homogeneous and not subject to self-selection bias, which complicates evaluations of voluntary social programs. In these respects, the conditions in our analysis were hospitable to comparison-group methods.

The tests consisted of multiple replications in which three different types of comparison groups (in-state comparison groups, out-of-state comparison groups, and multistate comparison groups) were used for two nonoverlapping time periods (the first two years after random assignment and the third through the fifth years after random assignment). Most of the tests were based on large samples of anywhere from 328 to 4,015 control-group members. In these respects, the conditions in our analysis were conducive to conducting meaningful and fair tests.

So what do we conclude from these tests? With respect to what non-experimental methods work best, we conclude that the best comparison groups are local and that simple differences of means and OLS regressions perform as well as more complex alternatives. Because these findings are consistent across many replications based on large samples of people from six different states, we believe that they would probably generalize to many other mandatory welfare-to-work programs.

With respect to what methods could replace random assignment, we conclude that there are probably none that work well enough in a single replication, because the magnitude of the mismatch bias for any given nonexperimental evaluation can be large. This added error component markedly reduces the likelihood that nonexperimental comparison-group methods could replicate major findings from randomized experiments such as NEWWS. Arguably more problematic is the fact that it is not possible to account for mismatch error through statistical tests or confidence intervals when nonexperimental comparison group methods are used.

Our results offer one ray of hope regarding nonexperimental methods. Although nonexperimental mismatch error can be quite large, it varies unpredictably across evaluations and has an apparent grand mean of 0. A nonexperimental evaluation that used several comparison groups might therefore be able to match a randomized experiment's impact estimate and statistical precision. It is important to recognize, however, that this claim rests on an empirical analysis that might not be generalizable to other settings. In contrast, statistical theory guarantees that random assignment produces impact estimates that are free of selection bias and nonexperimental mismatch error.

In summing up our case, we wish to emphasize that rarely, if ever, are the findings from a single study definitive by themselves, and the present analysis is no exception to this rule. When trying to draw conclusions about an issue, one should weigh all the relevant evidence. It is possible that comparison-group approaches can be used to construct valid counterfactuals for certain types of programs and certain types of data. Considered in conjunction with related research exploring nonexperimental comparison-group methods, however, the findings presented here suggest that such methods, regardless of their technical sophistication, are no substitute for randomized experiments in measuring the impacts of social and education programs. Thus, we believe that before nonexperimental comparison-group approaches can be accepted as the basis for major policy evaluations, their efficacy needs to be demonstrated by those who would rely on them.

Appendix: Replicating Key Findings from NEWWS Using Experimental and Nonexperimental Estimators

This appendix describes how we used our estimates of bias from nonexperimental comparison group methods to assess how well experimental and nonexperimental methods could replicate key findings from NEWWS.

Replicating the Net Impact Findings

We first examined how well experimental and nonexperimental methods could replicate key conclusions about whether the net impacts are likely to be positive for each of the four main categories of programs tested in NEWWS (Hamilton et al. 2001): job-search-first programs (one each in Atlanta, Grand Rapids, and Riverside); high-enforcement education-first programs (one each in Atlanta, Grand Rapids, and Riverside and two in Columbus); low-enforcement education-first programs (one each in Detroit and Oklahoma City); and the Portland program, which was employment-focused but used a mix of job search and education as initial activities.

This process had four steps:

1. *Estimate the NEWWS programs' net impacts and the standard errors of the impact estimates from the experimental data.* The estimated net impact and standard error for each program studied in NEWWS were obtained by regressing total earnings for the five-year follow-up period (expressed in 1996 dollars) on an indicator of whether each sample member was in the program group or the control group and on a series of baseline characteristics. For each of the three program types implemented by more than one NEWWS site, the estimated mean impact was computed as an equally weighted average of the impacts across sites, and the standard error of the mean impact was computed accordingly. The standard error of the mean impact for the high-enforcement education-first programs was adjusted for the fact that the two Columbus programs used the same control group.[12]

Findings from this analysis are reported in the top panel in table 5A.1. The first column in the panel lists the average experimental impact estimate for each type of program examined. The second column lists the estimated experimental standard error of these impact estimates. The third column lists the estimated nonexperimental error (discussed in the fourth step, below).

2. *Determine the likelihood that an experimental replication would produce a statistically significant net impact estimate from NEWWS.* Let m_i be the experimentally estimated impact for program approach i, and let se_i^2 be its estimated error variance (the square of its standard error). Because we focus our replication analysis on positive NEWWS impact estimates, assume that m_i is positive. Based on information from one experiment, the best guess is that another experiment run in the same place with the same type of program and the same sample sizes would yield a series of impact estimates centered on m_i with a variance of se_i^2. This implies that the probability that another experiment would produce an impact estimate that is positive and statistically different from 0 at the 0.05 significance level using a one-tailed Z test is:

$$\text{Prob}(m_i + \varepsilon_i > 1.6448 se_i), \tag{5A.1}$$

where ε_i is random sampling error.

The standard normal distribution is appropriate for computing this probability because experimental impact estimates have an asymptotically normal distribution whether they are regression-adjusted using OLS (as in NEWWS) or calculated as a simple difference between means (Amemiya 1985). A one-tailed test was used because we were interested in replications that would yield the same conclusions about which NEWWS programs had positive effects. The 0.05 statistical significance criterion was used because the impact estimates in NEWWS

Table 5A.1   Impact and Standard Error Estimates on Total Earnings over Five Years (in 1996 Dollars)

Type of Impact Estimate and NEWWS Program Approach	Estimate	Standard Error	
		Experimental	Nonexperimental
Net impacts			
Portland	5,034	1,327	2,967
Job-search-first	2,138	455	1,598
High-enforcement education-first	1,503	385	1,356
Low-enforcement education-first	770	432	1,926
Differential impacts			
Portland versus job-search-first	2,896	1,403	3,371
Portland versus high-enforcement education-first	3,531	1,382	3,263
Portland versus low-enforcement education-first	4,264	1,396	3,538
Job-search-first versus high-enforcement education-first	634	1,151	2,096
Job-search-first versus low-enforcement education-first	1,368	627	2,503
High- versus low-enforcement education-first	733	579	2,355

Source: Authors' calculations.

were tested using two-tailed tests and a 0.10 statistical significance criterion, and a positive estimate that is significantly different from 0 in a one-tailed test at the 0.05 level will also be significantly different from 0 in a two-tailed test at the 0.10 level.

3. *Determine the mismatch error variance that would result from using each nonexperimental estimator to measure the impacts of the NEWWS programs.* As noted in the body of the chapter, experimental replications that preserve the same conditions as the original experiment differ from one another solely because of random sampling error (which depends on the size of the analysis sample and the variation in the outcome measure across individual sample members). Nonexperimental replications, in contrast, are subject not only to random sampling error but

also to error arising from nonexperimental mismatch (which is independent of sample size and individual outcome variation). Therefore, the key to inferring the total variance for nonexperimental impact estimators is to estimate the variance of the mismatch error, which we denote σ_ω^2, and to add it to the variance of random sampling error for the experimental findings to be examined. Note that a specific nonexperimental impact estimate, m_i^n, can be written as:

$$m_i^n = \mu_i + v_i, \tag{5A.2}$$

where μ_i is the true impact and v_i is the total nonexperimental error. The total nonexperimental error can be expressed as:

$$v_i = \varepsilon_i + \omega_i, \tag{5A.3}$$

where ε_i is random sampling error and ω_i is nonexperimental mismatch error.

Because sampling error and mismatch error are independent of each other, the total variance of nonexperimental error for a series of studies that have the same variation in random sampling error can be expressed thus:

$$\sigma_v^2 = VAR(v) = VAR(\varepsilon) + VAR(\omega) = \sigma_\varepsilon^2 + \sigma_\omega^2 \tag{5A.4}$$

The corresponding expression for a series of nonexperimental studies that have different amounts of variation in random sampling error (because they have different sample sizes, different underlying variation in individual outcomes, or both) is:

$$\sigma_v^2 = VAR(v) = E[VAR(\varepsilon)] + VAR(\omega) = E(\sigma_\varepsilon^2) + \sigma_\omega^2 \tag{5A.5}$$

Rearranging terms in the latter expression yields:

$$\sigma_\omega^2 = \sigma_v^2 - E(\sigma_\varepsilon^2) \tag{5A.6}$$

Thus, to estimate the variance of nonexperimental mismatch error, σ_ω^2, we estimated the total nonexperimental error variance, σ_v^2, as the variance of the five in-state OLS bias estimates; estimated the average variance attributable to random sampling error, $E(\sigma_\varepsilon^2)$, as the mean of the estimated error variances for the five in-state bias estimates; and took the difference between these two estimates.

The first step in this process was to estimate the bias for each in-state comparison with respect to total five-year follow-up earnings, estimate its associated standard error, and obtain its implied error variance. These findings are displayed in the first three columns in table 5A.2. The next step was to compute the variance of the five bias estimates

Table 5A.2   Nonexperimental Mismatch Error for In-State Comparisons for Earnings over Five Years (in 1996 Dollars)

In-State Comparison	Bias Point Estimate	Standard Error of Bias Point Estimate	Variance of Bias Point Estimate	Variance Component
Oklahoma City	778	660	436,100	
Detroit	-2,867	1,206	1,454,837	
Riverside	551	922	849,872	
Michigan	-3,829	1,051	1,104,037	
Portland	3,206	1,534	2,351,712	
Total variance of bias point estimates				8,284,105
− Estimated variance from sampling error				1,239,311
= Variance attributable to nonexperimental mismatch error				7,044,793

Source: Authors' calculations.

(8,284,105) as an estimate of the total nonexperimental error variance, σ_v^2. (Because this was an estimate of the population variance, our computation reflected four—that is, n − 1—degrees of freedom.) The next step was to compute the mean of the five estimated error variances (1,239,311) as an estimate of the average variance of random sampling error, $E(\sigma_\varepsilon^2)$. The final step was to compute the difference between these two error variances as an estimate of the variance attributable to nonexperimental mismatch error (7,044,793).

4. *Determine the likelihood that a nonexperimental estimator would produce statistically significant net impacts where NEWWS produced such impacts.* The final step in our analysis was to determine the likelihood that a nonexperimental estimator would produce a statistically significant positive impact for a particular experimental impact finding, m_i, that was positive and statistically significant. Specifically, we asked: What is the probability that the nonexperimentally estimated impact would be positive and statistically significant at the 0.05 level in a one-tailed test, assuming that the true impact is equal to the experimentally estimated impact, m_i? Estimating this probability required an estimate of the total standard error of the corresponding nonexperimental estimator, se_n. We obtained this estimate by adding the estimated variance of mismatch error (7,044,793) to the estimated variance of random sampling error for the specific experimental finding and taking the square root of this sum. The estimated nonexperimental standard error for each type of program is listed in the third column in the top panel in table 5A.1.

We then computed the probability that a replicated estimate would be positive and statistically significant as:

$$\text{Prob}(m_i + v_i > 1.6448se_n), \tag{5A.7}$$

where v_i is a random variable from a normal distribution with a mean of 0 and standard deviation of se_n.

Replicating the Differential Impact Findings

Comparing the likelihoods of experimental and nonexperimental replications of the differential impact findings from NEWWS is a straightforward extension of the procedure for net impacts. Specifically, if estimates from two program types i and j have the distributions described above, then their difference also has an asymptotically normal distribution. Under the null hypothesis of no difference in impacts across models,

$$\sqrt{N}(m_i - m_j) \xrightarrow{\text{d}} N(0, V_i + V_j + 2C_{ij}),$$

where V_i and V_j are the variances of the estimates of the two program models and C_{ij} is their covariance. In NEWWS, all estimates are independent except when a common control group is used to estimate the impact, that is, except in the cases of the job-search-first programs in Atlanta, Grand Rapids, and Riverside (each of which shares a control group with its high-enforcement education-first counterpart) and the two Columbus programs (which share a control group with one another).

The bottom panel in table 5A.1 presents the experimental differential impact estimate, its associated standard error, and the estimated standard error of a nonexperimental estimator for the several program types that were compared. Using the same logic as that used for net impact estimates, the probability that a replication of the evaluation of two program types would produce a positive differential impact estimate that was statistically significant at the 0.05 level for a one-tailed test is:

$$\text{Prob}[(m_i - m_j) + v_{ij} > 1.6448se_{ij}], \tag{5A.8}$$

where se_{ij} is the estimated standard error of the differential impact estimate and v_{ij} is a random variable from a normal distribution with a mean of 0 and a standard deviation of se_{ij}.

Notes

1. This chapter focuses only on standard nonexperimental comparison-group designs (often called nonequivalent control group designs) for esti-

mating program impacts. It does not examine quasi-experimental approaches such as interrupted time-series analysis, regression discontinuity analysis, or point-displacement analysis (Campbell and Stanley 1963; Cook and Campbell 1979; and Shadish, Cook, and Campbell 2002).

2. In the literature on propensity scores, the term "balance" has a special meaning that grew out of Paul R. Rosenbaum and Donald B. Rubin's (1983) definition of the balancing score as "a function of the observed covariates x such that the conditional distribution of x given b(x) is the same for treated ($z = 1$) and control ($z = 0$) units" (42). This definition, which is used throughout this chapter, differs from the definitions used in other literatures and in other chapters in this volume.

3. The term fixed effect, which has different meanings in different literatures, is often a source of confusion. In keeping with the usual practice in economics, we use the term in this chapter to mean a component of an individual's outcome that does not change over time and therefore can be eliminated by differencing individual outcomes over time.

4. For an excellent early discussion of this issue in the context of evaluating employment and training programs, see Steven M. Director (1979).

5. The sites in the experimental sample were Atlanta, Georgia; Chicago, Illinois; Hartford, Connecticut; Jersey City, New Jersey; Newark, New Jersey; New York City; Oakland, California; Philadelphia; San Francisco; and Fond du Lac and Winnebago counties, Wisconsin.

6. Zhong Zhao (2004, 100) compared a number of matching estimators using Monte Carlo experiments and declared "no clear winner," although some estimators may be preferable under certain conditions.

7. All our analyses were conducted using SAS statistical software. A routine for doing propensity-score matching using the STATA software package, written by Edwin Leuven and Barbara Sianesi and called "psmatch2," can be downloaded from http://ideas.repec.org/c/boc/bocode/s432001 .html (accessed January 5, 2005).

8. The short-run bias of the random growth model was estimated from the following regression: $(y_{i,SR} - y_{i,-1}) - 1.75\,(y_{i,-1} - y_{i,-2}) = \alpha + \lambda C_i + \Sigma\gamma_j W_{ij} + \Sigma\delta_m X_{im} + \varepsilon_i$. An analogous expression was used to estimate the medium-run bias (Bloom et al. 2002, appendix A).

9. The members of the advisory panel were David Card (University of California, Berkeley), Rajeev Dehejia (Columbia University), Robinson Hollister (Swarthmore College), Guido Imbens (University of California, Berkeley), Robert LaLonde (University of Chicago), Robert Moffitt (Johns Hopkins University), and Philip Robins (University of Miami).

10. We learned about the value of using propensity-score balance tests to screen out inappropriate comparison groups from Donald Rubin's presentation in a session called "Are There Alternatives to Random Assignment?" at the November 2001 Research Conference of the Association for Public Policy Analysis and Management in Washington, D.C.

11. Our estimates differ slightly from those presented by Gayle Hamilton et al. (2001) because ours are reported in 1996 dollars, whereas theirs are reported in nominal dollars.

12. As already indicated, both the traditional case management group and the

integrated case management group in Columbus used high-enforcement education-first approaches. In calculations of the mean impact for the high-enforcement education-first program category, each of the two case management groups was included separately and was in this sense treated as a separate site.

References

Agodini, Roberto, and Mark Dynarski. 2004. "Are Experiments the Only Option? A Look at Dropout Prevention Programs." *Review of Economics and Statistics* 86(1): 180–94.

Amemiya, Takeshi. 1985. *Advanced Econometrics.* Cambridge, Mass.: Harvard University Press.

Ashenfelter, Orley. 1974. "The Effect of Manpower Training on Earnings: Preliminary Results." Industrial Relations Section working paper 60. Princeton: Princeton University.

———. 1978. "Estimating the Effects of Training Programs on Earnings." *Review of Economics and Statistics* 60(1): 47–57.

Ashenfelter, Orley, and David Card. 1985. "Using the Longitudinal Structure of Earnings to Estimate the Effect of Training Programs." *Review of Economics and Statistics* 67(4): 648–60.

Barnow, Burt S. 1987. "The Impact of CETA Programs on Earnings: A Review of the Literature." *Journal of Human Resources* 22(2): 157–93.

Barnow, Burt S., Glen G. Cain, and Arthur S. Goldberger. 1980. "Issues in the Analysis of Selectivity Bias." In *Evaluation Studies Review Annual,* edited by Ernst Stromsdorfer and George Farkas. Volume 5. San Francisco: Sage Publications.

Bassi, Laurie J. 1984. "Estimating the Effect of Training Programs with Non-Random Selection." *Review of Economics and Statistics* 66(1): 36–43.

Bell, Stephen H., Larry L. Orr, John D. Blomquist, and Glen G. Cain. 1995. *Program Applicants as a Comparison Group in Evaluating Training Programs.* Kalamazoo, Mich.: W. E. Upjohn Institute for Employment Research.

Bloom, Howard S., and Maureen A. McLaughlin. 1982. *CETA Training Programs—Do They Work for Adults?* Washington: U.S. Congressional Budget Office and National Commission for Employment Policy.

Bloom, Howard S., Larry L. Orr, George Cave, Stephen H. Bell, Fred Doolittle, and Winston Lin. 1997. "The Benefits and Costs of JTPA Programs: Key Findings from the National JTPA Study." *Journal of Human Resources* 32(3): 549–76.

Bloom, Howard S., Charles Michalopoulos, Carolyn J. Hill, and Ying Lei. 2002. *Can Nonexperimental Comparison Group Methods Match the Findings from a Random Assignment Evaluation of Mandatory Welfare-to-Work Programs?* New York: MDRC.

Campbell, Donald T., and Julian C. Stanley. 1963. *Experimental and Quasi-Experimental Design for Research.* Chicago: Rand McNally.

Commission on Behavioral and Social Sciences and Education. 1985. *Youth Employment and Training Programs: The YEDPA Years,* edited by Charles L. Betsey, Robinson G. Hollister, and Mary R. Papageorgiou. Washington, D.C.: National Academy Press.

Cook, Thomas D., and Donald T. Campbell. 1979. *Quasi-Experimentation: Design and Analysis Issues for Field Settings.* Chicago: Rand McNally.

Couch, Kenneth. 1992. "New Evidence on the Long-Term Effects of Employment and Training Programs." *Journal of Labor Economics* 10(4): 380–88.

Dehejia, Rajeev H., and Sadek Wahba. 1999. "Causal Effects in Nonexperimental Studies: Reevaluating the Evaluation of Training Programs." *Journal of the American Statistical Association* 94(448): 1053–62.

———. 2002. "Propensity Score Matching Methods for Nonexperimental Causal Studies." *Review of Economics and Statistics* 84(1): 151–61.

Director, Steven M. 1979. "Underadjustment Bias in the Evaluation of Manpower Training." *Evaluation Review* 3(May): 190–218.

Fraker, Thomas M., and Rebecca A. Maynard. 1987. "The Adequacy of Comparison Group Designs for Evaluations of Employment-Related Programs." *Journal of Human Resources* 22(2): 194–227.

Friedlander, Daniel, and Philip K. Robins. 1995. "Evaluating Program Evaluations: New Evidence on Commonly Used Nonexperimental Methods." *American Economic Review* 85(4): 923–37.

Glass, Gene V. 1976. "Primary, Secondary, and Meta-Analysis of Research." *Educational Researcher* 5(10): 3–8.

Glazerman, Steven, Dan M. Levy, and David Myers. 2003. "Nonexperimental versus Experimental Estimates of Earnings Impacts." *Annals of the American Academy of Political and Social Science* 589(September): 63–93.

Goldstein, Jon. 1972. *The Effectiveness of Manpower Training Programs: A Review of Research on the Impact on the Poor.* Washington: U.S. Government Printing Office.

Gronau, Reuben. 1974. "Wage Comparisons—A Selectivity Bias." *Journal of Political Economy* 82(6): 1119–43.

Hamilton, Gayle, and Thomas Brock. 1994. *The JOBS Evaluation: Early Lessons from Seven Sites.* Washington: U.S. Department of Health and Human Services and U.S. Department of Education.

Hamilton, Gayle, Stephen Freedman, Lisa Gennetian, Charles Michalopoulos, Johanna Walter, Diana Adams-Ciardullo, Anna Gassman-Pines, Sharon McGroder, Martha Zaslow, Jennifer Brooks, and Surjeet Ahluwalia. 2001. *How Effective Are Different Welfare-to-Work Approaches? Five-Year Adult and Child Impacts for Eleven Programs.* Washington: U.S. Department of Health and Human Services and U.S. Department of Education.

Heckman, James J. 1976. "The Common Structure of Statistical Models of Truncation, Sample Selection and Limited Dependent Variables and a Simple Estimator for Such Models." *Annals of Economic and Social Measurement* 5(4): 475–92.

———. 1978. "Dummy Endogenous Variables in a Simultaneous Equation System." *Econometrica* 46(4): 931–59.

Heckman, James J., and V. Joseph Hotz. 1989. "Choosing Among Alternative Nonexperimental Methods for Estimating the Impact of Social Programs: The Case of Manpower Training." *Journal of the American Statistical Association* 84(408): 862–74.

Heckman, James J., Hidehiko Ichimura, Jeffrey Smith, and Petra Todd. 1998. "Characterizing Selection Bias Using Experimental Data." *Econometrica* 66(5): 1017–98.

Heckman, James J., Hidehiko Ichimura, and Petra Todd. 1997. "Matching as an Econometric Evaluation Estimator: Evidence from Evaluating a Job Training Program." *Review of Economic Studies* 64(4): 605–54.

———. 1998. "Matching as an Econometric Evaluation Estimator." *Review of Economic Studies* 65(2): 261–94.

Heinsman, Donna T., and William R. Shadish. 1996. "Assignment Methods in Experimentation: When Do Nonrandomized Experiments Approximate Answers from Randomized Experiments?" *Psychological Methods* 1(2): 154–69.

Hirano, Keisuke, Guido W. Imbens, and Geert Ridder. 2003. "Efficient Estimation of Average Treatment Effects Using the Estimated Propensity Score." *Econometrica* 71(4): 1161–89.

Hollister, Robinson G., and Jennifer Hill. 1995. "Problems in the Evaluation of Community-Wide Initiatives." In *New Approaches to Evaluating Community Initiatives: Concepts, Methods, and Contexts,* edited by James P. Connell, Anne C. Kubisch, Lisbeth B. Schorr, and Carol H. Weiss. Washington, D.C.: Aspen Institute.

Hotz, V. Joseph, Guido W. Imbens, and Jacob A. Klerman. 2000. "The Long-Term Gains from GAIN: A Re-Analysis of the Impacts of the California GAIN Program." NBER working paper W8007. Cambridge, Mass.: National Bureau of Economic Research.

Hsiao, Cheng. 1990. *Analysis of Panel Data.* Cambridge: Cambridge University Press.

Joreskog, Karl G., and Dag Sorbom. 1988. *LISREL 7: A Guide to the Program and Applications.* Chicago: SPSS Inc.

LaLonde, Robert J. 1986. "Evaluating the Econometric Evaluations of Training Programs with Experimental Data." *American Economic Review* 76(4): 604–20.

Lipsey, Mark W., and David B. Wilson. 1993. "The Efficacy of Psychological, Educational, and Behavioral Treatment." *American Psychologist* 48(12): 1181–1209.

Maddala, G. S., and Lung-Fei Lee. 1976. "Recursive Models with Qualitative Endogenous Variables." *Annals of Economic and Social Measurement* 5(4): 525–45.

Michalopoulos, Charles, Howard S. Bloom, and Carolyn J. Hill. 2004. "Can Propensity-Score Methods Match the Findings from a Random Assignment Experiment of Mandatory Welfare-to-Work Programs?" *Review of Economics and Statistics* 86(1): 156–79.

Muthén, Bengt. 1994. "Multilevel Covariance Structure Analysis." *Sociological Methods and Research* 22(3): 376–98.

Muthén, Linda, and Bengt Muthén. 1998. *Mplus User's Guide.* Los Angeles: Muthén & Muthén.

Raudenbush, Stephen, and Anthony Bryk. 2002. *Hierarchical Linear Models: Applications and Data Analysis.* 2nd edition. Thousand Oaks, Calif.: Sage.

Rosenbaum, Paul R., and Donald B. Rubin. 1983. "The Central Role of the Propensity Score in Observational Studies for Causal Effects." *Biometrika* 70(1): 41–55.

Shadish, William R., Thomas D. Cook, and Donald T. Campbell. 2002. *Experimental and Quasi-Experimental Designs for Generalized Causal Inference.* Boston: Houghton Mifflin.

Smith, Jeffrey, and Petra Todd. 2005. "Does Matching Overcome LaLonde's Critique of Nonexperimental Estimators?" *Journal of Econometrics* 125(1–2): 305–53

Smith, Mary Lee, Gene V. Glass, and Thomas I. Miller. 1980. *The Benefits of Psychotherapy.* Baltimore: Johns Hopkins University Press.

Stromsdorfer, Ernst, Howard Bloom, Robert Boruch, Michael Borus, Judith Gueron, Alan Gustman, Peter Rossi, Fritz Scheuren, Marshall Smith, and Frank Stafford. 1985. *Recommendations of the Job Training Longitudinal Survey Research Advisory Panel.* Washington: U.S. Department of Labor.

U.S. Department of Labor. Bureau of Labor Statistics. 2002. Consumer Price Index. Available at: www.bls.gov/cpi (accessed January 5, 2005).

Vella, Francis. 1998. "Estimating Models with Sample Selection Bias: A Survey." *Journal of Human Resources* 33(1): 127–69.

Wilde, Elizabeth Ty, and Robinson Hollister. 2002. "How Close Is Close Enough? Testing Nonexperimental Estimates of Impact Against Experimental Estimates of Impact with Education Test Scores as Outcomes." Discussion paper 1242-02. University of Wisconsin, Institute for Research on Poverty. Available at: www.ssc.wisc.edu/irp/pubs/dp124202.pdf (accessed January 5, 2005).

Winship, Christopher, and Stephen L. Morgan. 1999. "The Estimation of Causal Effects from Observational Data." *Annual Review of Sociology* 25: 659–707.

Zhao, Zhong. 2004. "Using Matching to Estimate Treatment Effects: Data Requirements, Matching Metrics, and Monte Carlo Evidence." *Review of Economics and Statistics* 86(1): 91–107.

Index

Boldface numbers refer to figures and tables.

104–5; production function estimation, 43; for selection bias elimina-
tion, 178, 187, 190, 191, 202, **213,
214, 215,** 216, 217–18

participation, in program, 15–16,
19–22
Pearson, K., 8
peer-group models, 118
peer review, 211
Peirce, C., 11, 164n1
physicians, 121, 124, 165n12
Pindyck, R., 110n10
place-based interventions, 22–24, 115,
116–25, 152–57. *See also* cluster randomization
police patrol initiatives, 116
policy considerations, 8, 38, 75, 86–88
political issues, 123, 131
pooling, of data, 48, 68–69, 105–8
Porter, T., 28n2
Portland, Oreg., NEWWS site, 17,
196, 198, **201, 203–4,** 219, 220
prediction of future outcomes, 142,
178
predictive validity, 147, 148, 151
prejudice, 119
primary data, in cross-site experiments, 38, 39
production functions, 42–48
program impacts or effectiveness:
cluster randomization, 125–28, 142;
definition of, 173; intermediate vs.
ultimate outcomes, 16; measurement of, 39–40, 78–88
program implementation, 15, 17–19,
41, 53–56, **59**
program management, 70–71n3. *See
also* program implementation
program participation, 15–16, 19–22
PROGRESA program, 165n8
Project Independence (PI), 39
propensity-score balancing: comparison group method, **213, 214,** 216,
217; expectations of, 185–86; limitations of, 178; with longitudinal
data, 184–85; methods of, 202;
process of, 177; School Dropout

Prevention Experiment application, 190; Tennessee Class-Size
Experiment application, 191
propensity score-weighted least-
squares regression, 210, **213, 214**
psychophysics, 5
psychotherapy, effectiveness of, 2–3
public finance theory, 117
public health campaigns, 24
public housing, 119–20, 127, 152,
154–56, 164n3
public service and information campaigns, 121

Quercia, R., 165n6
Quetelet, A., 5, 6

race and ethnicity, welfare-to-work
program study, 29n5, **52, 65**
random-effects model, 43
random-growth models, 179, 209–10,
213, 214, 215, 216
randomized experiments: applications of, 1–3; basic description of,
14, 75; black box problem, 15–17,
77; compared to nonexperimental
estimates, 25–27; criticisms and
shortcomings, 15, 28–29n4; definition of, 1; future research, 19; as
gold standard in evaluation research, 12, 75; historical background, 3, 11–14; limitations of,
76–77; prevalence of, 12, 75; program implementation effects,
17–19; program participation effects, 19–20
Raudenbush, S., 71n7, 136, 143,
166n17
reading achievement, 131–32, 142,
144–46
reading programs, 43–44, 147
regression discontinuity, 10
reliability, cross-site experimental approach, 50, 57
repeated cross-section methodology,
154
researcher bias, protection from,
210–11